Liber Amicorum for the Rt. Hon. Lord Wilberforce,
PC, CMG, OBE, QC

LIBER AMICORUM FOR

The Rt. Hon. Lord Wilberforce,
PC, CMG, OBE, QC

EDITED BY
Professor Dr Maarten Bos
AND
Professor Ian Brownlie, QC, FBA

CLARENDON PRESS · OXFORD
1987

Oxford University Press, Walton Street, Oxford OX2 6DP
Oxford New York Toronto
Delhi Bombay Calcutta Madras Karachi
Petaling Jaya Singapore Hong Kong Tokyo
Nairobi Dar es Salaam Cape Town
Melbourne Auckland
and associated companies in
Beirut Berlin Ibadan Nicosia

Oxford is a trade mark of Oxford University Press

Published in the United States by Oxford University Press, New York

© Oxford University Press except where stated, 1987

All rights reserved. No part of this publication may be reproduced, stored in a retrieval system, or transmitted, in any form or by any means, electronic, mechanical photocopying, recording, or otherwise, without the prior permission of Oxford University Press.

British Library Cataloguing in Publication Data
Liber amicorum for Lord Wilberforce
1. International Law
I. Bos, Maarten II. Brownlie, Ian
III. Wilberforce, Richard Orme, Baron
341   JX3091
ISBN 0-19-825595-0

Library of Congress Cataloging-in-Publication Data
Liber Amicorum for the Rt. Hon. Lord Wilberforce.
Includes index.
1. International law. 2. Arbitration and award, International. 3. Wilberforce, Richard Orme Wilberforce, Baron, 1907-00. I. Bos, Maarten. II. Brownlie, Ian.
JX3091.F465 1987 341 87-3114
ISBN 0-19-825595-0

Printed and bound in Great Britain
by Cambrian News Ltd., Aberystwyth.

Contents

PART I: A Tribute to Lord Wilberforce by the Lord Chancellor

1. Richard Wilberforce: A Man for all Seasons   3
   The Rt. Hon. LORD HAILSHAM OF ST. MARYLEBONE PC, CH, FRS, D.C.L., Lord High Chancellor of England and Speaker of the House of Lords.

PART II: Public International Law

2. The General Assembly and the Problems of Enhancing the Effectiveness of the Non-use of Force in International Relations   13
   HE JUDGE TASLIM O. ELIAS, Member and former President of the International Court of Justice

3. Legal Issues Involved in the Potential Military Uses of Space Stations   23
   Professor Dr D. GOEDHUIS, LL.D, Chairman of the International Committee on Space Law of the International Law Association

4. Universal International Law in a Multicultural World   39
   HE Judge Sir ROBERT JENNINGS, QC, Member of the International Court of Justice, former Director of Studies of the International Law Association

5. Diversion of Waters and the Principle of Equitable Utilization: A Short Outline of a Complex Problem   53
   Judge EERO J. MANNER, Chairman of the Committee on International Water Resources of the International Law Association

6. Global Satellite Telecommunications: The End of a Dream?   61
   Professor NICOLAS MATEESCO MATTE, OC, QC, RSC, former President of the International Law Association, Director of the Centre for Research on Air and Space Law, McGill University

Contents

7. Lord Wilberforce and International Law — 77
   Professor CECIL J. OLMSTEAD, Chairman of the International Law Association

8. The Distinguishing Characteristics of the Concept of the Law of Nations as it Developed in Ancient India — 91
   HE Judge NAGENDRA SINGH, President of the International Court of Justice

PART III: Arbitration and Commercial Law

9. Commercial Dispute Resolution: The Changing Scene — 111
   The Rt. Hon. LORD JUSTICE KERR, Lord Justice of Appeal

10. State Corporations in International Relations — 131
    Dr F. A. MANN, CBE, FBA, Solicitor of the Supreme Court, London, Honorary Professor of Law at the University of Bonn

11. The New *Lex Mercatoria*: The First Twenty-five Years — 149
    The Rt. Hon. LORD JUSTICE MUSTILL, Lord Justice of Appeal

12. Fault in the Common Law of Contract — 185
    Professor G. H. TREITEL, QC, FBA, Vinerian Professor of English Law in the University of Oxford

PART IV: European Community Law

13. The Impact of Community Law on Indirect Taxation — 211
    N. P. M. ELLES, Chairman, Value Added Tax Appeals Tribunal

PART V: Public Law

14. Lord Wilberforce and Administrative Law — 235
    Professor D. G. T. WILLIAMS, Rouse Ball Professor of English Law in the University of Cambridge, President of Wolfson College, Cambridge

Index — 249

Preface by the Editors

The International Law Association, founded in 1873, held its 62nd Conference in Seoul, Korea. When on 30 August, 1986, its new President, Dr Thok-Kyu Limb, declared the Conference closed, one of the great periods in the Association's history came to a simultaneous end. The allusion is to the span of twenty-three years during which the Rt. Hon. Lord Wilberforce, PC, CMG, OBE, QC, filled the post of the Association's Executive Chairman.

In 1985 Lord Wilberforce decided to hand over the gavel to younger hands and to step down from a position he had held for a record number of years. Since he had done so with ever growing distinction, it was only with considerable reluctance that the Executive Council acceded to his request to be relieved of the burdens of an office which, indeed, over the years had become one of signal importance in the world of public and private international law.

Under Article II of the Constitution of the Association, 'the objects of the Association include the study, elucidation and advancement of international law, public and private, the study of comparative law, the making of proposals for the solution of conflicts of law, and for the unification of law, and the furthering of international understanding and goodwill'.

Article VII, furthermore, provides that, 'with the approval of the Executive Council, Branches consisting of not less than ten members may be formed'. At present, some forty Branches of the International Law Association are in existence all over the globe, counting several thousands of members in addition to those members registered directly with Headquarters, London.

It must be clear that the preparation of the biennial Conferences of an organization of such magnitude is a major task. It is the Executive Council's responsibility to see to it under the guidance of its Executive Chairman. Every single Conference held may be considered to represent the outcome of many years of dedicated labour, and not only on the Council's part, but on that of the Association's International Committees as well.

All this has to be kept in hand by an Executive Chairman whose qualities of character should enable him to be a driving force as much as an arbitrator, the embodiment of the Association's legal conscience in sometimes dramatic circumstances as much as a lawyer of practical insight.

Bringing to his Executive Chairmanship the unrivalled authority of the highest court of law in England, Lord Wilberforce for nearly a quarter of a century lent the Association the imprint of his great talents. His contribution to the Association's well-being in a stormy period of human history has been vital.

Adequate means to thank him for his service to the Association other than a lasting memory in the hearts of all those who witnessed his leadership are hard to find. All the Association as a learned society can do is but an approximation of the measure of its gratitude towards a man who for so many years, and so successfully, stood over its destiny and gave it lustre.

A mere token, therefore, is the *liber amicorum* which the Association is honoured now to place before him. Plans for it arose in 1985, and in 1986 letters of invitation were sent by the Editors to a limited number of potential contributors. All responded favourably and handed in their papers in a surprisingly short amount of time.

To all of them the Editors wish to express their sincere thanks for their co-operation in this act of homage.

It is their hope that the volume, which is to be made available to all members of the Association at a concessionary price, will be an exhortation to them to emulate Lord Wilberforce's example of dedication to it—dedication apparent once more in his acceptance of the title of Patron of the Association! Through the care of the Oxford University Press, however, the book will also be marketed to the legal profession at large, and the thought is cherished that this form of distribution, particularly, will bring even wider appreciation of the International Law Association's aim and work.

Notes regarding Lord Wilberforce's life and career are sufficiently to be found in Lord Hailsham's tribute, as well as in the contributions made by Professor Olmstead and Lord Justice Kerr. This is why the Editors thought they might dispense with any further detail in the Preface or elsewhere in the book.

A final word of thanks is due to the Oxford University Press, and in particular to Mr Richard Hart, whose never failing courtesy made it a pleasure to work with them.

Epe/Oxford
March, 1987

PART I

A Tribute to Lord Wilberforce by the Lord Chancellor

1

Richard Wilberforce: A Man for All Seasons

by THE RT. HON. LORD HAILSHAM OF ST. MARYLEBONE

I was originally asked by Professor Brownlie to contribute to this collection of tributes to one of the most distinguished and versatile lawyers of our own day almost as a potential biographer. This role the preoccupations of my present office compelled me to decline. My own selection was for a review of some of his more influential cases, and thus of his contribution to English judge-made law, and the principles and constraints to which it should be subject. I soon found that the very range of these cases, and the quotability of some of the crucial sentences in it would not only be beyond the scope of my availability for research, but would also very quickly reveal my own limitations as a lawyer and a judge. Yet to refuse Professor Brownlie's invitation on the ground of pressure of business would be, to say the least, discourteous, and to decline the opportunity to say something worthwhile about one of the friends in the legal world I most admire would be to miss an opportunity of which I am more than anxious to avail myself.

I have known Richard Wilberforce for sixty years, first as an undergraduate reading the same course of Honour Moderations and the ancient school of Greats; then as a colleague at All Souls, where we were elected in successive years as prize fellows, each, surprisingly in retrospect, having chosen law as our special subject; then as members of the Bar practising in different fields and with different ambitions and aspirations in mind. Later I appeared before him as a Judge of Appeal, particularly in the Lords and the Judicial Committee of the Privy Council; and finally I found myself sitting with him on both bodies as Lord Chancellor, or, when absent, confidently relying on his skill in my absence to preside over one or other of their divisions. Throughout this time, I believe he would allow me to say, that we have enjoyed a close, unbroken, and affectionate, though not necessarily intimate, personal relationship. Thus I am probably in a better position than anyone else to review his career and describe his talents and character, which I admire greatly. If what follows is considered inadequate or incomplete, these deficiencies must be ascribed not merely to the personal pressures constraining any holder of my present office, but at least in part to the width, flexibility, and depth of the man whom I am trying to describe.

The first thing I would like to say is that Lord Wilberforce is one of the supreme examples of the advantage in the upper reaches of the law enjoyed by a man who did not take his first degree in the Honour School of Jurisprudence. This is no criticism of that school in any of our universities. It is the main gate through which most practitioners enter the legal profession. It has produced academics and judges of the first quality throughout its history. But it does, I believe, say something of the nature of law itself. Law, I believe, is a subject which is best approached by persons who, by one means or another, have first acquired a perspective on life which is wider than the subject they are subsequently about to study or practise. It cannot be a coincidence that of the major figures in the law whom I have known at all closely, Richard Wilberforce read classics, with ancient history and philosophy, as did Lord Simon; Lord Diplock read chemistry; Lord Reid was already an expert on Scottish law before he came in later life to bring his immense talents to influence the English; and my father was, after school, largely self-educated, with a wide range of reading and social experience behind him. Lord Denning combined a first in mathematics with his first in law. Of all the Lord Chancellors in history, I believe only Lord Birkenhead got a first class in law; and the others who did study law as their first degree, did not, in fact, achieve first-class honours. Lord Wilberforce came to the law as a highly educated man in other fields, and this, throughout, has been his main contribution, both as a judge and as an occasional, but highly articulate and sometimes controversial, contributor to the general debates on legal subjects in the House of Lords in its capacity as a legislative or deliberative assembly.

Those who regard Lord Wilberforce as a conservative lawyer with liberal tendencies would, I believe, be perfectly correct in their estimation. He is acutely conscious of the limitations imposed on the judicial office. This he explained in his opinion in *Ainsworth* v. *National and Provincial Bank*,[1] when he refused to follow Lord Denning's 'creative' doctrine of the deserted wife's equity in deciding the question of 'whether the small proportion of deserted wives concerned can be given the protection which social considerations of humanity evidently indicate without injustice to third parties, and a radical departure from sound principles of real property law', and concluded that 'the wife's claim should have been recognised for what it is, a personal claim to support, which can be satisfied by the provision of a home, and not as something attaching to the property which can follow it into the trustee's hands'. The liberal tendency of his mind as exemplified by the first part of the analysis was no mere lip service. In the Matrimonial Home Bill, which followed the decision, and whose passage he supported in the House of Lords, he spoke of the legislative

---

[1] [1965] AC 1175.

proposal as 'exemplifying in a rather striking way the difference, the dividing line between cases where the law can be reformed by decisions of the Courts and other cases where the intervention by the legislature is concerned'.

Those who would regard Lord Wilberforce as a timidly conservative judge, rather than one who rightly discerned the dividing line between Parliamentary legislation and 'legislation' by judicial interpretation, reckon without his revolutionary decisions in revenue law, much criticized, but, in my belief, manifestly correct. In the most important of these, Lord Wilberforce was there confronted with an intensely artificial arrangement devised solely for the purpose of tax avoidance, and boldly rejected the argument which had recently dominated judicial thinking to the effect that a taxpayer was under no obligation so to arrange his affairs as to incur the maximum liability to tax. He dissipated the fog of fallacy surrounding this doctrine by the succinct pronouncement which I cannot forbear to quote:

I have a full respect for the principles which have been stated, but I do not consider that they should exclude the approach for which the Crown contends. That does not introduce a new principle. It would be to apply to new and sophisticated legal devices the undoubted power and duty of the Courts to determine their nature in law and to relate them to existing legislation. While the techniques of tax avoidance progress and are technically improved, the courts are not obliged to stand still. Such immobility must result either in loss of tax to the prejudice of other taxpayers or to Parliament's congestion or, most likely, to both. To force the courts to adopt, in relation to closely integrated situations, a step by step, dissecting, approach which the parties themselves may have negated, would be a denial rather than an affirmation of the true judicial process. In each case the facts must be established, and a legal analysis made: legislation cannot be required or even be desirable to enable the courts to arrive at a conclusion which corresponds with the parties' own intentions.

The capital gains tax was created to operate in the real world, not that of make-belief.[2]

There, I think, it was the Greats man speaking, rather than the Chancery judge. Typically, legal lawyers tend rather to tie themselves in knots when faced with a quasi-philosophical problem. To my mind, the Ramsay decision, which really revolved round the question of whether the reported cases compelled the House to adopt the 'single-step approach' contended for by the taxpayer, had a strange analogical resemblance to the logical conundrums, like Achilles and the tortoise, propounded by the ancient Greek philosophers, rather than a pure question of statutory interpretation or legal principle; and Lord Wilberforce's analysis was one of the considerable masterpieces of legal ratiocination attributable more to his general educational background than his Chancery experience or that as a

---

[2] W. T. Ramsey v. IRC [1982] Ac 326.

revenue judge. The Ramsay approach was a revolution in its time, and has since become part of established legal learning in revenue cases such as *Furniss* v. *Dawson*,[3] where the judgment was given by Lord Brightman.

Equally radical in its own way was Lord Wilberforce's leading judgment in *Miliangos* v. *Frank (Textiles) Ltd.*,[4] in which he overturned a whole series of decisions purporting to show that payment of damages or a specific sum could not be ordered by an English court in, or in terms of, a foreign currency. His closing words are also worthy of direct quotation:

My Lords, in conclusion I would say that, difficult as this whole matter undoubtedly is, if once a clear conclusion is reached as to what the law ought now to be, declaration of it by this House is appropriate. The law on this topic is judge-made: it has been built up over the years from case to case. It is entirely within this House's duty, in the course of administering justice, to give the law a new direction in a particular case where, on principle and in reason, it appears right to do so. I cannot accept the suggestion that because a rule is long established only legislation can change it—that may be so when the rule is so deeply entrenched that it has infected the whole legal system, or the choice of a new rule involves more far-reaching research than courts can carry out. A recent example of the House changing a very old established rule is *West Midland Baptist (Trust) Association (Inc.)* v. *Birmingham Corporation* [1970] AC 874. Lord Reid thought that it was proper to re-examine a judge-made rule of law based on an assumption of fact (as to the stability of money) when the rule was formulated but which was no longer true and which in many cases caused serious injustice. So in that case the House selected a new date and did not think it necessary or right to wait for legislation and I would not think it necessary or right here. Indeed, from some experience in the matter, I am led to doubt whether legislative reform, at least prompt and comprehensive reform, in this field of foreign currency obligation, is practicable. Questions as to the recovery of debts or of damages depend so much upon individual mixtures of facts and merits as to make them more suitable for progressive solutions in the courts. I think that we have an opportunity to reach such a solution here.

To assess Lord Wilberforce's contribution as a lawyer would be unrealistic without reference to two matters. The first is his maiden speech in 1965 in the House of Lords on the bill which established the Law Commission, in which, to my great satisfaction, although I was a member of the Commons at the time, he criticized the rather churlish reception given to the proposal by the Conservative opposition. Since it is now twenty-one years old, and since it marked an interim stage in Lord Wilberforce's thinking on law reform, the speech has a double interest. One would still, I imagine, endorse his rather astringent comment:

Almost everybody is his own armchair law reformer. Everybody has his hobby horse in the way of law reform and not always those subjects which catch the headlines are those which really call for attack.

[3] [1984] AC 474.   [4] [1984] AC 443.

There is also something almost prophetic, as well as illustrative of his own wide interests, extending far beyond his own Chancery speciality, in his selection of 'family relations' as one of the topics most likely to be candidates for attention by the Commission; and many would underwrite his selection of property rights and the position of children as particular matters for early consideration. He was speaking before the 1969 legislation, the consolidating statute of 1973, the Family and Matrimonial Proceedings Act of 1984, which brought into effect three of the Law Commission's most important reports, the Child Abduction Act of 1985, and the 1986 legislation setting our own United Kingdom house in order and enabling signature and ratification of two international conventions, the product in large part of the work of both Law Commissions, as well as the Matrimonial Homes Act 1967, which, however, was probably far from Lord Wilberforce's thought at the time.

More dated is the reference to the third edition of *Halsbury's Laws*, which repeated the error of the original General Editor in regarding this work as a work of 'inchoate codification' instead of what it is, a practitioner's encyclopaedia of English law. Generally at that time Lord Wilberforce himself was, it seems, like one of his own 'armchair law reformers' in failing to observe the inherent difficulties in the way of codification, which have led the Law Commissions largely to abandon, in favour of *ad hoc* reforms, their original plan of codification on the Continental model. The difficulties here lie more in the field of our deep-seated tradition of evolutionary development by judge-made law, our inherently long-winded and dilatory methods of Parliamentary legislation, and our strangely literalistic rules of the judicial interpretation of statute all of which have hitherto precluded an 'efficient and modern civil and criminal code' on the Continental model which Lord Wilberforce then envisaged.

The second matter to which I would make reference in assessing Lord Wilberforce's contribution is his long presidency (shared for the greater part of the time with Lord Diplock) of one of the two divisions in which it has become the tradition of the Appellate Committee of the Lords and the Judicial Committee of the Privy Council to sit. One very soon learns that it is one thing to be a good judge of law and come to a firm decision after hearing skilled argument, but that an added dimension is superimposed on the presiding judge of a court of five. At the time when my father was Lord Chancellor, he sat every day, but, since the early part of the war, the coincidence in hours between the House sitting as a deliberative chamber and the hearing of appeals led directly to the present structure of the Appellate Committee, and indirectly to the present procedure of two panels of five, with a report to the House for formal judgments, which is much more rational and works much better. An unfortunate consequence from the point of view of the Lord Chancellor is that he gets far less judicial experience than he would like. He cannot preside over both panels at once, and only spasmodically over either. He is therefore apt to lose contact with the Bar and bench—with the Bar because he becomes less acquainted with the quality of some of its leading members, with the bench because he acquires less experience of studying considered judgments in the light of probing criticism from its members and colleagues on the Appellate Committee.

The effective tenure by Lords Wilberforce and Diplock of office as vice-presidents of the Appellate Committee and the Judicial Committee of the Privy Council marked an end to the period, comparatively brief in time, when vice-presidents took their place in the centre chair merely by seniority in appointment. The original plan required viscounts to take precedence over Barons, a ridiculous position which could lead the junior appointment to take the chair over the most senior Lord of Appeal in Ordinary. But the choice of mere seniority was far too rigid, and this rigidity became apparent when, at least in the House of Lords, it came to be realized that, in a minority at least of Scottish appeals, it was desirable for the two Scottish Lords of Appeal to sit in the same panel. The position is, therefore, now by appointment following consultation with the Lords of Appeal.

It would be wrong to conclude an estimate of Lord Wilberforce either as a judge or as a man without some reference to his leisure pursuits, which sometimes illustrate both the breadth of his learning and the width of his knowledge of matters not always within the cognizance of a Chancery Judge. If anyone wishes to see an example of the breadth of his legal learning, let him look at his decision in *Catrim* v. *Carr*.[5] This was a decision on natural justice in domestic tribunals, particularly where an appellate jurisdiction is provided for by a society's own rules. That was a case in which I found myself sitting with Lord Wilberforce in a very subordinate position, during my period in opposition after my first term as Lord Chancellor. Lord Wilberforce's understanding of the social background against which the drama had been unfolded was obvious from the start, without being the least intrusive. But in my view, the opinion of the Board which he delivered out of a wealth of decided authorities is a masterpiece of judicial reasoning in a field currently expanding where knowledge of the background is as important as the juristic principles involved.

My own assessment of Lord Wilberforce is almost too high to be capable of being printed without raising a blush of embarrassment to his cheek. His personal virtue, his modest and generous character, his wide educational background, his eminent and versatile intellect, and the profundity and

[5] [1980] AC 574.

scholarly professionalism of his legal utterances really make him one of the most outstanding English lawyers of his age, and perhaps of any other. The fact that he is also a friend of sixty years enables me to record my appreciation with all the greater personal satisfaction.

PART II
Public International Law

2

The General Assembly and the Problems of Enhancing the Effectiveness of the Non-Use of Force in International Relations*

by JUDGE T. O. ELIAS

In December 1977, the General Assembly, on the recommendation of the Sixth Committee, adopted Resolution 32/150 entitled 'Conclusion of a World Treaty on the Non-Use of Force in International Relations'. It also established a 'Special Committee on Enhancing the Effectiveness of the Principle of Non-Use of Force in International Relations'[1] consisting of thirty-five member State.

The Committee has held annual sessions from 1977 up to September 1985, and the problems of enhancement of the effectiveness of the principle of non-use of force have been agitated in all meetings of the Committee. The various views may be summarized as follows.

At its inception, many representatives of States Members of the Committee welcomed the proposal of the Soviet Union to elaborate the Treaty of the Non-Use of Force as proposed in document A/AC.193/L.3, and the delegates welcomed the undertaking of this task of concluding a treaty, pointing out that the idea had met with the approval and support not only among the broader circles of world public opinion, but also among the overwhelming majority of member States. It was also stressed that the current *détente* in international relations provided propitious conditions for the conclusion of the proposed treaty. The view was expressed that the principle of the non-use of force had been recognized by virtually all States as one of the main foundations of international relations, had received legal confirmation in Article 2(4) of the Charter and had been authoritatively confirmed and developed in special international instruments as the

---

* The learned editors of this volume of essays in honour of Lord Wilberforce have, in their wisdom, imposed a limit of fifteen pages to the contribution that this writer might submit, in order to keep the entire book within proper perspective in view of the number envisaged. It therefore seems appropriate to choose a topic of some contemporary relevance within the framework of the United Nations system; I have elected to present an analysis of some of the problems of an aspect of international peace and security in the world of today, a subject which I regard as one dear to Lord Wilberforce's heart.

[1] A/32/500.

Declaration on Principles of International Law concerning Friendly Relations and Co-operation among States in accordance with the Charter of the United Nations, and in a number of bilateral treaties. Since then, there have been several wars and cases of armed conflict, and the development of nuclear weapons and a network of military alliances carrying with them the threat that such conflicts could escalate into world-wide nuclear war, have taken place. It was also emphasized that there were still active forces in the world striving to undermine the process of *détente*, whip up the arms race, create new types of lethal weapons, and strengthen the aggressive military blocs. The Conference of Ministers for Foreign Affairs Non-Aligned Countries held at Belgrade in July 1978 had expressed particular concern at the reversals in the process of *détente*.

During the Thirty-first session of the General Assembly, Mr Sy (Senegal) said that

> ... the question of the conclusion of a world treaty on the non-use of force in international relations had been raised for the first time by the Non-Aligned Movement at its summit conference at Lusaka in September 1970. In proposing the inclusion of that question in the agenda of the thirty-first session of the General Assembly and in submitting a draft treaty, the Soviet Union had taken up the same idea, giving it a more specific form.
>
> However, for most of the countries of the third world, which had often been victims of the use of force, it was urgent to promote the rule of law in international relations and the scrupulous observance by Member States of their obligations pursuant to the Charter. It was therefore necessary to continue and to perfect the various forms of action undertaken in the past with a view to developing and elaborating on the principles of the Charter.
>
> Moreover, the Charter had not been able to put a stop to the use of force in international relations and it had not been very effective in preventing the emergence of new, more subtle forms of the use of force, which used certain principles of the Charter as a front. Some countries had taken advantage of the general character of the prohibition set forth under Article 2, paragraph 4, of the Charter to justify their imperialist, colonialist, neo-colonialist and racist manoeuvres. The Soviet initiative should be encouraged and supported because it aimed at remedying the loopholes in the Charter.[2]

All these developments, it was pointed out, emphasized the timeliness of the Soviet initiative, indicating that the proposed treaty would exact a positive influence in strengthening international peace and security, lessening the danger of armed conflict, and contributing to the process of *détente* and international co-operation by increasing confidence among the States, as well as enhancing the role of the United Nations. It would help to eliminate colonial oppression and new colonial practices, and to realize the

[2] A/AC.193/SR.10, paras. 17, 20, 21.

right of every people to self-determination, economic independence, and full sovereignty over its natural resources.

The view was also expressed that the proposed treaty, far from weakening the relevant provisions of the Charter, would enhance their effectiveness, and that while it was time that the principle of non-use of force was enshrined in the Charter, the conclusion of international treaties and the establishment of binding juridical rules, which were principal aims of the Charter, would enhance the principle of international law. After all, many Charter principles and provisions had been progressively codified and developed since the inception of the United Nations, and a notable example in this direction was General Assembly Resolution 1815 (XVII) of 18 December 1962, in accordance with the requirements of Article 13, paragraph 1(*a*), of the Charter, which culminated in the adoption of the Declaration of Principles on International Law concerning Friendly Relations and Co-operation among States, in accordance with the Charter of the United Nations.[3]

At another stage of the discussions, the view was expressed that the treaty might have a negative influence on the legal force of the Charter, but it was pointed out that this would not necessarily be so, since a distinction could be drawn between the legal force of a principle and its effectiveness, and the proposed treaty, when merely confirming the legal force already possessed by the principle under consideration, would raise its effectiveness. It was observed that a strict fulfilment by States of their applications could not be automatically assessed merely as a result of being parties to a treaty, since the will of States presupposed a series of political factors not governed by international law. The argument in question reflected a nihilistic approach to international law and a belief in the freedom of States to act in accordance with changing circumstances. Many delegations argued that, although the world had been spared a third world war, it had nevertheless witnessed much violence; and while agreeing that member States were bound by the Charter to seek to remedy that situation, they expressed serious doubts as to the appropriateness of elaborating a treaty at all or adopting the course in the Soviet draft; indeed, some of them stressed that the objections and doubts should be carefully weighed.

For example, Mr Rosenstock (United States of America) expressed the view on 7 September 1978:

No amount of misquotation or partial quotations from the Committee's mandate could narrow its freedom of choice, and, ultimately, the Assembly's freedom of choice, with respect to those ways and means. The Committee could choose to elaborate a treaty or, if that did not seem the most prudent course to follow, it might devote its efforts to such other recommendations as it deemed appropriate. It

---

[3] Resolution 2625 (25).

was not required to pursue any one means of enhancing the effectiveness of the prohibition of the threat or use of force. It was required to consider all reasonable approaches to that end and it should not focus too early on one approach to the exclusion of others.

In the Soviet draft treaty in document A/AC.193/L.3 there were many curious departures from the Charter. For instance, language such as that in Article III of the draft, relating to treaties concluded by States, could hardly fail, at the present time, to raise concern about doctrines of limited sovereignty; it was to be hoped that a reference to treaties between members was not an attempt to use treaties obtained by the crudest forms of duress to enhance those tarnished doctrines.

Some members expressed the view that the principle of non-use of force was already stated with admirable clarity in the United Nations Charter, in particular in Article 2(4), and the clarity and scope of that provision were confirmed by the Declaration on Principles of International Law concerning Friendly Relations and Co-operation among States. In their view, the basic problem was that, because there was no rule prohibiting the use of force, or because some States were unaware of the existence of such a rule, if States were prepared to break that rule or to maintain that it did not exist, no amount of repetition of the injunction against the threat or use of force would deter them from breaking the rule. The instance was given of the Briand–Kellogg Pact of 1928, proposing the abolition of war as an instrument of national policy for States which showed that the technique proposed in the Soviet draft treaty had not been efficacious; and that in any case, it did not prevent the ultimate failure of the League of Nations, despite its proclamation of treaties on the use of force and the outlawing of war. It was concluded that the best lesson which could be learned from the Second World War was that the best hope for mankind lay in a comprehensive collective security system.

Another argument was that the principle of non-use of force was linked with the principle of the peaceful settlement of disputes and the right of self-defence, and was a component of the peace-keeping system established by the Charter in Articles 11 and 12, as well as in Chapter 7. It was said that the proposed treaty would be dangerous, since it would risk divesting the Security Council of its freedom of action, and would restrict its discretionary powers under Article 39; that was why texts of such political importance on the definition of aggression had been given the status of *recommendations*, not treaties. In this regard, the view was expressed that, if the Soviety Union had submitted a draft of a *resolution* or a solemn *declaration* of the General Assembly, then its initiative would have been more welcome. The parallel existence of the proposed treaty and the provisions of the Charter on the same subject would give the false impression that time had eroded the obligation already enshrined in

[4] A/AC.193/SR.10, paras. 2, 4.

Article 2(4). If the obligation set forth in Article 2(4) were to be not only reaffirmed, but also reformulated as in the proposed Soviet draft, there would be a risk of differing interpretations of the two formulae, which would open the way to new problems; and difficulties could arise as to the application of Article 103 of the Charter, especially where a conflict between the two parallel provisions was not obvious.[5] Mention was made, in this connection, of the problem of asserted or implied exception, or *reservations*, to the principle of non-use of force, including, *inter alia*, the assertion that armed struggle and assistance to those engaged in armed struggle was consistent with the Charter, and the all to frequent attempts of States guilty of encouraging the use of force by proxy or covertly to disclaim responsibility for the ensuing violence or even to justify uses of force, as well as the use of force across frontiers to ensure doctrinal orthodoxy.

In this connection, Mr Zehentner (Federal Republic of Germany) said that

> ... the Soviet Union had proposed that the Committee should draft a World Treaty on the Non-Use of Force in order to fulfil its mandate. The delegation of the Federal Republic of Germany respected the motives behind the Soviet proposal; however, there was considerable doubt in the Committee as to the appropriateness of that course, and the objectives and doubts of many delegations in that respect required careful consideration. It seemed a delicate undertaking for a binding convention to restrict itself wholly or in part to repeating the substantive content of basic rules and principles of the Charter. The prohibition of force contained in Article 2, paragraph 4, was not subject to the discretion of the parties. If the rule was made the subject of a convention, there was a danger that misunderstandings and misinterpretations would ensue. If member States chose not to ratify such a convention or to qualify their accession by resorting to reservations or interpretative explanations, it was not clear whether the problems thus raised could be solved by the provisions of Article 103 of the Charter, according to which the obligations of member States under the Charter prevailed over their obligations under other international agreements. Should the contents of a new treaty deviate from the Charter, however, the resultant complications would run counter to the desired end. It would be impossible to prevent a conflict between two different sets of rules intended to apply to one and the same situation.[6]

In similar vein was the argument of Ferrari-Bravo, the Italian representative, at the meeting of 1 September 1978, ending up with preferring a General Assembly *resolution* to a treaty.[7]

Another problem would certainly arise as to how to establish a list of types of actions to be included in, or excluded from, the prohibition of the

---

[5] Reference should be made here to I. Brownlie, 'International Law and the Activities of Armed Bands', *International and Comparative Law Quarterly* 7: (1958) 712–35.

[6] See A/AC. 193/SR. 12, para. 8, of 11 Sept. 1978.

[7] A/AC. 193/SR. 8, paras. 4, 10, 11.

use of force, and a number of States would abstain from becoming parties to the new instrument, moreover differential attitudes to the definition of what constitutes 'force' in such a new treaty, would certainly cast doubt on the value of Article 2(4) and weaken the principle which the Charter aimed at strengthening. There would then be different groups or classes of States adhering to, or not adhering to, the proposed treaty.

Many delegations supporting the Soviet initiative recalled that the question of the conclusion of a world treaty on the non-use of force in international relations had been raised for the first time by the Non-Aligned Movement at its summit conference at Lusaka in 1970. The argument was advanced that if a treaty on the non-use of force could be drafted which would not detract from the equivalent provisions of the Charter or prejudice their fundamental validity, but would enhance their application and remove the ambiguities and loopholes which had given rise to abuses in the past, such an instrument would make a valuable contribution to the legal regulations. This would be especially so since the principle of non-use of force in such a treaty could not be discussed without due regard to the fact that it formed part and parcel of a whole structure and philosophy of a world order based on the existence of the United Nations.

What is most needed is an adequate definition of the notion of force and use of force, covering, in addition to *military* force, *subversive* and *economic* coercion. Mr. Zehentner observed that

... Under Article 24 of the Charter, the Security Council was allowed a substantial amount of discretion in its task of maintaining international peace and security. The Charter provided no precise definition of such terms as threat to peace, breach of peace or act of aggression. The legal terms used in connexion with the prohibition of the use of force in Article 2, paragraph 4, also required interpretation; that was particularly true of the term force, which obviously involved several different kinds of force apart from military force.[8]

And he further observed that

It had become evident that the principle of renunciation of force in international relations could not be considered without simultaneously taking into account the fundamental right of all States to self-defence, whether individual or collective. Article 51 of the Charter clearly recognized that inherent right, while being less clear on its substantive content. History had shown that the obligation of States under Article 2, paragraph 4, had been violated time and again. The continued arms race showed that States were preparing themselves for the use of arms in the future as well. In order to counter the dangers inherent in that situation in the interests of international peace and security, a credible alternative must be offered to the solution of problems by force. That need was recognized in the Charter, which raised States' commitment to the peaceful settlement of disputes to the rank

[8] *Supra*, (n. 6), para. 6.

of a basic principle. Yet, neither that commitment nor its procedural elements as stipulated in Chapter IV of the Charter had yet been fully implemented. The obligation of States to settle international disputes by peaceful means was the logical corollary of the prohibition of the use of force. Well-functioning mechanisms and institutions for the peaceful settlement of disputes were certain to create confidence and to facilitate the observance of the principle of the renunciation of force.[9]

Reference was made in this connection to the recent declaration approved by the Conference of Ministers for Foreign Affairs of Non-Aligned Countries held at Belgrade in July 1978, which reiterated the need to eliminate the threat or use of force and pressure in international relations as one of the fundamental objectives of the policy of non-alignment, and deplored pressures such as outside support of terrorism, covert attempts to destabilize governments, and the use of mercenaries, defamatory press campaigns, and financial bodies to try to control international credit in ways which came close to interference in the internal affairs of States and to violation of the principle of non-intervention. With regard to subversion, the view was expressed that it should no longer be posible to condemn in words the use of force in international relations, while undertaking subversive action designed to destabilize whole regions or to set up hegemonic systems; a new international instrument on the non-use of force should contain a clear denunciation of direct or indirect outside intervention aimed at undermining the political independence or territorial integrity of States. It was further contended that such a treaty should emphasize territorial aspects of the non-use of force or the threat of force, such as prohibition of the occupation of the territory and other acts directed against the unity and territorial integrity of States, as well as the prohibition of the deployment of the armed forces of a State against the territory of another State.

The envisaged treaty should contain any express obligation of nuclear-weapon States to refrain from using nuclear weapons or threatening to use them against non-nuclear-weapon States, and to refrain from being the first to use such weapons. The treaty should also incorporate provisions of obligation of all States to adopt effective measures for disarmament, and so reduce the danger of a confrontation between them. The Proposal by a number of States that the legitimacy of the struggle of colonial and other dependent peoples for liberation should be recognized was countered by the view that the treaty would thereby contain provisions dealing with matters of the use of force not covered in the Charter, however much it might be necessary that there should be an express provision for the rights of peoples to wage a struggle, including an armed struggle in their pursuit of liberation from colonial domination.

[9] Ibid., para. 7.

The inclusion in a world treaty of all the elements in the foregoing paragraphs would represent a major step forward, and a number of delegations stressed the importance of the relationship between the Charter and such a new treaty, emphasizing that the particular form of any document to contain all these should be carefully and separately studied in later deliberations of the Special Committee. The method used in the case of the Declaration on Friendly Relations and the Final Act of the Conference on Security and Co-operation in Europe should be carefully studied. The Soviet draft treaty would in any case provide a useful institutional framework for the discussion of important problems such as the definition of the right of self-defence, which should not be invoked to justify the astronomical costs of the arms race and to reject such positive proposals as that calling for a small percentage of the money currently spent on armaments to be used to improve the well-being of the masses of the world. While the majority of developing countries believed that the exercise of the right of self-defence was not the only situation in which the use of force was permissible, and that there were other rights which must in the last resort be protected by force, they maintained, nevertheless, that armed reprisals to obtain satisfaction for injury and armed intervention as an instrument of national policy other than for self-defence were illegal under the Charter, and that the prevalent view with regard to the exceptions based on Article 51 had been that they should be interpreted strictly, and that the State which allegedly or in fact found itself threatened by war preparations by another State should have immediate recourse to the Security Council, rather than to have recourse to measures of anticipatory self-defence.

Many delegates consider as coming within the purview of the Special Committee problems relating to the elimination of poverty, ignorance, and injustice, the establishment of a more equitable economic order, arms control and disarmament, arms production and trade, and obstacles standing in the way of the exercise of the legitimate rights of peoples to self-determination. Some delegations take the view, however, that attempts to be all-embracing should be avoided, and that limits should be set to the Committee's task so that it could accomplish its mission more effectively.

In the last report of the Special Committee on Enhancing the Effectiveness of the Principle of Non-Use of Force in International Relations, it was noted that

the failure of the Sub-Committee to agree on even minimum steps to enhance the effectiveness of the Principle of the Non-Use of Force in International Relations could give the mistaken impression that doubt was being cast on the fundamental nature of the principle as a basic norm of international law, and yet, nothing was further from the truth.[10]

The report went on to note that

> if a positive notion could be sifted from the discussions, if a common denominator could be found among all representatives, however divergent their positions, it was precisely the firm conviction, which everyone seems to share, that the principle was a fundamental one, from which no derogation was possible.[11]

It was felt that the failure of the Sub-Committee might lead to a deterioration of the multilateral negotiating process, and to a lack of faith in the virtues and potentials of such a system as an effective way to achieve meaningful results in the international arena. The hope was expressed that there would be no need for a modification of the Special Committee's mandate, and that the language of its current mandate, together with the options contained in it, was flexible enough to accommodate the interests of all delegations, if a genuine spirit of negotiation and compromise was applied in good faith to its interpretation and implementation.[12]

---

[10] General Assembly, 40th Session, Suppl. 41 (A/40/41, 1985), p. 36, para. 152.
[11] Ibid.
[12] Ibid. p. 36, para. 153.

3

Legal Issues Involved in the Potential Military Uses of Space Stations

by PROFESSOR D. GOEDHUIS, LL. D

INTRODUCTION

Among the numerous programmes which have already been undertaken or contemplated in the utilization of the space environment is the crucial one aimed at the development of space stations. Whereas in many publications consideration has been given to the potential scientific and commercial uses of these stations, the question of their possible military requirements has not as yet received as much attention. The purpose of the present article is an enquiry into the attitudes of the main countries concerned with space development toward the potential military uses of these stations, and an examination of the legal rules prohibiting or permitting such uses.

The article will be divided in three parts. In the first, an effort will be made to give an impression of the present state of development of space stations. As will be seen, there are at this stage several factors which make it extremely difficult to obtain a clear picture of how and when the aim of constructing viable space stations can be achieved.

In the last year a string of misfortunes has befallen the Western World's space programmes. As far as the United States is concerned, the disaster to the Challenger space shuttle on 28 January 1986, and the following accidents with the Titan and Delta rockets, have faced the United States with the need to reassess its programme policy aimed at the development of an American space station, and, at the time of writing the present article, a new programme to cope with the fundamentally changed situation has been defined. As for the European programme, the failure of the European Ariane rocket, which was destroyed shortly after its launch on 30 May 1986, has resulted in a serious delay in the originally planned launching of such a station. It should be stressed, however, that these failures have not led to any lack of determination to proceed vigorously with the development of space stations on both sides of the Atlantic. Another question which has arisen in the aftermath of these failures concerns the effect they will have on international co-operation in the establishment and management of space stations, which the American Administration considers essential. On this question some comments will be made below.

In the second part of the article, consideration will be given to the attitudes of the United States and Western European and some other countries concerned with space development, including the Soviet Union, to the military uses of space stations. Finally, in the third part, the question of what is prohibited or permitted in the conduct of military uses of such stations will be examined.

I THE DEVELOPMENT OF SPACE STATIONS

(a) By the United States

On 25 January 1984, President Reagan announced the American goal of establishing the first manned space station in the next decade. He emphasized the need to foster and increase American co-operation in the programme with other countries. Although in the preceding decades the American Space Agency, NASA, had on several occasions considered the development of such a station, it was decided to concentrate first on the means of space transportation needed for putting a station into orbit. Priority was given to the development of the space shuttle, which was considered to be the sole means of transportation for the later development of such a station. In the early 1970s NASA started the development of the space shuttle, and several shuttles were launched with success; but then, on 28 January 1986, the Challenger shuttle exploded very shortly after launching. In the last half-year, American space experts have been considering how to minimize the effect of this failure on all American space programmes, including the development of space stations. However different the various suggestions on how to proceed in the altered situation may be, it is agreed unanimously that the policy of relying on the shuttle fleet alone as a means of space transportation must be abandoned.

In addition to the commitment to the use of expendable rockets, great pressure is being exerted for the development of an aerospace plane which, it is believed, would ultimately be available for at least some of the tasks which up till now have been carried out by the shuttle. This plane, projected to be a more efficient space transportation system, is being pursued as the key to the long-term crucial importance of the American role in world aeronautics. So far as the plans regarding the development of an American space plane is concerned, which could lead by the beginning of the next century, to a runway take-off spacecraft, it should also be mentioned that both the United Kingdom, with the development of a horizontal take-off and landing spacecraft (HOTOL) and France, with the project of the Hermes spacecraft, are pursuing the same objective.

(b) The role of Western European and Some Other Countries

Thanks to US support, Europe has achieved a technological level, which makes it capable of a partnership in the next big step in spaceflight, the permanent space station, a partnership including not only joint development of this new system, but also its full use.[1]

In August 1973, a 'Memorandum of Understanding' between NASA and a number of European countries was signed for a co-operative programme concerning the development, procurement, and use of a space laboratory (SKYLAB) in conjunction with the American space shuttle.[2] The European nations participating were West Germany, France, Italy, the Netherlands, Denmark, Austria, and Switzerland. It should be noted, however that, as SKYLAB is not a facility that can be used over a period of many years, it cannot be considered as a true space station.[3]

Two years later, in 1975, a European Space Agency (ESA) was established by merging the European Space Research Organization (ESRO) with the European Organization for the Development and Construction of Space Vehicle Launches (ELDO). The Convention regarding the establishment provided *inter alia* that ESA would be used exclusively for peaceful purposes to promote European space co-operation in scientific programmes and operational space application systems. It also provided that the Agency might co-operate with other international organizations and other governments. As to such co-operation, in April 1985 the Council to ESA decided to join the United States in design studies for a $12-billion manned space station planned for the mid 1990s. It was further agreed to authorize the spending of about $60 million on studies for a space laboratory unit, named 'Columbus', which could be plugged into the United States core of the projected space station.

ESA countries, while recognizing the importance of co-operating with NASA in the international space station programme, decided at the Rome Space Station Conference in January 1985 to evolve a long-term autonomous space capability. Consequently, ESA wanted to maintain the option of detaching the module from the space station for autonomous operations. On this issue, a dispute arose between ESA and NASA which, at the time of writing, has as yet not been resolved.

At present ESA is completing final studies for a new multi-billion-dollar programme encompassing space transportation, space stations, and tele-

---

[1] Dr Gottfried Greger, the West German Minister for Research and Technology, 'Europäische Erfahrungen und Perspectiven', *Space Stations*, ed. Böckstiegel (Carl Heymanns Verlag, 1985), 24.

[2] See Eileen Galloway, 'The Relevance of General Multilateral Space Conventions to Space Stations' in *Space Stations*, p. 51.

[3] On the SPACELAB, Europe's contribution to the US Space Transportation Programme, see M. Bourely, 'Agreements between States and with International Organizations', in *Space Stations*, pp. 71 ff.

communications projects, that will set the course for European space activity for the next ten to twenty years. This programme, to be presented for approval by its members in 1987, covers authorization for development of the Columbus space stations, the Ariane launcher, and the Hermes manned mini space plane.

As mentioned above, just as the United States was set back through the Challenger disaster, as well as the failure of the Delta and Titan vehicles, ESA's programme will be affected by the loss of Ariane V18, launched from French Guyana on 30 May 1986. Although this failure will strain Western launch capability, it is believed that Ariane flights could be resumed in 1987, and that the European programme might recover in about two years from the delays created.

Before ending the above—in view of the limited scope of the article—very incomplete remarks on the space station programme of non-Communist countries, one final remark should be made on a recent development towards international co-operation in the establishment of space stations. Japan's National Space Development Agency (NASDA) plans to form an international division called Space Station Integrated Project Center (SSIPC) to advance Japanese participation in the United States space station program.

(c) By the Soviet Union

The first low-orbiting space station, called Salyut 1, was launched by the Soviets in April 1971. Since that time, several other Salyut spacecraft have been launched, but as the Saluyt 7, which has been in orbit since 1982, was considered too small, a new type of orbital station was launched on 20 February 1986, constituting another important step towards the aim of a permanently manned complex in space. The launch of this station, named MIR ('Peace'), was timed to mark the opening of the five-yearly Communist Party Congress. A further development took place on 5 May 1986, when Soviet cosmonauts on the MIR station completed the new station to Salyut 7 in their Soyuz 16 transport vehicle. In view of the remarkable progress of the Soviet space station programme and of the failures of the American and European space transportation systems referred to above, the Soviets, at this stage, appear to have an important lead in the establishment of manned space stations. Although a leading British space expert, Mr Geoffrey Perry of the Kettering Space Observer Group, recently expressed the view that by the time the United States orbits a permanently manned space station in the 1990s, the Soviet Union will have had one for seven or eight years, it can be assumed that the United States will make every effort to close the present gap.

II. PRESENT ATTITUDES TOWARDS THE POTENTIAL MILITARY USES OF SPACE STATIONS

It is obvious that the question of the military uses of space stations cannot be considered without taking account of the military uses of all other areas of the space environment. As an in-depth enquiry in the various aspects of these uses would far exceed the confines of the present article, I will confine myself to the following remarks of a general nature regarding the present militarization of space.

As will be seen in the third part of the article, under the terms of the present legal rules applicable, outer space is only *partially* demilitarized, and between 70 and 80 per cent of all American and Soviety launchings of spacecraft serve military purposes. It should be noted that the Soviet Union has made several proposals to the United Nations aimed at banning *all* weapons in space. However, as long as military competition on land, on the sea, and in the air continues, it is unrealistic to expect that such competition in outer space can be avoided. It is therefore not surprising that the Soviet proposals received insufficient support.[1] So far as the potential military uses of space stations are concerned, I submit that a *complete* demilitarization of these stations is as unlikely to be achieved as a *complete* demilitarization of other areas of the space environment.

In this context some remarks should be made on the effect of SDI programme, announced by President Reagan will have on the militarization of space stations. An examination of the numerous highly complex issues arising in the research and deployment of defensive weapons in space lies outside the scope of this survey. Suffice it to say that President Reagan, notwithstanding the doubts expressed by a number of American scientific and political experts on the feasibility and negotiability of this programme, recently announced once more the firm determination of the Administration to proceed with his initiative. As for the Soviet position on SDI, whereas after President Reagan's announcement the Soviet Union at first indicated that no arms control would be possible unless the United States abandoned this programme, the latest arms control proposals demonstrate a shift in this position. In these proposals the Soviet Union offered to begin reducing its strategic nuclear forces if the United States agreed not to withdraw from the 1972 ABM Treaty for a period of about fifteen years. From this offer the conclusion can be drawn that the Soviet Union is prepared to accept that research on defensive weapons in space, under the terms of the ABM Treaty, is not prohibited. At a later stage some comments will be made on the *kind* of research which the Soviets might find acceptable. As will be mentioned below, the United States Administration appears to be convinced that, also in the context of SDI, certain military uses of space stations will be indispensable.

(a) *The United States*

Whereas at the beginning of 1984 the Department of Defence (DOD) expressed the view that there were no defence requirements for a space station, at a later stage it became convinced that military uses of these stations would be needed, in particular in the context of the SDI programme. Professor Nicolas Mattee, in an important article entitled 'Space Stations, a Peaceful Use for Humanity?', refers to the United States People Protection Act of 24 October 1983 which in Section 3(4) advocates the transfer to DOD of those space launch vehicles that are necessary for the conduct of national military space activities, including the deployment of space-based defence systems and Par. 5 of this section purports to order the immediate development of a manned space station capable of supporting both national security activities and other activities in space. This, according to Professor Matte, has been interpreted as a deliberate step towards SDI, and explains why the Reagan Administration is so keen on a manned space station.[5] Apart from functions which have both military and non-military objectives, such as remote sensing, reconnaissance, communication, weather observation, and others, the present position of the American Administration appears to be that purely military functions, including ballistic defence operations, as well as support of anti-satellite (ASATs) operations of space stations, are needed in the context of the SDI programme.[6]

(b) *European Nations*

In the first place, attention should be drawn to the address which President Mitterrand gave on 7 February 1984 to the two Houses of Parliament in The Hague, in which he called on Western European nations to begin their own work on an orbiting defensive space station. After his address, he stressed that his suggestion of such a European system was not meant to prise Western Europe from the United States. His proposal was apparently aimed as a hedge against the unavailability of a corresponding United States system.

In November 1985 the importance of building a European military platform was stressed by M. Pichaud, chief military space engineer for the French General Delegation for Armaments' ballistic missile office (DEN). He suggested that the platform proposed as a joint European project by

---

[4] In an address given 19 June 1984 to the Scientific Committee of both Houses of the British Parliament, the present writer made some detailed comments on this issue. See 'Science in Parliament', 42 (Oct. 1984): 25.

[5] See 'Annals of Air and Space Law', 10 (1985): 443.

[6] On the development of ASATs, see below. p. 34

President Mitterrand could be serviced and fuelled by the French Hermes space plane, which is at present being developed.

So far as West Germany is concerned, it should be noted that in December 1985 in Brussels, the West German Defence Minister, Manfred Woerner, began discussions with other European nations about the possibility of a 'European Defence Initiative' which would be an adjunct to the United States SDI.

At the time of writing, no official statements have yet become available on the question of what role—if any—a European defensive system in space would be assigned to a European space station. If the assertion made above that an SDI system would necessarily lead to certain military uses of space stations is correct, the conclusion may be drawn that, in the context of a European Defence Initiative, military uses of a similar kind on a possible European space station can hardly be avoided. However, there have been indications that a number of European countries favour an agreement which provides that space stations should only be used for exclusively peaceful purposes.[7]

(c) The Soviet attitude towards potential military uses of space stations

Reference was made above to Soviet proposals aimed at banning all weapons in outer space. These proposals obviously implied a complete demilitarization of space stations. Since a total disarmament in the space environment cannot be achieved independently of a general disarmament on earth, on the sea, and in the air, these proposals—as has been mentioned—have proved to be unacceptable. When President Reagan, on 25 January 1984, announced in his State of the Union message that the United States would establish its first manned space station, the Soviet news agency Tass said in an article published the following day, that the United States space station would become a tool of the military and suggested that Washington had already agreed to put the station at the disposal of the Pentagon. The Soviet assertion, made on several occasions, that its space stations would only be used for non-military purposes has been challenged in several American publications. In an article published in the American journal *Aviation Week and Space Technology*, it was postulated that the Soviets intended to provide a self-defence capability for their space stations which would include direct-energy weapons,[8] and in an article published in the American magazine *'Newsweek'*, it was stated that Unites States intelligence officials believe that cosmonauts on the Salyut 7

---

[7] In this context attention should be drawn to the ESA Convention, which provides that ESA will be used for exclusively peaceful purposes.

[8] *'Aviation Week and Space Technology'*, 11 June 1984.

space station had been experimenting with a laser programme similar to the one planned by the United States.[9]

Attention may also be drawn to the 1985 edition of the United States Department of Defence publication *'Soviet Military Power'*, according to which the Soviets have made known their plans to replace Salyut 7 with larger space complexes supporting twenty or more cosmonauts on a permanent basis. Such complex would enhance their space-based military support and war capabilities. Missions could include military research and development of orbit repair satellites, image interpretation, ASAT support operations, and ballistic missile defence operations. However that may be, it is difficult to imagine that the Soviets would not try to match any military uses of space stations which the United States might consider to be indispensable for its security.

III. LEGAL ASPECTS OF POTENTIAL MILITARY USES OF SPACE STATIONS

In response to the question of what kinds of military uses—if any—would be permitted on these stations, there are four treaties in particular, should be taken into account.

First, the two treaties related specifically to the uses of the space environment, namely, the Outer Space Treaty of 1967 and the Moon Treaty of 1979. As to the latter, it should be noted that in view of the ambiguities of certain of its provisions—to which reference will be made below—both the United States and the Soviet Union have refrained from its ratification.

Second, the two treaties applicable to general disarmament, namely the ABM Treaty of 1972 and the Test Ban Treaty of 1963.

Before focusing attention on the provisions of these treaties which are relevant to the military uses of space stations, some observations should be made on the legal status of such stations both in free space and on the moon.

In Article II of the Outer Space Treaty of 1967, it is stated that outer space, including the moon and other celestial bodies, is not subject to national appropriation by claim of sovereignty, by means of use or occupation, or by any other means. On the basis of this Article, it has been generally recognized that States cannot claim sovereignty over any kind of space station, regardless of whether it is itinerant in geostationary orbit or on the moon.[10] Although in December 1976, eight Equatorial Countries adopted in Bogotá a Declaration in which they claimed sovereignty over

---

[9] *'Newsweek'*, 11 Mar. 1985.
[10] See Professor Carl Q. Christol, 'Space Stations: Political, Practical and Legal Considerations.' *Hastings International and Comparative Law Review*, (Spring 1984), no. 3, pp. 530 ff.

space above their countries at the height at which geostationary satellites are placed in orbit, this thesis has been rejected by all other States, as well as by practically all legal experts.[11]

While under the terms of the Space Treaty no State can claim sovereignty over space stations, Article VIII stipulates that a State Party on whose registry an object launched in space is carried shall retain jurisdiction and control over such object. In this context the question of the interpretation of the term 'space object' arises. As it is generally agreed that a 'space object' is an object which is designed or intended for use or used in space, there can be no doubt that a space station is a space object, and that, as Professor Gorove has rightly remarked, all current law applicable to a space object would also apply to such a station.'[12]

Proceeding to an enquiry as to whether installation of *any* kind of weapons on space stations is permitted, the first question to be considered related to the interpretation of Article IV of the Space Treaty which has given rise to strong divergencies. First, it should be noted that under the terms of this Article, a different approach has been followed as to the carrying of weapons on objects placed in orbit around the Earth and those on the Moon and other celestial bodies. Whereas in the first paragraph it is laid down that States parties undertake not to place in orbit around the earth any objects carrying nuclear weapons or weapons of mass destruction, install such weapons on celestial bodies, or station them in any other manner, in the second paragraph it is stipulated that the moon and other celestial bodies shall be used exclusively for peaceful purposes, and that the establishment of military bases and the testing of any type of weapons are forbidden.

(*a*) *The Legal Position of Potential Military uses of Space Stations in Free Orbit.*

The first important conclusion which should be drawn from Article IV is that insofar as stations in free orbit are concerned, the carrying of weapons—apart from nuclear weapons and weapons of mass destruction—is not prohibited.

Before considering the *kind* of weapons, other than those just mentioned, which are not prohibited, some comments should be made on the interpretation of the term 'weapons of mass destruction'. As Mr

---

[11] On the Bogotá Declaration, see the article by the present writer, 'Influence of the Conquest of Outer Space on National Sovereignty', *Journal of Space Law,* (Spring 1978), 38 ff.

[12] Stephen Gorove, 'Legal Aspects of Stations in Space', in *Space Stations,* p. 151. On the disputes regarding the interpretation of the term 'jurisdiction' see E. Kamenitskaya, 'Large Space Systems: Some Problems of Jurisdiction', in *Proceedings of the 27th Colloquium of the Law of Outer Space*' (New York, 1985) 254 ff.

Jasentuliyana, Deputy Chief, Outer Space Division of the United Nations, has remarked, with the development of space stations, the lack of definition of this term might possibly become an important issue.[13] In his article entitled 'Art. IV of the 1967 Outer Space Treaty and Some Alternatives for Further Arms Control', Professor Gorove pointed out that both the United States and the Soviet Union regard atomic explosive weapons, radioactive-material weapons, lethal chemical and biological weapons, as well as any weapons developed in the future that have characteristics comparable to those of the atomic bomb or the other aforementioned weapons, as falling into the category of weapons of mass destruction.[14]

However, when the definition of this term was adverted to in the Conference of the Committee on Disarmament, speculations were made as to whether ASATs were covered by this term.[15] On this issue some comments will be made below.

In the preceding pages attention was drawn to functions which have both military and non-military objectives, such as remote sensing, reconnaissance, communication, weather observation, and others. It is submitted that there can be little doubt that such activities will also be carried out on space stations and that—as is generally recognized—operations like reconnaissance play an important role in the achievement of greater strategic stability.

So far as the question is concerned whether these functions are legally permissible, there are no rules so far adopted which would restrain or prohibit any of them. Among the host of issues which arise in the potential militarization of space stations, the most crucial one concerns the use of defensive weapons on these stations. Attention has been drawn above to the views expressed by both American and European space experts that, in the context of the SDI programme, support of ballistic missile operations of space stations cannot be avoided. When considering the legal position of such operations, it is the ABM Treaty of 1972 which has to be taken into account.

In the last few years the interpretations by the United States and the Soviet Union of several of the provisions of the Treaty have given rise to fundamental differences. Though—in the limited scope of the present article—it is not possible to go into a detailed examination of the discordance between the two Parties in the evaluation of the Treaty, the following comments may be made regarding their present positions on the

---

[13] *'Maintaining Outer Space for Peaceful Uses'*, ed. N. Jasentuliyana (UN University, 1984), 127.

[14] Ibid. *Space Stations*, p. 81.

[15] See D. P. O'Connell, *The Influence of Law on Sea Power* (Manchester University Press, 1975), 156.

most critical legal issues arising in this connection.[16] In Article V of the Treaty, it is provided that each party undertakes not to develop, test, or deploy ABM systems which *inter alia* are space-based. As research into such systems is not specified a general agreement exists in the United States that, on the basis of this Article, research on defensive weapons in space is allowed.

Although the Soviet Union had made several statements aimed at banning *all* research under the SDI programme, as a condition for reductions in offensive weapons, at the end of May 1986, it made a proposal indicating a highly important shift in attitude. In this proposal the Soviet Union offered to begin reducing its strategic forces if the United States agreed not to withdraw from the ABM Treaty for a period of about fifteen years. The proposal implied that laboratory research of defensive weapons in space would not be prohibited. Though the importance of this proposal should not be underrated, when one takes account of the American position on the *kind* of research which should be allowed, the arduous problems with which negotiators on this issue will be faced become clear.

As for the American position, it should be noted that both in official and non-official American circles, conflicting opinions have been expressed about the kind of research which would be permitted under the terms of the Treaty. In a study released in April 1985, the Pentagon expressed the view that the Treaty, while limiting anti-ballistic missiles, would nevertheless permit field tests of experimental devices to demonstrate technical feasibility. In this connection, the critical issue of the testing of X-ray lasers arises. On the basis of an agreed statement (D) attached to the Treaty, which provides that future ABM systems based on other physical principles would be subject to discussions, representatives of both the American DOD and the State Department suggested that the Treaty, in its present form, did not prohibit the testing of systems based on such principles.

This interpretation of the agreed statement was sharply criticized by several American experts, including Mr Gerard Smith, the chief American negotiator of the Treaty. Though members of the Administration considered the broad interpretation suggested by the Pentagon to be justified, they declared that this was a moot point since the Administration would structure the Treaty in accordance with the old restrictive interpretation.[17]

However, notwithstanding this undertaking the Administration decided

---

[16] For a detailed discussion of the attitudes of the United States and the Soviet Union to the meaning of the Treaty, see the article by the present writer, 'The Importance of Preserving and Strengthening the ABM Treaty of 1972' in *International Relations* (May 1986) 475 ff.

[17] For a detailed discussion of the American position, see ibid.

on 28 November 1985, to conduct a test in Nevada which centered on a nuclear X-ray laser.

It is submitted that X-ray laser tests, using nuclear explosions, would infringe both the terms of Article IV of the Space Treaty of 1967 and those laid down in Article I of the Test Ban Treaty of 1963. Tests of this kind would be illegal in the whole of the space environment, including space stations.

Another issue which has to be considered in the potential militarization of space stations concerns the emplacement of ASATs on such stations. As the use of such weapons in the space environment has not been covered by any Treaty so far concluded, it is submitted that—as long as they do not use nuclear explosions—emplacement of such weapons on space stations is legally permissible.

In view of the importance of protecting specialized high-altitude satellites, such as those used for arms control information and early warning of a strategic nuclear attack, debates have taken place in the last few years on the possibility of achieving a ban on ASATs in high orbit. Whereas a discussion of these debates would exceed the confines of the present article, some comments may be made on the latest attitudes of the United States, the Soviet Union, and some other countries concerned with space developments. In August 1985, President Reagan, in a Certificate to Congress, declared that the United States was endeavouring in good faith to negotiate with the Soviets a verifiable agreement with the strictest possible limitation on ASATs. So far as the Soviet Union is concerned apart from its proposal to ban all weapons in space—the one concrete deal which the Soviets most wanted out of Washington was a moratorium on the testing of ASATs. Although President Reagan, rejected such a moratorium, in the middle of December 1985, Congress passed a resolution halting United States tests of these weapons until 30 September 1986, unless the Soviets resumed testing before this time. Among the countries supporting proposals for banning ASATs destined to operate at high altitudes should be mentioned France and Canada.[18]

Though it cannot be expected that the two parties to the ABM Treaty will be able in the short term to reach an agreement on such a ban, as the prohibition of the use of ASATs aimed at destroying satellites in high orbit has been recognized to be in the strong mutual interest of both Parties, long-term negotiations on this issue might offer a reasonable chance of success. But until an agreement on such use is achieved, the emplacement of ASATs on space stations is not prohibited.[19]

---

[18] In Nov. 1984 the former Prime Minister of Canada, Mr Trudeau, called on NATO to support the French and Canadian proposal to ban the testing and deployment of ASATs destined to operate at high altitudes.

[19] For further comments on this subject, see below p. 37-8.

(b) The Rules Aimed at Preventing Militarization of Stations, on the Moon

Both Article IV (2) of the Space Treaty and Article III of the Moon Treaty have provided that the moon and other celestial bodies shall be used by all States parties for exclusively peaceful purposes. Neither of the two treaties has given an answer to the crucial question arising of the interpretation of this term and in the limited contest of the present article it is not possible to dwell on the very extensive literature devoted to this issue. It is important, however, to emphasize the extent to which the fundamental divergencies between the United States and the Soviet Union on the interpretation of this term have led, and will lead, to conflicts on the kind of military activities which would be allowed on lunar stations. The United States has insisted that the term prohibits only military *aggressive* purposes, whereas the Soviet Union has emphasized that the term bans *all* military activities.

In an article on the Moon Treaty, the present writer has drawn attention to the harmful consequences which the interpretation of 'peaceful purposes' as 'non-aggressive purposes' would entail.[20] In Article IV of the Space Treaty and Article II of the Moon Treaty, it has been laid down that the use of military personnel for scientific research and for '*any other peaceful purposes*' is not prohibited. The interpretation of the latter phrase as 'non-aggressive' purposes would mean that a lunar system could be used for all kinds of military purposes, as long as they could not be considered to be aggressive. But, in accepting such a position, one would necessarily come into conflict with another provision laid down in both articles, that the establishment of military bases, installations, and fortifications shall be forbidden.

Though great caution is required in speculating on the possibility of the two parties arriving at an agreement on interpretation of the term 'peaceful', it is difficult to see how such an agreement can—in the short term—be expected. Consequently, one may have strong doubts that the original aim of the authors of both Treaties to arrive at a *complete* demilitarization of the moon will be achieved. In the context of the development of defensive weapons in space, the question arises whether a role of lunar stations in such a development can be avoided.

It should be stressed however, that under the terms of both treaties referred to, the *testing* of any kind of weapons on lunar stations is prohibited. Even if one accepted the American view that non-aggressive uses of these stations would be allowed, the testing of such weapons would be illegal.

---

[20] 'Conflicts in the Interpretation of the Leading Principles of the Moon Treaty of 5 December 1979', *Netherlands International Law Review*, I (1981) 22 ff. On the Soviet Interpretration of the term, see Reginald V. Dekanozov, 'Mankin's Interests and the Use of Outer Space for Peaceful Purposes', in *Proceedings of the 27th Colloquium on the Law of Outer Space*, pp. 305 ff.

CONCLUDING REMARKS

On the basis of the above investigation of the present efforts to establish space stations and of the attitudes of a number of countries concerned with the development of these stations towards the permissibility of using them for military purposes, some tentative conclusions may be drawn.

It has been submitted that it would be unrealistic to expect that efforts to arrive at a *complete* demilitarization of space stations would offer a chance of success. Apart from functions, such as communication, intelligence collection, navigation, and others which serve both non-military and military purposes, space stations are likely to provide a medium for space-based or space-orientated weapons. It is difficult to imagine that, in the context of the development of defensive weapons in the space environment, emplacement of such weapons on space stations could be avoided.

So far as the legal position of the potential military uses of these stations is concerned, attention was drawn to the widely divergent interpretations of the rules so far adopted aimed at a limitation or prohibition of certain military uses of the whole space environment, including stations in itinerant geostationary orbit, as well as stations on the moon.

As these divergent interpretations have led, and will increasingly lead to conflicts between the main space powers, the question was examined whether the identification of their common interest in constraining certain military uses of space stations might lead to a strengthening of the rules so far adopted aimed at a limitation of these uses.

In view of the fact that this problem is of course closely connected with the problem of restraining the use of weapons in the space environment *in general,* reference was made to the recent proposals by both the Soviet Union and the United States aimed at reaching a compromise on the development and deployment of defensive weapons in the whole of the space environment.

On the 23 June 1986, the Soviets offered to begin reducing their strategic forces if the United States agreed to withdraw from the ABM Treaty for a period of about fifteen years. President Reagan, in his response to this offer, declared an intention to abide by the Treaty for at least five years or for seven years if there is an agreement to cut the long-range arsenals to extremely low levels.

As these proposals imply significant shifts in the positions of both parties in relation to these activities, their importance, demonstrating a willingness to make an effort to reach some form of accord on this issue, can hardly be overrated. While the Soviets have now renounced their original opposition to *any* kind of research under the terms of the Treaty and are prepared to allow laboratory research of defensive weapons in space, the United States for its part has abandoned its insistence that the SDI programme could not be used as a bargaining chip to obtain deep cuts in both sides' nuclear armaments.

But, however much these developments should be welcomed, it should be recognized that the negotiators will be faced with formidable obstacles in their efforts to achieve some form of accord on defensive weapons in space and that the negotiations can be expected to be of long duration. It should be noted that the American proposal makes no mention of whether the United States would abide by a *restrictive* interpretation of the Treaty, limiting SDI testing or wished a broader interpretation that permits everything short of deployment. Although, according to statements made by American officials, some testing would be allowed, it appears that Mr Paul Nitze, dispatched at the end of July 1986 to brief United States allies on President Reagan's proposal, has declared that the President had no intention of moving to the broader interpretation of research.[21] However that may be, the drawing of a line between laboratory and applied research on defensive weapons in space will be an arduous subject to be resolved, all the more so as there still appear to be internal divisions in the American Administration on this topic.

So far as the question of the emplacement of defensive weapons on space stations is concerned, it seems at least doubtful that, as long as no general agreement of such weapons in space is reached, such emplacement can be avoided. It has been mentioned above that a different approach has been followed in the Space Treaties regarding the military uses of free space and those of the moon, and some comments were made on the divergent interpretations of the term 'peaceful purposes' referred to in Article 4 (2) of the Space Treaty of 1967 and Article 3 of the Moon Treaty of 1979. *If* the United States interpretation of the term 'peaceful purposes' as 'non-aggressive purposes' is accepted (an interpretation which has been challenged above), the United States might possibly argue that emplacement of defensive weapons on lunar stations is not prohibited. It can be assumed, however, that, in view of the explicit prohibition of the testing of any kind of weapons on celestial bodies (which includes the moon) laid down in both treaties, States Parties will refrain from such testing.

Apart from a consideration of the potential emplacement of anti-missile weapons on space stations, attention was given also to the use of ASATs on these stations. It was submitted that, under the terms of the treaties so far adopted, emplacement of such weapons on space stations is not prohibited. Reference was made to President Reagan's Certification to Congress that the United States was endeavouring to negotiate with the Soviets a verifiable agreement with the strictest possible limitation of

[21] *Newsweek,* 4 Aug. 1986, p 5.

ASATs. As both the United States and the Soviet Union have recognized the crucial importance of constraining the development of ASATs destined to operate at high altitudes—the preservation of which has to be considered as vital to the maintenance of a strategic balance—an agreement on this issue might offer greater *short-term* prospects than those aimed at an agreement on the control of anti-missile weapons.

In the preceding pages, focus has been laid on the bilateral negotiations between the two leading Space Powers, who govern all major space activities and whose attitude will consequently, exercise a decisive influence on the efforts to strengthen the rules aimed at a control of the military uses in outer space, including those of space stations. However, as an increasing number of States are going to play a significant role in the establishment of these stations, it is obvious that there are vital interests of these States that will have to be taken into account in any negotiations. Consequently, the bilateral talks between the two main space powers, on the control of military activities on space stations, should proceed in parallel with negotiations on a multilateral level.

The question of the most appropriate medium to study such control has led to divergent opinions. This is too wide a subject for a detailed discussion in the present article. Suffice it to say that the most effective forum in dealing with this issue appears to be the Committee on Disarmament.[22]

Finally, the hope may be expressed that the crucial issues arising in the potential military uses of space stations will lead to a recognition of the need not to delay negotiations, both on a bilateral and a multilateral basis, aimed at some form of control of these uses.

By studying options which are available, and dispersing confusions and illusions, preparatory work can be done which can make an important contribution to a more speedy achievement of a consensus on this issue when a clearer picture of the technological and political effects of the establishment of space stations has been obtained.

---

[22] Though a number of States have expressed the view that the issues arising on arms control in space should be considered by the United Nations Committee on the Peaceful Uses of Outer Space, the United States has insisted that this problem is an issue which goes beyond the expertise and mandate of the Committee.

4

Universal International Law in a Multicultural World

by PROFESSOR SIR ROBERT Y. JENNINGS QC

It is an honour to have a place in this tribute to Richard Wilberforce. Distinguished both as scholar and practitioner, he has, in his leadership of the International Law Association, made an important contribution to the progress and development of international law. Since the International Law Association is above all a society that bridges political and cultural frontiers, it seems appropriate here to look at the place and functions of international law, in the still new context of the global society of States which make up the international community of the present time.

In the past four decades, since the end of the Second World War, the scope and content of international law has changed out of all recognition. It is not only that there is vastly more of it, and that it touches many more subjects. Perhaps the most important change is that the old, classical orthodoxy that international law was concerned only with the relations of States, and by its very nature, could not be concerned with individuals or even with corporations, has simply disappeared. It now seems astonishing that, only a few decades ago, the respectable view was that international law not only did not apply to individuals, but by its very nature could not do so. Nowadays, treaty-law affects the everyday life of people, and the more advanced the country, the more likely are people to find themselves subjected to international law in a myriad ways.

This change in the content and the nature of international law has wrought another change, in some ways even more significant: a great deal of this new kind of international law now finds its way before domestic courts. In the older rather slim, case books of international law, municipal court decisions certainly appeared; but they were predominantly cases about States and their governments, such as questions of recognition, status, or immunities and privileges. Now, however, the cases—usually important ones—in which a judge of a domestic high court may find himself faced with questions of international law, are considerable in number.

Another, even bigger change in the international law scene is, however, the sudden transformation of the commmunity of States in which international law has to operate. The increase in the number of newly created, independent States, during the period—the period of the great decolonization movement—has added to a former list of some sixty and odd States, something over a hundred new ones. This happened, moreover, in a relatively short period. Thus, now, and for the first time, the international community is global, comprising therefore groups of States between which there are great differences: differences between political ideologies certainly, and of course between different stages of economic development; but above all between different cultures and religions. This is a novel and fundamental problem for international law. Certainly, it is not the first time that international law has been challenged by new States. It happened, as is well known, when newly independent States of Latin America made their different views of international law felt at the Second Hague Conference of 1907, and have made important contributions to its development ever since then. Looking back on that time it is easy to see that the absorption of those States, and the impact of their different views and ambitions, has been a great strengthening of international law. The newly independent American States, however, were, as they still are, essentially European and Christian in their culture and traditions. It was natural, therefore, for them to work within a Europocentric international law, and to put their demands for change in terms, as it were, of amendments to that system.

The problem today is different, and much more difficult to resolve. An international law which is indubitably European and Christian in its historical origins, has suddenly to cope with a community of States and peoples in which there is no longer a shared cultural tradition. It has to be able to comprehend not only different cultures and traditions, but also some that are even more ancient, and representative of larger populations than those that belong to the European tradition. There are also other stresses, such as politico-ideological ones which divide even those who do belong to European history; but it remains doubtful whether, in the long run, these political stresses will prove more lasting in their effects than those arising from the absorption of different cultures into the international legal system. Furthermore, it is obvious that the very penetration of domestic law and courts by international legal problems, to which attention has been drawn above, must aggravate rather than assist in this problem of bridging the cultural, religious, economic, and socio-political frontiers. International law is no longer a matter essentially for foreign offices; it also depends increasingly upon the possibility of achieving some degree of consonance in the decisions of domestic courts in international questions.

In this difficult and dangerous situation it is vital above all to keep constantly in mind that the first and essential general principle of public international law is its quality of universality; that is to say, that it be recognized as a valid and applicable law in *all* countries, whatever their cultural, economic, socio-political, or religious histories and traditions. International law must now develop and change to make it more suited to the new and truly global community of States. It already provides a much-divided world with its one common bond; and it is not without significance that, in those departments of the law where the States of the Third World demand changes in the law, for example concerning investment, or the distribution of wealth and resources, or the availability of skills, those demands are made in the form of proposals for changes in the relevant international law. The 'New International Economic Order' is the most obvious example of this tendency. This acceptance of international law as the vehicle of change is one of the most hopeful signs of the present times.

It seems appropriate, therefore, at this juncture, to look a little more closely at the problem of a universal international law in a multicultural world.

It was a cardinal principle of Grotius's conception of international law that it must be universal. As the late Judge Sir Hersch Lauterpacht put it, in his article on the Grotian tradition, the central theme of Grotius's thesis was 'The subjection of the Totality of International Relations to the Rule of Law'. This was not only the central theme of the treatise but also 'its main characteristic. There are no lacunae in that subjection of States to the rule of law.'[1] The same principle is put in even broader terms than Grotius could have used in his time, in Lauterpacht's own treatise:

The notion of international law itself and of an international community under the rule of law is based on the assumption—which, upon analysis, is a statement of fact—that there exist rules and principles of international law of universal validity binding upon all subjects of international law, whether States or not, regardless of their race, religion, geographical situation, political creed or degree of civilization.[2]

All this is not to say, of course, that there is no room for regional variations, perhaps even in matters of principle. The classical example of that is Latin American international law. Every law, including the law within the sovereign State, readily accommodates such variations. Universality does not mean uniformity. It does mean, however, that such a regional international law, however variant, is a part of the system as a whole and not a separate system, and it ultimately derives its validity from the system as a whole. This must be so if only because States within a particular region or system of States must also live with other States of the world society. There must always be some basic universal element—some general fabric of law—that binds all mankind. To take an obvious example: there can be no question today of a Latin American law of outer space

---

[1] BYIL, XXIII (1946), p. 19.   [2] *Collected Papers*, i. 113.

distinct from and opposed to the system laid down by general international law. Nor can there be any question of an area of the globe where the writ of international law does not run. This follows from contemporary practical considerations as much as from principle. In the beginnings of air law it was possible to have one system (the Havana Convention) in the New World, and another (the Paris Convention) in the old: but that became obsolescent when Lindbergh flew over the Atlantic Ocean.

Here, however, there is an important distinction. The postulate of universality, though logically necessary to any system of law that claims to be a true international law, may fall short of the full realization of universality in fact. Or it may take the form of an assumption—whether a justified assumption or not is beside the point for present purposes—of superior power, or superior culture or civilization by one group of States, so that international law then takes the form of a legal sanction for the subjection more or less of some peoples to others. In those circumstances the notion of 'the subjection of the totality of international relations to international law' takes on a very different appearance depending upon whether one views it from the point of view of the dominating or the dominated culture. As we shall see in a moment, Europocentric international law certainly over a long period illustrated this sort of flawed universality. And it has not been without competitors in this respect. Socialist international law, and more recently some forms of Islamic fundamentalism, have sometimes seemed to understand universality in a mono-cultural sense.

But now we come to the main problem. The main stock of modern international law, as a matter not of a theory but of historical fact, is one that not only had its origins in Europe and in the traditions of European Christendom; it is also an historical fact that European powers had at least until relatively recently a predominant influence over the formation and content of the rules of accepted international law. It was put succinctly by Sir Leoline Jenkins at the time of the beginnings of the system: 'By the law of nations I do not mean Civil Imperial Law but the generally received customs among the European Governments which are most renowned for their justice, valour and civility.' And this continued till recently. One need only think of the Declaration of Paris of 1863 when rules of naval warfare intimately and powerfully affecting neutral States were, in effect, decided upon, declared, and enforced by European naval and potentially belligerent powers. That great international lawyer John Westlake, who flourished not all that long ago, was able to say that for the evidence of customary law 'It is enough to show that the general *consensus* of opinion within the limits of European civilization is in favour of the rule'.[3] (Even in these periods, however, it is important not to exaggerate the idea of

[3] *International Law,* i, (1904), 16.

European hegemony. Both North American and Latin America, though admittedly themselves of European cultural origins, had already by the beginning of the twentieth century had a decisive influence on the shape of international law.)

It is not, surprising therefore, that the large body of newly independent States that have emerged since the Second World War in what may be called the decolonization decades, have seen a contradiction between the Europocentric content of much of traditional, and particularly perhaps customary, international law, and the essence of true universality which, in the language of Article 9 of the Statute of the International Court of Justice, would seem to require the 'representation of the main forms of civilization and of the principal legal systems of the world'. This dissatisfaction tended at first even to take the form of a tendency to reject customary law altogether and an expression of willingness only to recognize new treaty law which the new State had itself had the opportunity to accept or reject. But this attitude involved logical difficulties, including a rejection of the basic notion of international law, and was fairly rapidly abandoned; not least because States very quickly found themselves needing to argue their own cases on the basis of the old law. As Fitzmaurice put it: '. . . a distinction must be drawn between the question of how a particular rule came into being, and the source from which it derives its binding character when once it is in being. The first may occur through the consent of States; the second can never be said to arise from that consent without entailing a denial of the principle of the rule of law.'[4]

This problem has, however, been with us some time now. Many of the particular questions affected by this essentially doctrinal controversy have perforce had to be resolved in one way or another. So it is perhaps not too soon now to try to see it in the light of historical analysis rather than of dispute and polemic.

First I want to suggest certain propositions that seem to me, though I put them forward with all possible diffidence as one not at all expert in legal history, to be if not finally incontrovertible, at any rate sufficiently correct for working purposes. The first is so important that it must be stated even at the risk of seeming to state the obvious: that no person or institution can stand aside from its own history, or wholly shed its influence. Any change must begin from the place where history has placed us. An attempt to ignore, or discard, that history must result only in a corresponding failure of awareness of the extent to which historical shackles are being worn. In the anonymous saw which Fitzmaurice quotes in his remarkable article in the future of international law: 'Life must be lived forward but understood backwards.'[5]

[4] *Hague Recueil*, 1957, ii. 17.
[5] *Livve du Centenaire, 1873-1973*, Annuaire de l'Institut de Dróit International, p. 205.

Now, it is a fact of history that the fabric of modern international law was woven on the warp of a European tradition and nothing can alter that fact. It is doubtless interesting and instructive that scholarship has shown that systems of international law also existed, even long before Grotius, in other parts of the world and other civilizations. Yet it remains true that it was the system fathered by Grotius which provided the stock of the general system—that waxed and prevailed ineluctably with the waxing and prevailing of Europe itself. Fitzmaurice put it very clearly in the article already referred to:

Although it would be quite wrong to think that most of the great natural principles of law, and many of the principles governing relations between States, were not also to be found beneath other skies and in other climes than those of Europe, it was nevertheless out of these interwoven strands of the common European heritage and order that the particular body of rules we know as international law grew; . . .[6]

But there is also another very important parallel factor in this historical equation that is frequently forgotten. That Europocentric system of international law was called into being in the seventeenth century precisely to meet the needs of the new society of independent nation States which, in the ferment in Europe of renaissance and reformation, had displaced the former ideas of a united christendom organized not vertically but horizontally in a feudal stratification. Let me quote part of the remainder of Fitzmaurice's sentence:

. . . ; but—and here is something that is not always borne in mind, and of happy augury, perhaps, for our own times—it was not until the feudal system began to break up, and the Byzantine empire of the East ended after the fall of Constantinople to the Ottoman Turks, and Luther had nailed his remonstrances to the church door at Wittenberg, a process that culminated in the Peace of Westphalia (1648) that ended the wars of religion, and the final emergence of the nation-State—that this evolution of the international legal system, as we have come to know it since, really began to get under way . . .

Now it is also the case that the post-Second-World-War explosion of new nation-States which emerged from former colonial States, or at any rate from dependent States in one form or another, is in a significant sense a continuation and perhaps even a completion of that evolution of the nation-State world, which required and produced the original European international law. So that, insofar as it is itself the product of the juxtaposition of sovereign, independent nation-States, classical international law, with its roots in the period and place of the first emergence of that particular problem, is peculiarly apposite to the position of the latest band of recruits, from other continents and cultures, to an international society in which all members are either such nation-States, or are eager to

[6] Ibid., p. 210.

achieve that status as soon as may be; and indeed there was, it must be acknowledged, in this fulfilment of an ambition, even a considerable element of imitation. The former colonial territories wanted to be as their masters had been. Freedom and equality to them spelled out the sovereign nation-State. Thus, it was, it is submitted, inescapable that the newly enlarged society of States should begin with the common stock of traditional international law, for historical and sociological as well as reasons of legal principle.

Not that the post-Second-World-War emergence of new sovereign States into the international Society of States was the first time this happened. It had happened in the eighteenth century when the United States became independent of Europe and very quickly began to exert novel pressures for changes in the traditional international law system. It happened at the beginning of the nineteenth century when the many States of South and Central America gained their independence of Spain and Portugal, and took a significant role in the fashioning of new international law, notably in the Second Hague Conference in 1907 when they sought changes in the old system and also engrafted onto it a regional system of international law which remains importantly different to this day; but which in no way denies, or has ever sought to deny, the Grotian postulate of the subjection of the totality of international relations to the rule of law. It happened also in the later part of the nineteenth century when relations with Japan, China, and the Ottoman Empire, began to be conducted on the basis of international law (the latter change indeed having been made formally in Article 7 of the Treaty of Paris in 1856).

Those experiences, which we can now look back upon, of previous augmentations of the society of nation-States do, however, show very clearly that whilst it is inevitable that the new members of that society must start by taking international law as they find it, yet it is also true that more or less rapid change in that law, resulting directly from the new situation is likewise both inescapable and right. The process is illuminated by a wise remark of a writer of long before these developments took place, Thomas Hobbes: 'The legislator is he not by whose authority the laws were first made, but by whose authority they now continue to be law.' This is a seventeenth century anticipation of the principle of the intertemporal law, and of the importance of the distinction between "the creation of rights and the existence of rights".[7]

This latest and possibly last big expansion of membership of the international society of nation-States, which followed on the end of the Second-World-War, is now some decades old, and we can already begin to observe some of the results. It is typical of a slice of real history, as

[7] Huber in the *Palmas* case, RIAA, ii. 845.

opposed to theorizing and doctrine, that the new developments in the law have tended to be products of the summed forces of the old and the new, and have not by any means been as desired or prophesied by either the conservative or the radical theories which surfaced when the problem was first presented. Certainly that notion that a newly independent State should be bound only by treaties, and by those treaties to which it has itself agreed in the exercise of its new-found sovereignty, has had a marked and radical impact on the recently codified law governing State succession, where the 'pick and choose' doctrine is now strongly entrenched. And, of course, when it is a question of the novation or abrogation of treaties of a predecessor State, that innovative thesis is clearly apposite.

Nevertheless, a modern State cannot live by a basket of picked and chosen treaties alone. The fabric of law on which the treaties are imprinted is still the common international customary law, inseparable from its history, though, largely as a result of the impact of the new States on the international society, more plastic and quicker to reflect change and new developments than at any previous period of the development of international law.

The fact of legal life is well illustrated in the Third United Nations Conference on the Law of the Sea, and of the cardinal importance in that conference of the legal principle that the resources of the sea-floor and seabed beyond the area of national jurisdiction are 'the common heritage of mankind'. This principle, as is well-known, was enunciated and promulgated by resolution of the General Assembly of the United Nations in 1970 (res. 2749 (XXV), of 17 December 1970). It is interesting to see what the so-called 'group of 77', which at the conference comprised most if not all of the newly independent States, made of this principle in their formal statement of 15 September, 1978 'Declaring the Position of the Group of 77 on Unilateral Legislation affecting the Resources of the Deep Seabed'. That Declaration asserts that the General Assembly resolution of 1970 '. . . was not a recommendation simply inviting States to behave in a certain way . . . it was a solemn pronouncement by the most representative organ of the international community declaring that the resources of the seabed beyond national jurisdiction are the common heritage of mankind as a whole, and that they can only be exploited under an international regime and not unilaterally appropriated".[8]

There is no need here to go into the difficult questions of the resolutions of the General Assembly, much less of the meaning of the freedom of the Seas in this connection. Nor is it necessary to consider the meaning of the common heritage of mankind. It is sufficient for the purposes of the present discussion to point out that here is a group of the new States asserting the existence of a universal rule of international law wholly

---

[8] See *Third United Nations Conference on the Law of the Sea, Documents,* viii (1985), 38.

independent of any treaty that the Conference might produce. It is an assertion or proposition of law to which the Grotian thesis of the subjection of the totality of international relations to the rule of law is crucial.

That is only the most dramatic of the many instances which could be found in virtually every department of international law, where new States have argued and relied on the axiom of the universal binding force of rules of customary law or of general principles of law. It was, of course, bound to be thus: the innovator must have material to innovate.

Looking back on developments since the Second World War, it is possible now to appreciate that the moment when the international legal system first began to be challenged by some of the newly independent States as being too Europocentric was also the moment when the international legal system was for the first time becoming in fact, and not merely theoretically, universal. Traditional international law, especially in the late 19th Century and early 20th Century, had been somewhat uneasy as to how relations with peoples which had State systems not recognizably in the European mould, should be governed. Thus the concepts of territory as *res nullius,* or as subject to the acquisition of territorial title by occupation, were not by any means always confined to uninhabited areas. There had been notable hesitations in dealings with the countries of the far east and, of course, with the Turks. The assumption of crucial differences was written into the Statute of the International Court of Justice in Article 38(c), which speaks of the general principles of law 'recognized by civilized nations': obviously intended to indicate a technical difference in forms of legal and governmental organization (as W. E. Hall puts it when he speaks of 'countries *differently* civilized'.[9] The consequences of this former ambivalance towards those peoples not organized in recognizable sovereign nation-States, linger still in, for example, the unresolved controversies regarding the Indian native peoples of North America and their relationship to land.

Thus we can now see that the moment when new States of the Third World were inclined to make a gesture of rejection of the historical international legal system, was precisely the moment when it first truly comprehended the world system of States and began to shed its parochialism. This had been most importantly and dramatically asserted in the United Nations Charter, the rights and obligations of which are in universal terms; and which in this respect may be compared with the restricted character of its predecessor the League of Nations. The logical necessity of this development was stated without qualification by the late Judge Lauterpacht:

It follows from the nature of the purpose of the international organization of states conceived as the supreme organ of international law and as an embodiment of the

---

[9] *Hall's International Law* (8th ed. 1924), 47, emphasis added.

ultimate solidarity of interests of all States, that it must be universal in character. This means not only that the international organization must be open to all members of the international community. It means also that its membership must be compulsory on all states, and that there must be no legal possibility either of withdrawal from or expulsion from the organization.'[10]

It has also since then become clear that the inclination of new States to reject customary law and to opt solely for accepted treaties—even though, as we have seen, it left its mark strongly on the law and practice of State succession at that time—whatever its merits or demerits as a policy stance at the time it was mooted, is now clearly abandoned. Whatever else ultimately proceeds from the Third United Nations Conference on the Law of the Sea, it is certain that the former sharp and simple dichotomy between 'customary' law and treaties, is no longer viable: this quite apart from the logical problem which was always apparent, that the binding force, and much else, of treaty is derived from customary law. Indeed, the new States had, long before that, demonstrated their acceptance of a universal customary international law by the importance they began to attach to the idea of a *jus cogens*.

The post-Second-World-War establishment of a universal international law and the eventual realization and acceptance of this fact, is not the end of the problem but rather the beginning. The problems resulting from the emergence of so many new sovereign nation-States into the international Society, are both more numerous, more complicated, and sometimes more intractable, than was commonly supposed twenty or thirty years ago. Only a small selection of those problems can be referred to here.

First let it be said with no uncertain voice that the subjection of the totality of international relations in the greatly enlarged international community to a universal international law does not at all mean that international law is or could be a monolithic, much less a Europocentric monolithic, system. On the contrary, as more and more aspects of international law reach down through the State to corporations to other legal entities and to individuals, so international law has more and more to take into account and allow for differences of municipal law, differences of legal tradition, and differences of culture; for these differences are facts with which the international system has to deal; and it will fail adequately to do so in so far as it proves insufficiently flexible to allow for adjustment to the different situations. An obvious example, illustrated from the jurisprudence of the International Court of Justice itself, is the question of territorial title to desert areas inhabited by nomadic tribes (see *Western Sahara* case).[11] Unless the law can in such a case take account of a

---

[10] Oppenheim, *International*, 8th ed. by Lauterpacht), 372.
[11] ICJ Reports 1975, p. 3.

relationship of peoples with land that is entirely and essentially different from that of western land law and, indeed, different from the standard international law treatment of possession and user in relation to the acquisition and exercise of territorial sovereignty—though equally valid and almost certainly more ancient—it would be impossible to do justice in a territorial or boundary dispute concerning such areas. The International Court in the Western Sahara case had no difficulty in appreciating those differences of law and culture and of taking them into account in its decision. In thus comprehending a different legal tradition and culture it was aserting, not negating, the Grotian subjection of the totality of international relations to international law. It seems to the writer, indeed, that at the present juncture in the development of the international legal system it may be more important to stress the imperative need to develop international law to comprehend within itself the rich diversity of cultures, civilizations and legal traditions, than to concentrate on what might be called the 'common law of mankind approach' which sees importance in those general notions which, so long as they are stated in sufficiently general terms, are undoubtedly but hardly surprisingly to be found in all systems.

There is another problem that very much concerns the future structure of international law. The large number of newly emerged nation-States, which formerly were, many of them, colonial territories, have naturally and inescapably been preoccupied with the protection of their new sovereignty and the rights that go with it. It was symptomatic of this attitude that their first reaction to problems of investment, the flow of capital and credit, and the distribution of resources, should be the assertion as a basic principle of their sovereignty over the resources of the land with which nature had endowed them. At the time this was doubtless thought of as a demand for change, as in a sense it was; but it was at the same time, in jurisprudential terms conservative if not reactionary; for the definition and protection of sovereign independence was the primary concern of classical international law. Where international law, even modern international law, is relatively undeveloped is in international institutions that are something more than mere instrumentalities whereby sovereign States can associate and work together. The separateness of sovereign States is still the factor which dominates the international scene, and most international law, even that concerning individuals, is mediated and applied through the instrumentality of the State, its governmental machine, its courts, or its municipal law. This is why it is so interesting that, in respect of the resources of the deep-sea and sea-bed beyond national jurisdiction, the Third World has become devoted not to the assertion of the rights of sovereign States over natural resources but to the creation of an international instrumentality which would itself have crucial capacities over the resources: a truly radical method of resolution in which the international community has hitherto had little experience, but which is logically the next stage of the evolution of international organization. It was indeed the novelty of this proposal that attracted some of the criticism; for example, it was said with some truth that it would be an instrumentality with 'powers surpassing the combined powers of the Security Council, IMCO, ICAO, WHO, WMO, ITU, GATT, and IAEE'[12]

Another problem, which must be the last it is possible even to mention within the limits of this short paper, is that of international law making and changing. Here again there are inevitably reflected the tensions between sovereign independence and political, economic, and indeed legal, interdependence; and there is the inescapable dilemma of the law-maker between the need for predictability and stability and the need for change. But in this respect international law has developed quite remarkably in the last few decades. The success of the International Law Commission in the codification and progressive development of large and important areas of traditional law was the first big change. The second has probably been the experience of the Third United Nations Conference on the Law of the Sea: this is not the place to attempt to predict the results of this remarkable experiment in law-making, but there can be no doubt that the whole process of international law making and changiang will need to be reassessed as a result of that experience. It is not without significance that this was also the first major attempt at international legislation in which the new States of the Third World had been able to play a full part.

Thus, this period of the decades immediately following the Second World War has been one of rapid development in international law; perhaps necessarily so in a time which has also seen an important augmentation of the interdependence of States, as well as the most important increase in the number of them that has ever happened in the history of the modern world. Though it began with attempts by new States to repudiate aspects of traditional international law as being alien in origin and temper, it can now be seen that it was in fact the time when international law was to become for the first time truly universal in the Grotian sense. This in turn has made the more important the proper representation of the main forms of civilization and principal legal systems of the world. For universality does not mean uniformity but rather richness of variety and diversity.

Finally, it must be said that, for this process of change and adaptation of the law to suit changing needs of a changed society of States, the accurate and meticulous study of the history of international law (which, be it said, is not the same as the history of doctrines), including its European origins, is an essential tool. If one may cite not an international lawyer but one of

[12] UN Doc. A/AC. B8/SR, p. 9.

the greatest of all legal historians, F. W. Maitland, whose work on the history of English land law, dispelling mythical explanations and establishing the true and often long obsolete reasons of policy which gave rise to legal rules, thus made practicable the great reformation of English Land law in the Law of Property Acts of 1926:

If at one time it seemed likely, that the historical spirit (the spirit which strove to understand the classical jurisprudence of Rome and the Twelve Tables, and the Lex Salica, and law of all ages and climes) was fatalistic and inimical to reform, that time already lies in the past . . . Nowadays we may see the office of historical research as that of explaining, and therefore lightening, the pressure that the past must exercise upon the present, and the present upon the future. Today we study the day before yesterday, in order that yesterday may not paralyse today, and today may not paralyse tomorrow.[13]

That message is no less true for the state of international law today.

[13] Maitland, *Collected papers,* iii. 438.

5

Diversion of Waters and the Principle of Equitable Utilization: A Short Outline of a Complex Problem

by JUDGE EERO J. MANNER

Diversion of water out of a watercourse may serve various purposes: water-supply, irrigation, power production, and so forth. In most cases undertakings of this kind are covered by national water-laws. Used as a term of international law, 'diversion' usually means transfer of water from a watercourse into the same or another watercourse, usually within the territory of another State. Either one or both of those watercourses may be international in the meaning defined later on.

In a letter to the International Law Association dated 10 October 1952, the then President of the American Branch of the Association, Professor Clyde Eagleton, presented some views on the future work of the Association. Among other topics suggested for study, Professor Eagleton mentioned 'the international law concerning the diversion of waters in international rivers', a subject to which, up to then, insufficient attention had been given. He referred to a number of disputes in progress, and pointed out that the question would become more important 'as technical assistance is given to under-developed countries'. The letter does not make it quite clear whether Professor Eagleton had in mind the transfer of water from, or into, an international river as a specified hydro-electrical undertaking, or whether his suggestion referred to the uses of the waters of international watercourses in general. Anyhow, his initiative provoked a lively response at the 1954 Edinburgh Conference,[1] and a committee was set up under his chairmanship to examine the principles of the law of international watercourses.[2] Since then, the International Law Association has been engaged in that very comprehensive and complicated task. During the last three decades it had adopted a number of rules, articles and recommendations on the subject, prepared by two successive committees.[3] The most important and also generally best-known results of that activity

[1] See *Report of the Forty-sixth Conference* (Edinburgh, 1954), 309–38.
[2] That Committee on the Law of the Uses of the Waters of International River Basins and Interoceanic Canals, later called 'The Rivers Committee', originally had nine members. Its membership was completed in 1957 after it had submitted its first Report to the Dubrovnik Conference (1956).
[3] The Rivers Committee, then under the chairmanship of Professor Cecil J. Olmstead (United States), submitted its final Report to the 1966 Helsinki Conference: see the Report of

are the Helsinki Rules on the Uses of the Waters of International Rivers, adopted by the Association in 1966 and printed in numerous publications.[4]

The Helsinki Rules are a somewhat arbitrary combination of general rules and principles, on the one hand, and specific provisions on certain uses of waters on the other hand. They are not intended as such to regulate in detail the entire field of the international law of waters. But in spite of this reservation, the Helsinki Rules are still considered to be one of the main sources of the law of international watercourses at its present stage of development. Their leading principles are worthy of careful examination, even though the Rules do not solve all pending problems concerning the use of international watercourses.

Apart from some references in the commentary, the Helsinki Rules do not contain any express provisions on diversion of waters. On that account it has been asked whether the Rules are applicable to undertakings of this kind and, particularly, whether diversion of waters out of, or into, an international drainage basin would be allowable under the principle of equitable utilization.

The 1967 ILA Committee on International Water Resources Law has been well aware of the importance of the above questions, but during its arduous working programme, the Committee was not able to examine them more profoundly. After a preliminary study, some members of the Committee came to the conclusion that such diversion would be permissible, provided that the states concerned apply *mutatis mutandis,* the Helsinki Rules with respect to the installations and works required for its execution. The Committee felt, however, that the subject needed further study, and pointed out that in view of increasing technical possibilities of diverting water from one basin to another, some additional legal rules might be necessary.[5]

It is not possible, within this short essay, to examine in detail the international legal premisses of the diversion concerned. Some conclusions may nevertheless, be drawn on the basis of the principles of the Helsinki Rules and taking account of the special characteristics of such undertakings.

The leading principles of the Helsinki Rules are firmly connected with the concept of the international drainage basin. According to Article II of

---

that Conference, pp. 447–533. On the recommendation of the Conference a new 'Committee on International Water Resources Law' was set up in 1967, to study topics that still needed to be examined. A survey of the work of the Committee is included in its Report to the 1986 Seoul Conference, Part I.

[4] First published with introduction and comments as a separate booklet by the ILA in 1967. Some of the comprehensive materials collected for the preparation of the Rules is contained in *The Law of International Drainage Basins,* ed. Garreston, Hayton and Olmstead (New York, 1967).

[5] See the Report of the Committee to the 1986 Seoul Conference, Part I.

the Rules, such a basin is 'a geographical area extending over two or more States determined by the watershed limits of the system of waters . . . flowing into a common terminus'. Article IV of the Rules prescribes that each basin State is entitled to a reasonable and equitable share in the beneficial uses of the waters of the basin. That provision implies the *principle of equitable utilization,* a natural application of the notion of *'coherence'*, based upon the hydrological unity of the basin, and introduced and elaborated by the Austrian jurist Count Edmund Hartig.[6] The same idea appears also, as an agreed principle, in the 1958 ILA New York Resolution, according to which 'a system of rivers and lakes in a drainage basin should be treated as an integrated whole (and not piece-meal).'[7]

There is no doubt that the principle of equitable utilization must be regarded as the maxim of the Helsinki Rules. But as a legal rule it appears to be somewhat vague, and its implementation and application in practical cases are not without problems. As to the question whether the Helsinki Rules and, especially, the principle of equitable utilization, have reference to diversion of waters, no generally applicable answer seems to be possible. Since diversion may take place in various circumstances and by applying different technical arrangements, its legal premises vary from case to case.[8] A distinction must also be made between the basin from which, and the basin into which, water is diverted. Technically as well as legally the act of diverting water out of a watercourse, the transfer of that water, and finally its discharge into the receiving basin, are to be separated from each other.

Water may be diverted out of an international drainage basin into another such basin, or into a basin under national jurisdiction. In other cases water may be transferred from a watercourse under national jurisdiction into another national or an international drainage basin. Water might also be divered from one part of a drainage basin into another part of the same basin.[9] Passing over the less essential details, some general observations can be made concerning these various alternatives.

Generally speaking, diversion of water, as far as its technical nature, objectives, and hydrological consequences are concerned, is compatible with other water-related undertakings that would have corresponding effects within the basin. The fact that the Helsinki Rules do not expressly mention diversion of waters should not be understood as a negative

---

[6] Edmund Hartig, *Ein neuer Ausgangspunkt für internationale wasserrechtliche Regelungen: das Kohärenzprinzip, Wasser- und Energiewirtschaft* (Zurich, 1958).

[7] *Report of the Forty-eight Conference* (New York, 1958), 72–102.

[8] Some examples of diversion projects in North America are presented in Anthony Scott, *'The Economics of Water Export Policy'* (mimeographed, 1985).

[9] In the well-known *Lake Lanoux* arbitration case between France and Spain (1957), the former asserted in defence of its scheme that the diverted water was returned to the same watercourse.

attitude towards this kind of measure. On the other hand, the application of the Helsinki Rules to diversion of waters is limited by the Rules themselves, in so far as they deal with international drainage basins and have no reference to basins under national jurisdiction.

If water is diverted *out of* an international drainage basin by one of its basin States, the undertaking may, to that degree fall under the rule of equitable utilization. Accordingly, the undertaking State has to prove whether its project can be included in its share in the beneficial uses of waters of the basin.

As to diversion of water *into* an international drainage basin, there might be some problems. First, it can be asked whether this kind of discharge of water into another basin can be regarded as a beneficial use of its waters. Secondly, so far the receiving basin is concerned, the undertaking State may in such a case refer to the principle of equitable utilization only if it happens to be a basin State of that basin too. In practice, however, a project for diverting water from an international drainage basin into another such basin is hardly realizable without an agreement between all the basin States of both the basins concerned.

The *transfer* of water from one basin to another may be carried out by digging a new bed or canal between the two water systems. The legal nature of such a measure is not always easy to determine. An artificial link between two drainage basins, often crossing broad areas of land, can hardly be legally a part of either one of the basins it joins. The principle of equitable utilization, even if it concerns the basins, cannot be extended to cover the artificial waterway between them. Linking the basins may also raise the question of whether it would influence the international status of those watercourses. In other words, would it be possible to link together *legally* two international water systems or incorporate a watercourse under national jurisdiction with an international drainage basin? An affirmative answer to these questions would not correspond with the leading principles of the Helsinki Rules. An international drainage basin is not only a geographical entity: essentially and legally it is a water system of common interest, bound together by the notion of coherence. The legal composition of such a basin cannot be changed, nor the circle of its basin States extended simply by linking basins together (save in exceptional cases—for example for restoring historically established circumstances.[10]

The above-mentioned observations concern the applicability of the principle of equitable utilization with regard to the diversion of waters in

---

[10] It is not always self-evident how the limits of an international drainage basin should be drawn. This problem came up in connection with negotiations concerning the boundary-river treaty between Finland and Sweden. The river Tornio, which is part of an international drainage basin, is linked with the river Kalix in Sweden by a narrow canal made for floating timber many centuries ago. It was agreed that this kind of minor bifurcation could not change the status of the river Kalix as a watercourse under national jurisdiction.

general. In any particular case the application of the Helsinki Rules requires a careful consideration of all pertinent circumstances and relevant factors that must be taken into account in determining whether the undertaking constitutes a beneficial use in the sense of the provisions of the Rules and what in this case is a reasonable and equitable share (Article V). One essential factor to be taken into account in that determination concerns the territorial applicability of the principle of equitable utilization. Article IV of the Helsinki Rules prescribes that each basin State is entitled to the equitable and reasonable share in the beneficial uses of the waters of the basin *within its territory*. The wording of the Article may not be entirely unambiguous, but its meaning seems to be clear. The reference to the territory of the undertaking State proves that the principle of equitable utilization is not opposed to territorial jurisdiction.[11] On the other hand, it indicates that the right prescribed in this article does not include permission to carry out extraterritorial activities. However, that conclusion does not mean that application of the principle of equitable utilization would be excluded in cases of projects that required extraterritorial works or arrangements.

A distinction must be made between extraterritorial *measures* (such as construction of dams etc.) and *effects* beyond the boundaries of the undertaking State. The above-mentioned interpretation of Article IV refers, at least primarily, to extraterritorial measures, and leaves the question of extraterritorial effects without any definite answer. Such effects, although not necessarily injurious, are not uncommon in practice. Because a drainage basin reacts as a hydrological unit, a change in one part of it, caused by diversion, for example, may influence the water conditions in other parts of it. Injurious extraterritorial effects within the territories of other basin States may in some cases be covered by the principle of equitable utilization, and could become allowable through its application. But where conditions for such an application do not exist, the matter is not easy to settle. Obviously, general principles of law concerning the limits of the rights of the basin States to use the basin and its waters should be applied, but those principles are still contested and under development.[12]

Hydraulic works and installations needed for diverting or otherwise utilizing the waters of an international drainage basin must, for technical reasons, often be extended beyond the boundaries of the undertaking State. If there is no rule, treaty, or binding custom providing otherwise, all

[11] The conclusion that the principle of equitable utilization is not opposed to territorial jurisdiction (althoug it in a way 'softens' it) is not inconsistent with the principle of coherence. Coherence does not imply territorial unity; on the contrary, it presupposes that the basin is divided into areas under separate territorial jurisdiction.

[12] The Helsinki Rules do not contain any specific provisions defining the legal limits of the rights of basin States to use the basin and its waters; and consequently there is in the Rules no direct prohibition concerning injurious activities other than pollution. A rule prescribing the said limits was however, already in the ILA New York Resolution of 1958 (Agreed

questions connected with such measures should be regulated by agreement between the States concerned. The same might apply, *mutatis mutandis,* to undertakings giving rise to extraterritorial effects which exceed the above-mentioned limits of the rights of the basin States to use the basin and its waters. It must be observed that a basin State is not obliged to permit the other State to use its territory or to agree to any injurious activity. In order to come to an agreement, the basin States concerned must negotiate in order to reconcile their conflicting interests. The decisive question, however, is whether there exists an obligation to negotiate.

The international law of our time recognizes, and operates with, an obligation to negotiate. Starting with Article 33(1) of the United Nations Charter and the Declaration on Principles of International Law concerning Friendly Relations and Co-operation among States, there are numerous resolutions of international organizations, conventions, and treaties, all referring to an obligation to negotiate. The importance of negotiation as the most common, but still effective, procedure for settling disputes has been emphasized by eminent jurists, courts, and tribunals.[13] Obviously a majority of disputes are settled by negotiation. As to the law of international watercourses, the Institute of International Law in its 1961 Salzburg Resolution recommends that where objection is made to works or to utilization of the waters of a watercourse, the States should enter into negotiations with a view to reaching an agreement within a reasonable time.[14] In keeping with that recommendation, Article 30 of the Helsinki Rules prescribes that 'in case of a dispute between States as to their legal rights or other interests . . . they should seek a solution by negotiation.' Finally, it should be mentioned that the ILA Committee on International Water Resources Law has in its Report to the 1986 Seol Conference, dealt with problems connected with extraterritorial operations and works or installations within the territory of a co-basin State. The Committee recommends that 'the States concerned shall use their best endeavours with the view to reaching a just and reasonable arrangement in accordance with the principle of equitable utilization'. Although negotiations are not expressly mentioned in that recommendation, they must be regarded as an essential part of the 'best endeavours'.[15]

There is no doubt that the duty to negotiate should also concern

Recommendations, 1). A provision dealing with the same subject is included also in the 1961 Salzburg Resolution of the Institute of International Law. Further to be noted are Proposition 4 on the Law of International Rivers adopted in 1973 by the Asian–African Legal Consultative Committee and the Draft Articles contained in the reports of the International Law Commission on the Law of Non-navigational Uses of International Watercourses (Article 8 in the 1981 Report and Article 9 in the 1982 and 1983 Reports). See also the 1986 Report of the ILA Committee on International Water Resources Law (Complementary rules applicable to International Water Resources, Article I).

[13] Max Sörensen, *Manual of the Public International Law* (New York, 1968), 679.
[14] Articles 6 and 7.   [15] Draft Article II and comments.

extraterritorial works and installations needed for utilizing the waters of an international drainage basin. Moreover, the principle of equitable utilization seems to support that conclusion. As mentioned earlier, it is true that Article IV of the Helsinki Rules does not justify extraterritorial operations. On the other hand, neither the said Article nor the territorial jurisdiction of the basin States limits in other respects the implementation of the principle of equitable utilization. The principle is not merely a rule to be applied in case of disputes between neighbouring States, but rather an international legal order for regulating in a just and reasonable manner the uses of the waters of international drainage basins in their entirety. Because the Helsinki Rules do not contain any definite procedural norms concerning the implementation, in concrete cases, of the principle of equitable utilization, negotiations conducted with a view to reaching necessary agreements would often be the decisive factor.

The implementation of the principle of equitable utilization is often in practice not possible without affecting the territories of the neighbouring States. This is particularly true of measures necessary for utilizing boundary-rivers, where the boundary-line does not always divide the flow of water equally between the riparian States. A reasonable and equitable sharing of those waters therefore often requires an extension of dams or other installations over the boundary-line, or presupposes utilization of water resources within the territory of a neighbouring State.

It must be stressed that the above-mentioned situations are not rare exceptions. On the contrary, the necessity of using neighbouring territory and its water resources appears as an essential feature of equitable utilization. In this sense it may be said that there is an extraterritorial element, based upon both legal and physical considerations, in the right of the basin State to an equitable share in the beneficial uses of the waters of an international drainage basin. Recognition of that fact and a reciprocal understanding of the importance of neighbourly co-operation may facilitate the reaching of just and reasonable agreements in accordance with the principle of equitable utilization.

6

Global Satellite Telecommunications: The End of a Dream?

by PROFESSOR NICOLAS MATEESCO MATTE, OC, QC, FRSC

INTRODUCTION

In these times of international uncertainty and concern over the future of mankind, co-operation between peoples is more essential than ever before. Two areas of activity, among others, have contributed to such co-operation: international organizations and telecommunications. The former have provided a forum in which co-operation can and must be effected; whereas the latter, especially in the light of technological advances, has provided a means of facilitating it. The International Telecommunications Organization (INTELSAT) contributes significantly to international co-operation in both regards.

INTELSAT was created with the idea that satellite communications should be available to the nations of the world, as soon as practicable, on a global and non-discriminatory basis.[1]

The outcome of long and complicated negotiations, INTELSAT has accomplished this goal, and, in the process, has shown that States can learn to put aside their differences and consider their collective actions in the light of mutual trust and interest. Also, having successfully created a global telecommunications network, it has become an important tool for achieving mutual understanding among States.

Neither the development of telecommunications technology nor the interests of States have remained static since the founding of INTELSAT. Recently, however, increasing pressures threatened its successful management of international telecommunications, pressures that come from competing international networks—this mainly the consequence of United States policies towards deregulation and privatization—and from competing technologies, such as fibre-optic cables. This essay will examine the threat to INTELSAT and its goal of harmonizing international satellite telecommunciations.

---

[1] Preamble, Agreement Relating to the International Telecommunications Satellite Organization 'INTELSAT' 23: 4 *UST* 3813 (1972) (The INTELSAT Convention).

INTELSAT—THE DREAM

Satellite communications had its beginnings in 1962, when Telstar was launched, thus bringing to reality a device proposed two decades earlier by Arthur C. Clarke as an 'Extraterrestrial Relay'.[2] The communications satellite was recognized from the outset of the space age as a force in international telecommunications, providing, economically, the capacity to meet current and future demands for this service.[3] The challenge was to establish a global network that would be both effective and accessible.

President Kennedy, in a February 1962 letter to the United States Congress, proposed the legislative creation of a new Communications Satellite Corporation (COMSAT). In that letter the objectives of COMSAT were stated as including:

... the assurance of global coverage; co-operation with other countries; expeditious development of an operational system; the provision of service to economically less developed countries as well as industrialised countries.[4]

At that time the United States was the only state in the world capable of providing the satellites for such a system, and this initiative comprised a scarcely veiled implication that the United States would unilaterally create a global telecommunications network.[5] Many nations became concerned at this prospect, perceiving threats to existing international telecommunications links. There was an intense fear, for example, that if the United States had control of the satellite system, auxiliary equipment compatible with that system would also be American, thus endangering the telecommunications equipment industries of other states. At the same time the Americans would, of course, require the co-operation of other States to effectuate their system, for communication needs a receiver as much as a broadcaster. These factors precipitated the first inter-governmental discussions on creating a world communications network, in October 1962. Talks took place primarily between the Americans and the Europeans, but there was also broader international interest. This interest was expressed in the form of United Nations Resolution 1721, which stated that 'communications by means of satellites should be available to the nations of the world as soon as practicable on a global and non-discriminatory basis'.[6] It became apparent that some form of international organization was needed that could set up this network while at the same time satisfying political demands and needs, both national and international.

---

[2] See *Wireless World* (Oct. 1945); cited in A. C. Clark, 'Voices from the Sky', in *The INTELSAT Global Satellite System,* Progress in Astronautics and Aeronautics, 93 (New York, 1984), 8.

[3] See D. Wilson, 'Space Business: The History of INTELSAT' in *The Year Book of World Affairs 1971* New York, Praeger), 72, 72–7

[4] Published in London by USIS as A-17401-AC (7 Feb.1962); cited in *Year Book 1971*, p.75.

[5] *Ibid.* 5.

[6] United Nations General Assembly, Resolution 1721 (XIV), 3 Jan. 1962.

The stage was now set for formal negotiations to create a global satellite telecommunications network, and they began in Rome in February 1964. Participation by States representing nearly 80 per cent of international communications traffic went a long way towards assuring that any resulting agreement would be both economically and politically viable. As a result, on 20 August, 1964, interim arrangements were adopted for the establishment and operation of a global commercial satellite communications network. These arrangements were formalized in two interrelated agreements: the Interim Agreement signed by States and a Special Agreement signed by governments or their designated telecommunications entities, public or private.[7] Thus INTELSAT was born.

The interim arrangements established and operated—on a commercial basis, a single global satellite telecommunications network, which involved applying and developing the most advanced communications satellite technology. A four-year interim period of operation was established because of the uncertainty and immaturity of the satellite technology with which the network operated. It was clear, however, that if the technology were to prove itself, the interim agreements could be renegotiated to reach a more permanent arrangement.

The product of long and complicated negotiations during three plenipotentiary conferences in 1969, 1970, and 1971, definitive arrangements superseded the interim ones on 12 February, 1973.[8] Again, two documents constitute the agreement: An Agreement Relating to the International Telecommunications Organization (INTELSAT Convention) open for signature by States and an Operating Agreement Relating to the International Telecommunications Satellite Orgnization (Operating Agreement) open for signature by governments or a telecommunications entity designated by them.[9]

The prime objective of INTELSAT was to provide, on a commercial basis, the space segment required for international telecommunications services. These services must be of high quality and reliability, and must be available on a non-discriminatory basis world-wide.[10] Under specific circumstances INTELSAT also provides domestic services to States that

---

[7] Agreement Establishing Interim Arrangements for a Global Commercial Communications Satellite System and 'Special Agreement', 15: 2 UST 1705 (1964).

[8] For a detailed account of the different approaches taken for the negotiations of the INTELSAT definitive agreements, see P. D. Trooboff, 'INTELSAT, Approaches to the Renegotiation' (1968) 9 *Harv. Int J* 1

[9] INTELSAT Convention (*supra*, n. 1) and the Operating Agreement Relating to the International Telecommunications Satellite Organization 'INTELSAT' 23: 4 UST 4091 (1972).

[10] INTELSAT Convention, Article 3(a). It should be noted that, though the intention was to create a single global system, this goal was not accomplished from the outset because of Soviet bloc non-participation and insistence upon creating INTERSPUTNIK as a separate system.

have geographically separate territories,[11] and it may provide separate satellites or associated facilities for domestic, international, or special services as long as its own space segment for international service is not adversely affected.[12] INTELSAT thus has the scope and the legal power to operate a global network for telecommunications of all kinds.

It has been a particularly successful kind of international organization, unique at the time of its inception and clearly illustrating international co-operation.[13] In order to achieve an efficient communications network, certain compromises were reached by the international joint venturers in the organization. The result is that there are four organs to INTELSAT: the Assembly of Parties, the Meeting of Signatories, the Board of Governors, and the Executive, headed by the Director-general.

The Assembly of Parties, which meets every two years, is the principal organ, and is composed of all the member States party to the INTELSAT Agreement.[14] The member States each have one vote in decisions of the Assembly, and the Assembly has a mandate to oversee 'those aspects of INTELSAT which are primarily of interest to the Parties as sovereign states'. This includes INTELSAT's general policy and long-term objectives.[15] It allows all member States, including the small user states, to have significant input into INTELSAT's long-term policies and to protect their own interests. The powers of the Assembly are limited to those of recommendation only. In commercial matters, INTELSAT as a commercial enterprise, could not be allowed to have its objectives the target of political controversies. Thus, while the Assembly of Parties is the principal organ, it is not the supreme organ.

The Meeting of Signatories is composed of all the signatories, and each has one vote. It represents the member States at the participatory level through their telecommunications entities, whether public or private. Its functions and powers relate mainly to the major interests of the signatories as investors, the financial, technical, and operational aspects of INTELSAT.[16] All members have an equal opportunity to influence and participate in these important aspects of INTELSAT.

INTELSAT's principal managing organ is the Board of Governors. It is responsible for the design, development, construction, operation and

---

[11] This includes countries separated by territory under the jurisdiction of another state or by the high seas. See INTELSAT Convention, Article 3(e).

[12] *Ibid.*

[13] The International Maritime Satellite Organization (IMMARSAT) is now another such international body, successful enough to count among its members the USSR. For more detail on IMMARSAT, see N. M. Matte (*infra,* n. 18) 149 ff.

[14] INTELSAT Convention, Article 7(a).

[15] *Ibid.*, Article 7(b).

[16] *Ibid.*, Article 8(b). The Meeting of Signatories convenes ordinarily once each calendar year, but it may also convene extraordinarily (Article 7(d)).

maintenance of the INTELSAT space segment.[17] Consequently, it has extensive and far-reaching powers. This was the most difficult organ to negotiate definitive arrangements for providing equitable representation on the Board for the low investment signatories in all geographical areas. The resulting Board is one with three categories of governors and a weighted voting system.[18]

Each governor controls a number of votes, equal to the investment share of the signatory or group of signatories that he represents.[19] The investment share, determined annually, is based on how much a signatory utilizes the space segment, and thus the procedure encourages greater utilization of INTELSAT.[20]. It follows the commercial practice of allowing those with the greater investment to have the most influence, while the categories of governors give significant input to the 'minority shareholders'.

The fourth organ, the Executive, headed by a Director-general, handles the everyday management functions of INTELSAT, acting in accordance with the policies and directives of the Board.[21] Initially the United States signatory, COMSAT, provided this management function, but, since 1979, INTELSAT has done it with its own staff under the Director-general. This, too, illustrates successful international compromise, since the Americans entered the definitive agreement negotiations pressing hard for COMSAT as INTELSAT's manager.

INTELSAT, through its approach of international co-operation, has

---

[17] *Ibid.*, Article 10(a).
[18] *Ibid.*, Article 9(a), which reads as follows:

(a) The Board of Governors shall be composed of:

  (i) one Governor representing each Signatory whose invesment share is not less than the minimum investment share as determined in accordance with paragraph (b) of this Article;
  (ii) one Governor representing each group of any two or more Signatories not represented pursuant to subparagraph (i) of this paragraph whose combined investment share is not less than the minimum investment share as determined in accordance with paragraph (b) of this Article and which have agreed to be so represented;
  (iii) one Governor representing any group of at least five Signatories not represented pursuant to subparagraph (i) of (ii) of this paragraph from any one of the regions defined by the Plenipotentiary Conference of the International telecommunication Union, held at Montreux in 1965, regardless of the total number of Governors under this category shall not exceed two for any region defined by the Union or five for all such regions.

See also N. M. Matte, *Aerospace Law: Telecommunications Satellites* (Toronto, 1982), 118 and 257.

[19] INTELSAT Convention, Article 9. The Board meets as often as necessary, but at least four times a year.

[20] *Ibid.*, Article 9(b).

[21] *Ibid.*, Article ii(b).

been highly successful; 110 signatories make up its membership.[22] The global satellite network it operates carries roughly two-thirds of the world's overseas telecommunications traffic, using state-of-the art satellites of the INTELSAT V and VA series. Telephone, telegraph, telex, television, data, and facsimile services are provided to 170 countries, territories, and possessions, and recent trends find INTELSAT moving into more specialized business services.[23]

Contributing also to INTELSAT's success has been its monopoly position for delivering international satellite telecommunication to the participating States. By the Convention, the member States may only establish, acquire, or utilize other space segment facilities if those facilities are technically compatible[24] with INTELSAT's, and regional systems can be approved only if no 'significant economic harm' will result to INTELSAT.[25] The Board of Governors is charged with evaluating such competition, making recommendations regarding compatability, and further regarding the assurance that 'such facilities shall not prejudice the establishment of direct telecommunication links through the INTELSAT space segment among all the participants.'[26]

Through the international co-operation of its members, INTELSAT is about to achieve the goal of an effective and economical global telecommunications network. The final aim may be imperilled, as mentioned, by recent moves towards deregulation and privatization in international telecommunications and by competing technologies.

THE THREAT

The dream of a universal telecommunications network accessible on a non-discriminatory basis is threatened by two sources of competition. The first source of threat—and the one with the highest profile—is the move by the United States towards the establishment by private corporations of international satellite telecommunications services. The second source—potentially the one that can do the most long-term harm—is the advance of telecommunications cable technology into fibre optics.

---

[22] See *INTELSAT News*, 1/1 (1985) 5.

[23] *Ibid.*; see also R. R. Colino, 'A Chronicle of Police and Procedure: The Formation of the Reagan Administration Policy on International Satellite Telecommunications', (1985) 13 Journal of Space Law, 103, 106.

[24] INTELSAT Convention, Article 14(c). The importance of technical co-ordination for the functioning of a communications satellite system cannot be overstressed. It is the nature of electromagnetic radiation that signals carried on near frequencies interfere with each other if they coincide and thus abrogate their usefulness and economic harm results.

[25] INTELSAT Convention, Article 14(d).

[26] *Ibid.*

The threat to INTELSAT from private satellite networks is that it challenges the INTELSAT monopoly, which is seen to be important to its success. This threat, however, is just the latest of a number of incursions into this monopoly. Potentially competitive satellite systems have always had to be considered in the execution of the INTELSAT objectives. The INTELSAT Convention specifically addresses the issue. It makes provision for co-ordination but does not ban alternate systems.[27] As a result, domestic, regional, and specialized satellite networks have been established that cannot help but compete with INTELSAT.

At the time of the negotiation of the definitive INTELSAT Agreements, there was pressure to limit regional satellite systems, especially those that could eventually become competitive. This was one of the basic aims of the United States,[28] but the concurrent development of domestic, privately owned satellites within the United States weakened the American position against regionals, and the present compromise form of the Convention came into being.

Now, regional systems exist. Some, like the European Communications Satellite (EUTELSAT) system, were approved under the Article 14(d) co-ordination provisions, because it carries traffic that would otherwise be transmitted via terrestrial means[29] and clearly pose no threat of significant harm. Others, such as ARABSAT and PALAPA were also approved and were held not be of significant harm to INTELSAT,[30] even though the INTELSAT network could have been utilized. These periodic approvals result from the lack of a definition of 'economic harm' in the INTELSAT Agreement. Thus, the existence of potentially competing regional networks has set a precedent against the maintenance of the INTELSAT monopoly.

This precedent has been further entrenched with the establishment of a global specialized service satellite network, namely the International Maritime Satellite Organization (INMARSAT).[31] When the idea of

---

[27] *Ibid.*, Article 14(c), (d), and (e).

[28] Wilson (*supra*, n. 3), 84.

[29] The Interim EUTELSAT Agreement was signed 13 May, 1977, creating a separate intra-European satellite system operated on a commercial basis. Its general structure is similar to that of INTELSAT. The Agreement became definitive 1 Sept. 1985, when the ratification of France became effective. See N. M. Matte (*supra*, n. 18), 155–7.

[30] ARABSAT was brought into being by an April 1976 Agreement between the member States of the Arab League, with the purpose of providing a communications network for the fulfilment on the Arab League Charter. For the text of the ARABSAT agreement see N. Jasentuliyana and R. S. K. Lee (eds.), *Manual of Space Law*, 1979. II. 345. ff. The political nature of the creation of the ARABSAT system eased its passage through co-ordination procedures where it was found not to cause 'significant economic harm' to INTELSAT, despite the fact that its functions could have been carried out through INTELSAT. For further detail see Matte, (*supra*, n. 18), 157 ff.

[31] Founded by the Convention on the International Maritime Satellite Organization 'INMARSAT', 31: 1 UST 1 (1979) (The INMARSAT Convention).

maritime services was initially conceived, COMSAT staked a claim for INTELSAT in the field, asserting that it was the only international organization expressly granted authority to provide the space segment capacity for such a service. This position met with opposition, from a number of States that preferred a separate system, devoted to maritime services.[32] Due to a number of factors, which are beyond the scope of this essay—the separate system prevailed and in July of 1979, INMARSAT came into being.[33] The ramifications for INTELSAT are that limitations have been put on the scope of its own communications services, and the field of specialized satellite services has been open to separate networks. On the other hand, the emergence of INMARSAT, an international telecommunications organization patterned closely on INTELSAT and including the USSR, something yet to happen in INTELSAT, cannot but bode well for the continued internationalization of telecommunications.

While these regional and specialized networks constituted exceptions to INTELSAT's perceived role as the provider of international telecommunications 'No overt "challenge" to the exclusive role of INTELSAT for long distance international, trans-oceanic and intercontinental purposes had emerged until 1983.'[34]

In 1983 all this changed. Orion Satellite Corporation (Orion) filed before the United States Federal Communications Commission (FCC) an application which proposed the establishment of a communications satellite network separate from INTELSAT and authorized to provide international services to Europe.[35] This application was followed closely by three others proposing transatlantic services[36] and one by the Pan American Satellite Corporation (PANAMSAT) for a system to provide, *inter alia,* services between the United States and countries in Latin America.[37] Spawned in the atmosphere of deregulation currently existing in the United States, these applications found the FCC predisposed to act favourably towards them. This touched off a domestic debate between those who favour deregulatory objectives and those concerned with the consequences any tampering would have on the successful international institution INTELSAT.

[32] S. A. Levy, 'INTELSAT: Technology, Politics and the Transformation of a Regime' (1975) 29 *International Organization* 678.

[33] See Matte, *supra,* n. 18, 107 ff.

[34] See Colino, *supra,* n. 23.

[35] Application of Orion Satellite Corporation, File No. CSS-83-002-P, 11 Mar. 1983.

[36] International Satellite, Inc. (ISI), File No. CSS-83-004-P (LA); RCA American Communications, Inc. (RCA Americom), File No. I-T-C-84-085; Cygnus Satellite Company (Cygnus), File No. CSS-84-002-P (LA).

[37] File No. CSS-84-004-P(LA). Intended to provide domestic service in various Latin American countries, and service between New York and Miami and Latin America, it may also have 'incidental' transatlantic service to Spain.

Global Satellite Communications

Adding fuel to this debate, the executive branch of the United States Government modified its long-held view of the position INTELSAT should hold in international telecommunications. President Reagan announced on 28 November 1984: 'I hereby determine that separate international communications satellite systems are required in the national interest. The United States . . . shall consult with INTELSAT regarding such separate systems as are authorised by the Federal Communications Commission.[38]

The FCC reached a decision on separate systems on 25 July, 1985 when it authorized three pending applications for private international telecommunications networks[39] on the grounds of the public interest standard of the Communications Act of 1934.[40] Regarding the impact of such networks on INTELSAT, the FCC stated that 'limited injection of satellite facilities competition into international communications should bring to the world some of the dynamism that characterizes the U.S. domestic data processing telecommunications sector.[41]

INTELSAT perceives that the threat presented by separate communications satellite networks is that they may increase costs to users of INTELSAT by reducing the revenues it receives from the lucrative transatlantic market; this, in turn, could impede non-discriminatory access to INTELSAT, making costs to developing countries prohibitive. INTELSAT also fears that the separate systems could derogate from its global network and leave it a thin-route system.[42]

From the time of the initial Orion application to the FCC, INTELSAT and member States have expressed their concerns over the impact of the shift in American policy allowing separate international communication satellite systems. In April 1983, the then Director-general of INTELSAT, Santiago Astrain, warned that favourable United States action on the Orion application could open the floodgates, and result in a proliferation of such systems that would undermine INTELSAT's single global network.[43] This set the tone for INTELSAT's attitude, which found further expression in decisions of the Assembly of Parties and the Meeting of Signatories.

---

[38] Presidential Determination No. 85-2, 28 Nov. 1984, (1984) 49 *Federal Regulations* 46987.

[39] At this time conditional authorizations were granted to ISI, PANAMSAT, and RCA Americom. Action on the Cygnus and Orion applciations was deferred, and action on the recently presented Financial Satellite Corporation (FINANSAT) applciation was to be considered at a later date, but see *infra*, n. 47 and accompanying text.

[40] 47 USCA, ch. 5.

[41] See *FCC News*, 25 July, 1985: 'Commission Supports Presidential Determination that Alternative International Satellite Systems are in the National Interest (CC Docket 84-1299).' The Report and order were released 3 Sept. 1985; FCC 85-399.

[42] See Colino (*supra*, n. 34), 115; and Anon., 'Criticism of U.S. Separate Satellite Decision Rebutted' (Sept.–Oct. 1985) 6 *Chronicles of Int. Comm.* 3.

[43] Colino (*supra*, n. 34), 113.

In October 1983, the Assembly unanimously adopted a decision which, *inter alia*, urged all parties to ensure that their INTELSAT commitments were fulfilled and to reaffirm the importance of the parties being willing to refrain from actions that would jeopardize the INTELSAT system.[44] The fourteenth Meeting of Signatories, in April 1984, went even further and voted unanimously to urge all INTELSAT Signatories to refrain from entering into any arrangements which may lead to the establishment and subsequent use of [separate systems] to carry traffic to or from their respective countries.[45] The Assembly reiterated its concerns at its January 1985 meeting, by reaffirming the resolutions of the previous Assembly and the fourteenth Meeting of Signatories. It also urged all INTELSAT Parties to express their concerns to the United States Government.[46]

The United States Administration is proceeding with its policy of separate international communications systems, albeit within certain limits. To date, six companies have been given tentative authorizations by the FCC for separate systems.[47] In authorizing these companies, the FCC set out restrictions aimed at protecting INTELSAT, most of whose business comes from full-time international voice services. United States operators are limited to the provisions of private-line international services through the sale of long-term lease of transponders. They are also prohibited from any interconnection with public-switched message systems.[48]

In April of 1986, the FCC reaffirmed its endorsement of separate networks and modified its initial guide-lines and restrictions. The systems are now allowed to provide occasional-use television service under long-term contracts and to ancillary domestic communications service. More restrictively, the FCC has placed a one-year limitation on conditional grants, which means that the companies will have to act quickly in establishing their networks.[49]

Of the six companies that have so far received authorization one (RCA) has since dropped plans to launch a system. Four others, all with plans for trans-atlantic service, are proceeding, but have yet to establish authorization on the other side of the Atlantic. The sixth, PANAMSAT, while not without difficulties, is moving towards an operational system serving parts of Latin America. Negotiations continue with investors so that FCC financial requirements may be met; contractual arrangements are being finalized for satellite construction and launch and the sale of transponders;

---

[44] INTELSAT document AP-8-3, para 21.
[45] INTELSAT document MS-14-3, para. 22.
[46] INTELSAT documents AP-9-4, paras. 106, 107, and AP-9-3, para. 13.
[47] Orion, ISI, Cygnus, RCA Americom, Finansat, and PANAMSAT.
[48] FCC Report 85-399, 1985.
[49] 'FCC: Still Supporting Separate Systems' (May 1986), *Satellite Communications* 10.

and the United States and Peruvian governments are submitting a formal consultation request to INTELSAT.[50]

The threat to INTELSAT from separate satellite communications networks, private or otherwise, must be placed in perspective. While many of INTELSAT's fears are well founded, they are subject to mitigating circumstances. These fears represent the 'worst case' scenario, and the mere recognition of the potential harm has set in motion actions that will reduce any such harm.

The enthusiasm of the FCC for separate systems has been tempered by limitations on the type and scope of services which separate system operators can provide. The FCC and all their applicants urge that the services to be provided compete only minimally with INTELSAT's most lucrative ones (international voice telecommunications) and pose no threat to it. INTELSAT, which intends to move into some of these service markets, sees the competition as a threat to its provision of specialized services through its global network; but, as previously pointed out, INTELSAT's exclusive rights to provide such services have already been abrogated by the formation of INMARSAT.

The economic factors certainly at the present time, favour INTELSAT. As stated recently by the Director-general of INTELSAT.

Satellite communications is far from a risk-free activity. It can be expected that potential sources of financing will require that potential system operators obtain, at a minimum, launch and initial operating insurance. [And in light of recent failures] it becomes very doubtful if insurance can be obtained, leaving organizations to self-insure.[51]

However, all the economic problems INTELSAT forecasts for its own services will apply equally to the separate systems, and there is currently a surplus of transponder space available on the transatlantic route. INTELSAT is thus able to price competitively any new services it wishes to provide, at the same time, separate networks are entering a 'soft' market against a well-established, both in hardware and reputation, competitor.

There is also the question of co-ordination with INTELSAT.[53] As evidenced by the PANAMSAT bid to set up a separate system, there is a concerted effort on the part of these potential operators to effectuate co-ordination. In the end, however, separate systems must make arrange-

---

[50] The United States and Peruvian governments submitted a formal request for consultation under Article 14 of the INTELSAT Convention on 16 May, 1986, [for] the use of five transponders on PANAMSAT's proposed private international satellite system. See (19 May, 1986) 52(20) *Telecommunications Reports* 43.
[51] Colino (*supra*, n. 34), 154.
[52] See *infra*, n. 55.
[53] INTELSAT Convention, Article 14(d).

ments with governments outside the United States and the views of those States on the INTELSAT co-ordination procedure and the advisability of separate systems will determine the answer to this question.[54]

The second source of threat to the single global INTELSAT network—one that has for several decades co-existed well with INTELSAT—is the undersea cable network and, specifically, its advance into fibre-optic transmission cables. A new generation of fibre-optic submarine cables is expected to become operational beginning in 1988. TAT-8, co-financed by American and European telecommunications entities,[55] will, initially, provide for the translatlantic route, with a capacity equivalent to 40,000 voice circuits. Fibre-optic cables have the potential of providing efficient, reliable, and versatile communication routes. There is every reason to believe that fibre-optic technology, now in its infancy, will provide more and more capacity and that the number of cables laid will multiply.

Possessing a number of advantages over satellites as conduits for information—such as longer service life, comparative ease of repair, and potentially superior transmission quality—fibre-optic cables represent a significant element of competition to INTELSAT in all areas of service it provides. INTELSAT and its United States signatory have both acknowledged fibre-optic cable to be the principal threat in the future; but, as compared with efforts to curb separate system activities, little has yet been done to meet the threat—though some of INTELSAT's pricing policy[56] to meet separate system competition will be helpful when facing cable competition.

In attempting to meet the potential threat of fibre-optic cable, INTELSAT lacks one of its best weapons: there are no obligations on INTELSAT member States or signatories to co-ordinate cable systems with INTELSAT. Thus, INTELSAT has no internal power to limit this form of competition. To face the threat, it will have to compete directly, pricing its services to meet market demands.

CONCLUSION

From its inception in 1964 (consolidated by definitive agreements in 1974), INTELSAT has been extremely successful. A strong international orga-

---

[54] For detail on the European stance against balkanization by the introduction of separate systems, see Caruso, A., *Dérégulation et dérèglement dans les télécommunications par satellite: y a-t-il une différence?*, 6 *Journées internationales de l'IDATE*, (Montpellier, 24–26 Oct. 1984).

[55] See application of AT&T, FCC File No. I-T-C-84-072, S-C-L-84-001 (6 Feb., 1984), 20. An agreement was signed in May 1986 for a ninth transatlantic fibre-optic digital cable, TAT-9. See 52 (21) *Telecommunications Reporter* (1986) 21.

[56] INTELSAT is moving to restructure its pricing. For example, at the 62nd Board meeting in April 1985, it approved a 15 per cent reduction for full-time television leases. See 51 (14) *Telecommunications Reporter* (1985) 44.

nization has come into being, founded on the principles of international co-operation and the common heritage of mankind, as well as on a sound commercial principle. It has been able to provide, on a non-discriminatory basis, a dependable communications link world-wide. Moreover, it has been a vital factor in the transfer of communications technology. Most of INTELSAT's goals have been achieved, the principal exception being that a single global system is not in existence (INTERSPUTNIK being an example of an alternative system). INTELSAT does however, enjoy a near monopoly, in international satellite telecommunications; one that has had only recently, to meet the threat of competition.

As we have seen the threat to INTELSAT's continued successful commercial achievements comes from two sources. The first is competing separate international satellite systems, particularly privately (and for the most part United States) owned ones. These private separate networks have been proposed to enter the most lucrative markets, especially the transatlantic one. INTELSAT perceives this threat as harmful economically to itself because revenues lost from the transatlantic services would adversely affect user costs in less well used services, jeopardizing the non-discriminatory provision of services. The fledgling private satellite network operators argue that they are merely filling a gap in current services and are thus not detrimental to INTELSAT. On the contrary they claim that any competition they offer INTELSAT can only be good for it.

Separate systems are not a new phenomenon. Several regional networks, PALAPA, ARABSAT, EUTELSAT, are extant. Indeed, despite INTELSAT's stated goal of a single global system, its constitutive agreements sanction such competing networks, if they are compatible with INTELSAT. The existence of these separate networks establishes a precedent for co-existence with INTELSAT. Furthermore, the creation of INMARSAT to handle specialized maritime telecommunications globally indicates that INTELSAT has little claim to a monopoly over all types of satellite communications services, leaving the door open for other competing systems.

The second threat, and, for the future, clearly the greater of the two, comes from the development of fibre-optic telecommunications cables. This new technology has the potential of being better than satellites for carrying international communications traffic, and may tip the economic balance currently established between cable and satellite services. Fibre-optic cable will be used on the transatlantic route, presenting the same economic threat as private satellite systems. The difference, however, is that, in this case, INTELSAT will have to meet the competition head on. This is because the constitutive agreements of INTELSAT do not give it power to seek co-ordination with cable networks.

INTELSAT's reactions to these threats have been immediate, though directed for the most part at the separate satellite systems. To meet this perceived threat, the INTELSAT assembly has adopted resolutions urging the member States to refrain from making arrangements which would allow the establishment of separate systems. The organization is also actively opposing private initiatives in the United States, contesting them through national regulatory procedures. However, six such systems have been authorized by the FCC. Furthermore, the real challenge seems more likely to come from fibre-optic cable, and the competitive adjustments that INTELSAT is reluctant to adopt with respect to separate satellite systems may be the best way to maintain the goals of the organization.

The current trends to balkanization and deregulation in the world, which pose a threat to INTELSAT, will not, in the face of its impressive record of co-operation, diminish this organization, at least in the short term.

The real issue, however, is the effect that the threat has had, and will have, on INTELSAT's aim of a single global satellite telecommunications system. The Soviet bloc represents the only major hold-out from a truly global system and its inclusion would go a long way towards the INTELSAT dream. This is not out of the question: Soviet participation in INMARSAT may indicate a willingness on their part to be included in INTELSAT, much as the Soviet Union came to join the International Civil Aviation Organization in 1968, thus recognizing its usefulness in an important field of activity.

All that is lacking is political will, although that too seems to be increasing, as the beneficial economic results of INTELSAT activities appear more favourable each year.[57] Inclusion of the Soviet bloc, while a necessary step, will not, however, overcome the precedents already established with regard to regional separate systems and separate specialized networks. Thus, the new private systems, as long as they are economically and politically viable, will be there along with separate fibre-optic cable networks. INTELSAT will have to meet this challenge, but through its co-operative resources moving towards a more balanced international co-operation.

In aiming at assuming global telecommunications, while becoming by far the largest and most successful international organization in this field, INTELSAT did not succeed in its goal of being the only such system. Will decentralized regional or national ventures, assisted by the deregulation movement encouraged mainly by the United States Administration and by new technologies, put an end to the dream of benefits for mankind that INTELSAT's world-wide activities have already provided, and will continue to provide, in the future?

[57] See Matte (*supra*, n. 18), 144–5.

The answer is premature. It depends on competitive factors whose usefulness and magnitude remain to be proven. Yet, in the years to come, INTELSAT will remain an example of success as an international organization based upon a co-operative spirit and a new form of commercial venture. Its impressive achievements are due to the bold and practical way in which States' sensibilities and proclaimed fundamental principles, such as absolute sovereignty, *de facto* equality, and independence, have been reconsidered, readjusted and limited, in order to achieve a new breed of international co-operation, where the equitable sharing in benefits was facilitated by introducing a new form of co-participation and decisions, through a weighted vote and three-tiered co-ordination. Next to the ITU, whose venerable existence has been the result of *nécessité fait loi*, INTELSAT's continued experience represents an important force for continued excellent services, and, even more, a very rewarding example of new international rules, reflecting technological and economic progress and, as such, of political desire to promote worldwide development and peace.

7

Lord Wilberforce and International Law

by PROFESSOR CECIL J. OLMSTEAD

The influence of Lord Wilberforce on the development of the law generally has been constructive and strong indeed, although the full impact of his accomplishments will be determined only in years to come. His opinions have touched all areas of the law, from family law to international law. In the area of international law, public and private, opinions of Lord Wilberforce range from the effect in foreign jurisdictions of the laws of unrecognized states, to sovereign or state immunity and the applicability of the act of state doctrine. This article reviews and comments on selected Wilberforce opinions in the area of international law with emphasis on those dealing with jurisdiction, sovereign immunity and the act of state doctrine.

EFFECT OF LAWS OF UNRECOGNIZED STATES

An interesting judgement by Lord Wilberforce rather early in his tenure as Lord of Appeal in Ordinary was rendered in the case of *Carl-Zeiss-Stiftung v. Rayner & Keeler Limited and Others*.[1] From the international law perspective, the question presented involved the effect, if any, to be accorded a legislative act of an unrecognized government. The facts pertinent to this issue were that the *Stiftung* had been established in Jena, Germany, in 1891 and had since carried on its operations under the law and regulation of the authority in effective control of the geographic area in which Jena was situated. In July 1945, the Soviet Union took over from the United States the occupation of East Germany, including the province of Thuringia, where Jena was located. Despite the change of occupying power, the local administrative authority continued. In 1952, the government of East Germany passed a law dividing Thuringia into three districts, one of which, Gera, included Jena. As a result, a new body, the Council of Gera, assumed administrative authority in the area, including the administration of Carl-Zeiss-Stiftung. Subsequently, a proceeding was brought in the United Kingdom in the name of the Stiftung, which purported to act on the authority of the Council of Gera. Respondents

[1] [1967] AC 853 (HL).

contended that this Council relied for its creation upon a legislative act of the government of East Germany, unrecognized by the British government, so that any authority of the Council to proceed in a British court was a nullity.

Interestingly, Lord Wilberforce, through what might be termed an indirect rather than a direct route, gave effect to the legislative act of the East German government establishing the Council of Gera to the extent of permitting the Stiftung to maintain the action. Instead of approaching the issue directly by deciding what effect might be given to the law of the East German government, he reasoned that the British government considered the Soviet Union to be the *de jure* governing authority in that part of Germany where Jena was located and that the law establishing the Council of Gera was effective because it had been adopted by a government acting under the effective control and authority of the Soviet Union. Thus, by viewing this law as the legislative act of the Soviet Union, Lord Wilberforce was able to conclude that the East German Zeiss entity was authorized to proceed in its action in the British court.

Lord Wilberforce made reference to the US doctrine whereby courts in the United States generally will give effect to acts of a regime unrecognized as the government of a state, if those acts apply within the territory under control of that regime and relate only to domestic matters.[2] Not withstanding the absence of this practice under English law, Lord Wilberforce observed that neither did English law absolutely preclude giving effect to acts of unrecognized regimes in all cases. Finding it unnecessary to invoke such a doctrine to resolve the case, he suggested that it should be viewed as an open question in the future.[3] It seems clear that at the time of the events under consideration in the *Carl-Zeiss-Stiftung* case, the regime of East Germany failed to meet the minimum criteria for recognition as a government since it was not in effective control of the territory and population where it was located.[4] Moreover, Her Majesty's

---

[2] *See Restatement (Second) of Foreign Relations Law,* § 110 (1965); *Restatement of Foreign Relations Law* (Rev.), § 205, Tent. Final Draft (15 July 1985). Thus, United States courts have not automatically treated the acts of unrecognized regimes as a nullity. For example, in *Salimoff* v *Standard Oil Co.,* 262 NY 220 (Ct. App. 1963), the court held that a nationalization decree of the Soviet Union (recognized as a *de facto* government) was effective to pass title to property that was located in the Soviet Union at the time the decree was issued, although the property was later sold to United States corporations. The court in *Danivnas* v *Simutis,* 481 F. Supp. 132 (SDNY 1987) made a distinction between the kinds of acts of an unrecognized sovereign that will be given effect (private acts) and those that will not be (political acts). The litigation involved claims to a decedent's estate. The court gave effect to the 'certificate of right to inherit' issued by Lithuania and approved by an official of the Soviet Union, to the extent that it determined the rights of Lithuanian citizens. It refused to hold that the certificate was determinative of the rights of all heirs because to do so 'would approach, if not actually reach, a political act, since it would affect persons and property located in countries other than Lithuania' (481 F. Supp. at 135).

[3] [1967] AC at 954.

[4] The United States has adhered to the generally accepted principle in international law

Government had indicated to the courts that it did not recognize the East German entity either *de facto* or *de jure*. Clearly, the Soviet occupying forces were in effective control. In view of this lack of effective control by the East German authorities, it is doubtful that US courts would have given any effect to the legislative act of the East German Government.[5] Failure, however, to resolve the case by recognizing that East Germany had a legal system which was operative within the territory under Soviet occupation would have left in question resolution of the basic issue in the litigation, namely, how the Carl-Zeiss or the Zeiss trade name in the United Kingdom could be utilized. Thus, permitting the East German entity access to the courts provided the setting whereby the case was subsequently settled.[6]

A similar case arose in courts in the United States wherein the plaintiffs, the Carl-Zeiss-Stiftung, located in the Federal Republic of Germany, brought a trademark infringement action against VEB Carl Zeiss Jena, located in East Germany.[7] The United States courts found that the West German entity was the legal successor to the original foundation established in Jena, and therefore it was entitled to the exclusive use of the trademarks.[8] Since the court found that plaintiff, the West German foundation, was the true owner of the trade name and trademark in question, it was unnecessary to consider the effect of the act of the unrecognized East German government even as to matters within the territory where it was located. Although the court stated the general US rule that '[n]ormally the acts of an unrecognized regime which pertain to its purely local, private and domestic affairs will be given effect', it found that

---

that before a revolutionary regime will be recognized as a legitimate government, the recognizing state must find that the unrecognized regime is 'in control of the territory and population of the state' or that it controls a substantial part of the territory and population and exhibits a reasonable likelihood of displacing the previous government *Restatement (Second) of Foreign Relations Law*, § 101 and comment a (1965). Similarly, the revised draft of the Restatement adopts the position that a State is required 'to treat as the government of another State a regime that is in effective control of that state', unless that control is obtained in violation of international law. Formal recognition is not mandated. Moreover, treating a regime as a government does not require according it the right to bring an action in United States courts. *Restatement of Foreign Relations Law* (Rev.), § 203 and comment b, Tent. Final Draft (15 July 1985).

[5] *See Carl Zeiss Stiffung v V.E.B. Carl Zeiss, Jena,* 293 F. Supp. 892, 912 (SDNY 1968), *modified*, 433 F. 2d 686 (2d Cir. 1970). 'As far as our Government has been concerned, sovereign power in East Germany has been exclusively exercised by the Soviet Union through its agency or instrumentality, the government of East Germany, which remains unrecognized by us as an independent state'.

[6] After further proceedings in English courts, the matter was settled between the parties, with the West German entity and/or East German entity using the Zeiss name in various countries. In the United Kingdom for example, both use the name, whereas in the United States only the West German entity has rights to the name.

[7] *Supra* n. 5   [8] 293 F. Supp. at 897; 433 F. 2d at 698.

the East German act would have effect beyond its borders and thus did not fall within the general rule.[9] In the case of the East German authority, it seems questionable whether the general rule would have been applied in any case, since it was a surrogate for the Soviet Union with no independent and effective control.

In subsequent proceedings in the English action, Mr. Justice Buckley is reported by the opinion in the US Court of Appeals to have interpreted the Wilberforce opinion only to have authorized the East German Carl-Zeiss-Stiftung 'to instruct solicitors and sue as a plaintiff...'[10]

Viewed in this light, there is no fundamental difference between the Wilberforce opinion and the US decisions. Both permitted the East German entity to appear in court; in the British as a party plaintiff and in the United States as an appellant.[11] It should also be noted that in the United States suits by corporations owned by an unrecognized government have been allowed[12] Although the proceedings in the United Kingdom and the United States appear to have reached desirable results, neither faced up to the basic underlying issue, namely, what effect should a court accord the act of an unrecognized government taken within its territory? Surely, the answer must be to give such acts effect where they affect persons, things, or transactions within such a government's territory. If the act purports to have extraterritorial effect, it should not be enforced unless it is consistent with the public policy and law of the forum.[13] Since international law is a part of the law of civilized states, acts of state carried out by an unrecognized government which are in violation of that law should not be shielded from judicial scrutiny even if the effects of such acts are limited to the territory in which it purports to govern.[14] Finally, as to the *Zeiss* case, it is doubtful that East Germany in 1952 met the basic requirements of

---

[9] 293 F. Supp. at 900-01.

[10] 433 F. 2d 686, 701. See *Carl-Zeiss-Stiftung* v. *Rayner & Keeler Limited and Others,* [1970] 1Ch. 506.

[11] But cf. *Russian Socialist Federated Soviet Republic* v. *Cibrario,* 235 NY 255, 139 NE 259 (1923) (only a recognized government may be a plaintiff in New York courts).

[12] See e.g. *The Maret,* 145 F 2d. 431, 439 (3d Cir. 1944). See, *Restatement of Foreign Relations Law* (Rev.) § 205 comment A, Tent. Final Draft (15 July 1985). But see *Federal Republic of German* v. *Elicofon,* 358F. Supp. 747, 757 (EDNY 1972), where an East German museum was denied leave to intervene since it was found to be an arm of the East German government.

[13] See *United States* v. *Belmont,* 301 US 324 (1937); *Banco Nacional de Cuba* v. *Chemical Bank,* 658 F. 2d 903, 908 (2d Cir. 1981). See also *Republic of Iraq* v. *First Nat. City Bank,* 3241 F. Supp. 567 (SDNY), *aff'd,* 353 F. 2d 47, 51 (2d Cir. 1965), *cert. denied,* 382 US 1027 (1966).

[14] Cf. Olmstead, 'Nationalization of Foreign Property Interests, Particularly Those Subject to Agreements with the State', 32 NYUL Rev. 1122, 1135-6 (1957), discussing a sovereign's obligation to perform its contracts with private persons, and noting that 'the concept of sovereignty originally did not have the extreme meaning or impact that has sometimes been attached to it in more recent eras'.

statehood: a government that exercises effective control over a defined territory and population, and the ability to conduct independent foreign relations.[15]

SOVEREIGN IMMUNITY

One of the most controversial cases which arose in the House of Lords during the period of Lord Wilberforce's service was that of *Marble Islands* v. *I Congreso del Partido,* involving a defence of sovereign immunity.[16] In September of 1973, actions were brought against the vessel, *I Congreso,* owned by the Republic of Cuba and found in the United Kingdom where she had been built. These actions were brought to secure payment of claims for two cargoes of sugar purchased from Cubazucar, a Cuban State trading entity, and allegedly converted by the Cuban State Shipping Agency, Mambisa.

The owners of the cargo, a Chilean company, claimed that following a *coup d'etat* in Chile in which a military government under General Pinochet took power, Mambisa refused, on instruction of the Cuban government, to deliver the sugar and indeed interrupted the delivery from one vessel, the *Playa Larga,* which was in progress in the port of Valparaiso, Chile. On further orders from the Cuban government, that vessel departed port and joined its sister ship, *Marble Islands,* at sea, which was carrying the other cargo. Subsequently, the *Playa Larga* returned to Cuba, where the remains of the cargo were sold and *Marble Islands* was arrested at the Panama Canal on application of the cargo owners. After breaking arrest, *Marble Islands* proceeded to Haiphong, North Vietnam, where the cargo was sold to another Cuban state enterprise and on instructions of the government donated to the people of North Vietnam as part of Cuba's assistance programme. During the Pacific voyage, the ownership and flag of this vessel were transferred to the government of Cuba, it having been owned formerly by a Liechtenstein coproration and having Somali registration.

The issue presented was whether these alledged conversions of the cargoes were governmental acts clothed with the defence of sovereign immunity, or commercial transactions which under the restrictive theory of immunity would not be immune. Since the operative facts took place before the United Kingdom State Immunity Act of 1978 entered into force, the issue was approached under customary international law.

---

[15] See *Restatement of Foreign Relations Law* (Rev.) § 201, Tent. Final Draft (15 July, 1985), which defines 'state' as follows: 'Under international law, a 'state' is an entity which has a defined territory and permanent population, under the control of its government, and which engages in, or has the capacity to engage in, formal relations with other such entities'.
[16] [1983] AC 244 (HL).

As to *Playa Larga,* there was full agreement among the Law Lords with Lord Wilberforce's opinion that the transaction was commercial in nature and that no defence of sovereign immunity would avail the defendants. While this result may appear almost axiomatic in 1987, following enactment of the British statute, it was by no means clear at the time of the decision that the Lords would overturn established precedent and adopt the restrictive theory of immunity. In adopting the general view that commercial transactions entered into by a state or its entity deprive it of immunity, Lord Wilberforce went to some length in explaining that the 'relevant act' giving rise to the claim must be of a commercial nature rather than of a governmental nature and that it must remain of that nature throughout the entire transaction. He rejected the notion that 'once a trader' initially in a transaction made the stae 'always a trader' throughout the transaction.[17] Thus, he reasoned that a state could initiate a transaction of a commercial nature, but take some subsequent action within the whole context of the transaction which would be governmental in nature.[18] As to the *Playa Larga,* Lord Wilberforce concluded that the actions taken by the Cuban government in interrupting the unloading of its cargo and instructing her to leave the Chilean port were not such governmental acts as to give rise to a defence of sovereign immunity, but rather were acts which a private seller could have taken. Interestingly, the motive for these acts was political in nature—dissatisfaction with the Pinochet government which had displaced by force a government favoured by Cuba.

The *Marble Islands* case presented the Lords with a more difficult question of differentiating between acts *jure imperii* and those *jure gestionis,* Indeed, the Lords divided on the characterizations of the Cuban government's acts after it purchased the vessel from its former owners. Lord Wilberforce took the view that, when the Cuban government directed the cargo to be donated to the people of North Vietnam, this constituted a sovereign act [19] for which a claim of sovereign immunity was proper to shield it from judicial proceedings. In other words, that act broke the continuity of commercial actions. Lord Diplock, speaking for a majority in the *Marble Islands* case, concluded that the Cuban government itself had treated the transaction of selling the cargo to another government entity as being a private law transaction not covered by a defense of sovereign immunity.[20]

These cases are of significance for at least two reasons. First, the *Playa Larga* case adopts the restrictive theory of sovereign immunity as a matter of general international law. This result and the reasoning underlying it will surely be persuasive with courts where legislation has not been enacted adopting the restrictive theory. Second, the opinions are of immense value

[17] *Ibid* at 263. [18] *Ibid.*
[19] *Ibid* at 271-2. [20] *Ibid.* at 274-5.

in dealing with the difficult issue of determining the distinction between commercial acts and government acts. While the Lords differed as to the characterization of Cuba's acts as commercial or governmental regarding the cargo on the *Marble Islands,* the approaches of all to the issue reflect a case-by-case consideration rather than the adoption of an inflexible formula which could lead to unforseeable results in difficult cases. On the other hand, the reasoning of Lord Wilberforce that the act of the Cuban government in transferring title of the cargo of sugar to another of its owned corporations and then donating it to the North Vietnamese people as being peculiarly governmental in nature seems questionable. Could not a private person have taken similar action if that person had been sympathetic to North Vietnam?

During the post-World War II decades, there has been a sea-change regarding the doctrine of sovereign immunity. The increasing entry of states or their entities into commercial activities has led to the realization that recognition of broad immunity in cases of governmental involvement in commercial transactions would be inequitable to private entities. Even with the changes, however, governments continue to enjoy advantages over those private entities with which they do business. For example, prejudgement attachment or other protective remedies arising out of commercial activities generally are not available in proceedings against a government, whereas a government would not be precluded from attaching assets of a private party.[21]. Also, certain types of governmental

---

[21] For example, the Foreign Sovereign Immunities Act of 1976 provides for exceptions to the general rule of immunity from attachment prior to entry of judgement only where the foreign State has explicitly waived its immunity or the attachment is for the purpose of securing satisfaction of a judgement that may be entered against the foreign State and is not being employed as a means of obtaining jurisdiction. 28 USC, § 1610 (d) (1) N(2) (1982). The Draft Articles for a Convention on State Immunity, as approved by the International Law Association at Montreal, expressly permit prejudgement attachment:

> In exceptional circumstances, a tribunal of the forum State may order interim measures against the property of a foreign State available under this convention for attachment, arrest, or execution, including pre-judgement attachment of assets and injunctive relief, if a party presents a *prima facie* case that such assets within the territorial limits of the foreign State may be removed, dissipated or otherwise dealt with by the foreign State before the tribunal renders judgement and there is a reasonable probability that such action will frustrate execution of any judgement.

(Article VIII (D).) Section 13 (2) (a) of the United Kingdom State Immunity Act would apparently preclude interim relief such as prejudgement attachment against a State. One commentator has observed what 'When the Bill was being debated in Parliament, Lord Wilberforce attempted, unsuccessfully, to secure passage of an amendment that would permit certain exceptions to the general rule of immunity from execution. Though he was concerned primarily with situations in which the entity sought to be enjoined was not a State, he expressed the view that 'the courts ought not to be deprived of the power to freeze assets in this country where there is a genuine and properly constituted dispute in which State may be involved' Crawford, 'Execution of Judgements and Sovereign Immunity', 75 Am. J. Int'l L. 820, 869 n. 251 (1981), quoting 389 Parl. Deb., HL (5th ser.), cols. 1935-8 (1978).

assets are immune from execution of a judgement whereas private assets are fully subject to execution.[22].

It should be the policy of the law to place a government which enters the commercial or business arena on the same plane of legal accountability as is a private party. Sovereign or State immunity is a vestige of an earlier historical era; it has no place in today's commercial world. The anomaly of the situation is that many of those governments which rely heavily upon the immunity doctrine are governments which today are different indeed in political and economic theory from those governments of the earlier era whose practice gave rise to the doctrine.

ACT OF STATE

In one of the most litigated cases in modern times, Lord Wilberforce, speaking for a unanimous Court, resolved the decade-long dispute between two American oil companies, Buttes Gas and Oil Company and Occidental Petroleum Corporation, regarding rights to an oil concession in the Arabian Gulf where a significant discovery had been made.[23] Buttes held a concession from the emirate of Sharjah, while Occidental held rights from the emirate of Umm al Qaiwan (UAQ). These two emirates and Iran each claimed that the site of the discovery, approximately nine miles from the island of Abu Musa, lay on the seabed underlying its territorial waters. Buttes's concession, issued in 1969, was based upon a decree of the Ruler of Sharjah made in September of that year extending Sharjah's territorial sea from three to twelve miles. Although Iran claimed territorial rights on the island of Abu Musa, Sharjah, UAQ, and the United Kingdom all recognized sovereignty of Sharjah over that island. Occidental's claim to the discovery area was based upon a map attached to its concession depicting the area as underlying UAQ territorial waters. Although Buttes denied any knowledge of Occidental's map, Occidental contended that the Sharjah decree was actually made in 1970 and fraudulently backdated, through collusion of Buttes and Sharjah, to a time prior to Occidental's concession so as to give Buttes the appearance of prior right in the area. The chief executive of Occidental made public that contention in a press conference in London in October of 1970, whereupon Buttes brought an action for slander against Occidental and its chief executive officer. The latter parties counterclaimed charging the plaintiff with a fraudulent conspiracy to cheat and defraud Occidental and to cause Her Majesty's Government to act unlawfully to injure Occidental. Buttes sought an order based upon the act of State doctrine that the court should not excercise jurisdiction because Occidental's counterclaim involved acts of Sharjah, UAQ, Iran, and the United Kingdom which it characterized as acts of State.

[22] *See* Foreign Sovereign Immunities Act of 1976, 28 USC, § 1611 (1982).
[23] *Buttes Gas & Oil Co v Hammer and Others*, [1982] AC 888 (HL).

After years of legal battle, in 1981 the case reached the House of Lords. This consideration of Lord Wilberforce's opinion in the matter will focus upon his treatment of the act of State doctrine, which he properly characterized as 'a generally confused topic'.[24] After rejecting Occidental's arguments as being beside the point that the Sharjah decree extending its territorial sea to twelve miles permitted re-examination on the ground that it was contrary to international law or public policy and that such a decree need be recognized only in the territory of the acting state, Lord Wilberforce turned to the fundamental issue in the dispute, 'whether . . . there exists in English law a more general principle that the courts will not adjudicate upon the transactions of foreign sovereign states'.[25] Significantly, he stated that he wished to avoid becoming embroiled in 'terminology' and thus to consider whether there is an applicable principle, not as some variety of 'act of state', but as 'one for judicial restraint or abstention'.[26]

Following a full review of English and American cases from *Blad* v *Bamfield* (1673-4) 3 (Swans. 602) through *Banco Nacional de Cuba* v. *Sabbatino*, 376 US 398 (1964), Lord Wilberforce concluded that the counterclaim of Occidental would put 'to trial non-justiciable issues'[27] since their resolution would involve consideration and adjudication respecting transactions or arrangements between sovereign States: Sharjah, UAQ, and the United Kingdom, as well as conduct and agreements with respect to Iran.[28]

Surely Lord Wilberforce's result was the correct one in the circumstances of this case. To have explored in the course of trial the delicate arrangements between the four sovereign States and then to have made determinations regarding them would have taken the Lords into areas where any decision on the merits could have led to quite unforeseeable consequences. For a moment, suppose that an English court had reached a decision as to which of the three Gulf States had jurisdiction over the area and thus authority to issue a concession. Would the other States have abided by that decision? Would Britain have sought to compel adherence to its decision? To speculate as to answers to such questions would be fraught with uncertainty.

On the other hand, extension of the 'act of State' doctrine is to be resisted. Indeed, its restriction is particularly to be desired in cases where the foreign act of state is in violation of international law or of an agreement with the State, or where the act would affect property outside the territory of the acting State.[29] Thus, it is helpful that the decision did

---

[24] Ibid at 930.   [25] *Ibid* at 931.   [26] *Ibid.*
[27] *Ibid* at 938. For recent treatment and discussions in US law, *see Restatement of Foreign Relations Law* (Rev.) § 469, Tent, Final Draft (15 July, 1985).
[28] *Ibid* at 937-8.
[29] See generally, Olmstead (*supra*, n. 14).

not rest squarely upon the act of state doctrine.[30] Utilization of the doctrine of *forum non conveniens* could have been a basis to dismiss these proceedings without risking extension of the act of state doctrine in subsequent cases.[31]

The courts of one State are not appropriate to determine boundaries between two or more foreign States. The determination of boundaries between adjacent or, indeed, opposite States is a highly sensitive matter. Determination is normally reached by agreement between the States concerned or by an international tribunal whose jurisdiction has been acknowledged by such States.

In the case of *Hesperides Hotels Limited* v. *Misftizade*,[32] involving a suit in England for conspiracy to procure acts of trespass in a foreign country, Lord Wilberforce pointed out that the doctrine of *forum non conveniens* was not fully developed in England.[33] The *Hesperides* case rested upon an alleged trespass to foreign land. He found a long-standing rule that English courts would not adjudicate a case based upon a trespass to foreign land. Because of the delicacy of the issues involved in determining such an issue, Lord Wilberforce concluded that any change in the rule should be by legislation, rather than by court decision.

Judicial development of the doctrine of *forum non conveniens*, however, as a basis for refusing to hear cases based upon foreign boundaries or foreign trespass would appear a proper function for the courts. In the United States and other common law countries, the doctrine is a product of common law development and provides courts with a basis for restraint which avoids application of 'confused' doctrines such as act of State.[34]

---

[30] See Reporters' Note 12 to *Restatement of Foreign Relations Law* (Rev.) § 469 (*supra* n. 28), where it is stated that 'the House of Lords decided in 1981 to adopt the American view of the act of state doctrine...' citing *Buttes Gas & Oil Co.* v. *Hammer*. This appears to be a misconstruction of Lord Wilberforce's rationale.

[31] English law has never embraced the doctrine of *forum non conveniens* as it is applied in the United States. See *infra*, n. 36. Lord Wilberforce made this quite clear in his opinion in *The Atlantic Star*, [1974] AC 436 (HL). He emphasized that the American doctrine constitutes a radical departure from the discretionary doctrine applied in Great Britain, which holds that it may be appropriate to stay the proceedings in some cases, but only where the defendant can establish that (1) the stay would not cause injustice to the plaintiff; and (2) the exercise of jurisdiction would be so unfairly prejudicial to the defendant as to the 'oppressive' and 'vexatious'.

[32] [1979] AC 474 (HL).

[33] *Ibid.* at 537. See *The Atlantic Star*, [1974] A.C. 436, and see *supra*, n. 32.

[34] As it developed in the United States as a doctrine of judicial discretion, the general rule is that a court will not exercise its jurisdiction 'if it is a seriously inconvenient forum for the trial of the action' and there is another, 'more appropriate forum available to the plaintiff' (*Restatement (Second) of Conflicts,* § 84 (1971). Thus, before dismissing the suit, the court will consider the plaintiff's right to decide where to bring suit and the availability of an alternative forum. The court will also take into account the public interests, such as administrative difficulties arising out of congested dockets, and whether in a given case it is more appropriate to have the case tried in a forum that will not be required to become involved in complex

The real mischief of the act of state doctrine lies in its recent extension to a vast range of cases where a foreign government has had some involvement. Lord Wilberforce is to be applauded for not invoking the act of State doctrine to dispose of *Buttes*. His formulation of a concept of judicial restraint to avoid an examination of government-to-government arrangements and agreements does not constitute an extension of the act of State doctrine, and because of the uniqueness of the facts and circumstances of *Buttes* may require at most only occasional application of such a concept.

As a policy consideration, it would be anomalous to adopt the restrictive doctrine of sovereign immunity if an extended doctrine of act of state were to become its successor.

EXTRATERRITORIALITY

Lord Wilberforce had occasion to consider a case involving an effort of a United States Court to obtain evidence and documents situated in the United Kingdom and to obtain testimony from persons in the United Kingdom, some of whom were citizens of that country, through deposition.[35] In a proceeding in the United States District Court for the Eastern District of Virginia, the defendant, Westinghouse, contended that because of 'commercial impracticability' occasioned by an alleged uranium producers' cartel it had been unable to supply uranium pursuant to its contracts with plaintiffs. In the Virginia proceedings, letters rogatory were addressed to the High Court of Justice in England which sought the examination of nine named persons, present or former directors and employees of the British companies, Rio Tinto Zinc and its services

---

conflicts of law questions. See Piper Aircraft Co. v. *Reyno*, 454 US 235 (1981); *Gulf Oil Corp. v. Gilbert*, 330 US 501, 508 (1947).

A case that perhaps best illustrates the application of the *forum non conveniens* doctrine in the context of international litigation is *In re Union Carbide Corp. Gas Plant Disaster at Bhopal, India in December, 1984*, 634 F. Supp. 842 (SDNY 1986). On a motion of the corporate owner, the US District Court for the Southern District of New York invoked the doctrine to dismiss the claims of thousands of Indians who had suffered injury as a result of a massive gas leak at a pesticide manufacturing plant in Bhopal, India. As a preliminary matter, the court observed that while a plaintiff's choice of forum is normally accorded great deference because it is assumed to be the most convenient, the presumption applied with 'less than maximum force' where foreign plaintiffs were suing in US courts (634 F. Supp. at 845). After a detailed analysis of the Indian legal system, the court concluded that there was available to the plaintiffs an adequate forum in India (*Ibid.* at 852). The court then balanced the private interests (such as ease of access to sources of proof and witnesses, and the ability of the jury to view the location of the accident) against the public interests (administrative difficulties and the probable application of Indian law). In its consideration of the public interests at stake, the court determined that the interests of India in the litigation were far more significant than those of the United States. On balance, both the public and private interests involved led the court to conclude that 'the Indian legal system is in a far better position than the American courts to determine the cause of the tragic event and thereby fix liability' (*Ibid.* at 866). On the grounds of *forum non conveniens*, the case was dismissed.

[35] *Rio Tinto Zinc v. Westinghouse* [1978] AC 547 (HL).

company, or such other director or other person knowledgeable of the facts as to the evidence sought. A lengthy schedule of documents alleged to be in Rio Tinto's possession was also sought. The Rio Tinto companies and seven of nine named persons appealed to the House of Lords to have the order giving effect to the letters rogatory set aside or discharged. Subsequently, the District Court in Virginia was advised by the US Department of Justice that the evidence of the witnesses was required for a grand jury investigating possible violations of US antitrust laws.

In concluding that effect should not be given to the letters rogatory, Lord Wilberforce carefully considered the jurisdictional aspects of the US effort to obtain testimony and evidence from British nationals located outside the United States respecting conduct which took place outside the United States. Having received an intervention from the British Attorney General to the effect that the US antitrust investigatory procedures undertaken in the United Kingdom against persons outside the United States who are not US citizens would infringe the jurisdiction and sovereignty of the United Kingdom, Lord Wilberforce found that while the United States sought to advance its public interest by enforcing its antitrust policy and law, the United Kingdom also had a public interest at stake, namely, assuring its sovereignty.[36] He pointed out that '[I]t is axiomatic that in antitrust matters the policy of one state may be to defend what it is the policy of another state to attack'.[37]

This case is another illustration of the conflict that has arisen over efforts of the United States to extend its jurisdiction to aliens located outside its territory and to conduct occuring outside its territory. *Rio Tinto* is a classic example of conduct occurring abroad which may have an effect in the territory of another State.[38] If a cartel had been found to exist and if its conduct had effects upon the US economy, then under the effects doctrine the United States would have been entitled to exercise its antitrust jurisdiction.[39] If the United States had jurisdiction to prescribe its law with respect to Rio Tinto, its directors and employees, then it should have jurisdiction to order the production of documents and testimony.[40] However, the issue of whether the State has prescriptive jurisdiction over the person or conduct based on the effects doctrine is a matter of great controversy in the international community. The effects doctrine as applied to the regulation of restrictive business practices appears to have

---

[36] *Ibid.* at 616-17.   [37] *Ibid.* at 617.

[38] For a discussion of the problem, see *Restatement of Foreign Relations Law* (Rev.), Tent. Final Draft (15 July, 1985, Introductory Note Chap. 1. Part IV, at 345-8.

[39] *Restatement (Second) of Foreign Relations Law,* § 18 (1965); *Restatement of Foreign Relations Law* (Rev.) § 402, Tent. Final Draft (15 July, 1985).

[40] See Jennings, *Extraterritorial Jurisdiction and the United States Antitrust Laws,* 33 Brit. YB Int'l L. 146 (1957); Collins, 'International Aspects of Obtaining Evidence Abroad', in *Extraterritorial Application of Laws and Responses Thereto* 184, 186 (1984).

been accepted in the European Community and in at least some of its member States,[41] but by no means all of them.

So long as Britain and the United States maintain conflicting positions on the effects of doctrine, it is apparent that jurisdictional issues will arise and these will affect private litigants. Moderation and restraint should be practised by courts and enforcement authorities to ameliorate the effects of differences of view as to bases for prescriptive jurisdiction.[42]

CONCLUSION

To attempt to do justice to Lord Wilberforce's outstanding contributions to the development of international law within the confines of a single article is impossible. This article touches upon a sample of his judicial work in the area of international law. It should, however, be sufficient to whet the appetite of the reader for more and to indicate the range and depth of Lord Wilberforce's analytical skills and legal craftsmanship in but one area of the law which will long reflect the stamp of his judicial expertise.[43]

---

[41] See, *Imperial Chemical Industries, Ltd.* v. *Commission* (the Dyestuffs case), 11 Common Mkt. L. Rev. 557 (Ct. of Justice 1972); and see *The Law Against Restraints on Competition of the Federal Republic of Germany*, § 98 (2), which expressly adopts the effects doctrine of jurisdiction.

[42] See, *Restatement of Foreign Relations Law* (Rev.) § 403, Tent. Final Draft (15 July, 1985).

[43] For a collection of House of Lords opinions of Lord Wilberforce, see *Selected House of Lords Judgments of Lord Wilberforce* (Philippine Branch of the International Law Association, Manila, November 1983).

8

The Distinguishable Characheristics of the Concept of the Law as it Developed in Ancient India

by PRESIDENT NAGENDRA SINGH

I. A TRIBUTE

It is always a unique opportunity to write in honour of a great jurist, whose contribution to both national and international law has been outstanding. I write to emphasize the latter branch of the law, which Lord Wilberforce has sponsored as his personal endeavour, not connected with the high national office which he holds as a member of the House of Lords.

As chairman of one of the most important non-governmental organizations (NGOs) in the world, Lord Wilberforce has been responsible not only for popularising and promoting the subject of international law by encouraging the opening of new branches of the International Law Association (ILA) in distant corners of the globe, but also for the progressive development of that vital law which regulates inter-State conduct. This he has done by encouraging the formation of separate committees of the ILA on different subjects and aspects of international law. The services rendered by Lord Wilberforce have been unparallelled in this direction.

I contribute this article in sincere admiration of his legal personality, which has emphasized the universality of international law. This aspect is indeed vital to the development of international law in the right direction. Whatever the effect of different legal philosophies of national laws of numerous nation States, the regime of international law is universal; and no nation can develop its own parochial concepts of inter-State regulation based on national interest and a chauvinistic outlook, as that would be disastrous to the world community. This article is dedicated to the law whose welfare lies in its universality, and also to the ILA and its Chairman Lord Wilberforce, who have spared no pains to promote that aspect in relation to international law. The noble Lord has adored that law throughout his life and thereby won the admiration of many of his friends, who hold him in high esteem among the jurists of the world as a well-wisher and promoter of the law, which alone can one day bring peace on earth.

THE ANCIENT INDIAN CONCEPT OF INTER-STATE LAW
Universality of Application

If the concept of the law of nations comprises a body of rules, whether customary or written, which States in their intercourse with each other consider as binding, it would perhaps not be quite accurate to observe as Oppenheim has done, that international law 'in its origin is essentially a product of Christian civilization and began gradually to grow from the second half of the middle ages'.[1] Apart from the fact that Christian civilization may not have quite enjoyed a monopoly in regard to prescription of rules to govern inter-State conduct, it is submitted that the concept of Christendom itself hampered the development of international law on the broad basis on which it exists today. For example, the principle that the rules of civilized conduct among nations applied to States within Christendom alone, and that nothing of a binding nature could govern the relations of a Christian state with a non-Christian state, did lasting damage to the development of the correct concept of modern international law, which recognizes political entities irrespective of their religious beliefs. Even in the thirties of the present century, Mussolini's Italy, when using expanding bullets in its war with Ethiopia, took the plea that as the latter was outside Christendom, the recognized rules of warfare could not apply to the Italo-Ethiopian conflict of 1936. Nor was the concept of the medieval Muslim law of nations outside India universal in character, since it was 'primarily concerned with regulating the relations of entities and nations within a limited area and within one civilization'.[2] However, ancient India and subsequently later medieval India under Muslim rule was fortunate in remaining free from prejudices which would limit the application of the law of nations to one's own civilization.

If we probe the history of ancient India, we find that no distinction between believers and non-believers was recognized in regard to inter-State conduct, and even when the former were involved in a war to the death within or without Aryavarta, or whether it was a just and righteous war ('Dharma Yuddha') or an unjust war ('Adharma Yuddha'), it was expressly enjoined by the sacred laws of Dharmasastra that all belligerents at all times and in all circumstances must adhere to the accepted rules of warfare.

A study of the *Smrtis* would undoubtedly reveal that ancient India had a highly developed system pertaining to the laws and rules of war, based on considerations of humanity and chivalry. The rules of warfare applied even if the struggle was in the nature of a civil war, which is again in conformity

---

[1] Oppennheim, *International Law*, 8th ed. (1955), i. 6.
[2] Majid Khadduri, *War and Peace in the Law of Islam* (1955).

The Law of Nations in Ancient India

with the modern concept of recognition of belligerency and insurgency—for example, the Geneva Conventions of 1949 or the latest Red Cross Convention of 1977. Again, the general rules of warfare as prescribed by the Code of Manu which came later (200 BC–100 BC), or by other lawgivers, were governed by the principles of humanity and chivalry. For example, Manu lays down : 'one who surrenders or is without arms or is sleeping or is naked, or with hair untied (i.e., unprepared) or is an on-looker (non-combatant) must never be killed', irrespective of whether the opponent was a believer or Arya, or a Yavana (alien non-believer), or whether he was fighting a just war or not.[3] The dictates of humanity coupled with consideration of universality of application irrespective of caste, creed, or political colour, helped the development of the law of war in ancient India on a basis as it is known today.

Again, the distinction between combatants and non-combatants and the rule forbidding weapons of destruction was not only formulated, but there are examples of its recognition in ancient India.

A classic example of the observance of the rules of warfare is to be seen when Lakshmana, in the war against Ravana, the demon king, was forbidden by Rama, the king of Ayodya, to use a weapon of war which would destroy the entire race of the enemy, including those who did not bear arms, because such destruction *en masse* was forbidden by the ancient laws of war, even though Ravana was fighting an unjust war with an unrighteous objective and himself was classed as a devil-demon, and hence could be considered outside the then world of civilization.[4] Another such example is to be found in the *Mahabharata* when Arjuna, observing the laws of war, refrained from using the *'pasupathastra'*, a hyper-destructive weapon, because when the fight was restricted to ordinary conventional weapons, the use of extraordinary or unconventional types was not even moral, let alone in conformity with religion or the recognized laws of warfare.[5] This unique concept contributed to inter-State law in the field of belligerent relations has yet to win recognition from the sovereign States of the world, though jurists are prepared to press for its acceptance today.

Moreover, the Indian customary laws governing inter-State conduct described by the *Smrtis* and based on principles of chivalry governed the conduct of administration of enemy-occupied territory and also prescribed the treatment to be meted out to a defeated king in the following words of Manu:

When a king has conquered a foreign foe, he shall make a prince of that country (not of his own) the king there, and (Vishnu adds., iii, 49) he shall not destroy the royal race of his foe unless that royal race be ignoble birth. He is to honour the gods and the customs of the conquered country and grant exemption from taxation (for a time) (Manu, vii, 201).[6]

[3] *Manusmrti*, vii. 91, 92.
[5] *Mahabharata, Udyog Parva*, 194. 12.
[4] Ramayana, *Yuddha Kanda Sloka*, 39.
[6] *Cambridge History of India*, i, 290.

The above treatment was prescribed for the enemy king irrespective of whether he belonged to Indian or foreign civilization, as is clear from the treaty signed between Seleukos and Chandragupta Maurya in 305 BC, when the former, accepting defeat, retired and concluded a humiliating peace.[7] However, Chandragupta accorded to Seleukos the treatment of an independent foreign sovereign. The rules governing this particular aspect were so well known and well established that the Macedonian world-conqueror Alexander the Great learnt of them in detail while waiting on the banks of the Hydaspes in the summer of 326 BC planning to give battle to the Indian king Paurava, or Poros. It is possible that Alexander, having heard of the chivalrous rules of warfare recognized by the Indian warrior class, had perhaps made up his mind before the battle began to treat Paurava according to the Indian concept of law on the subject. Thus, after the battle of Hydaspes had been fought and won, victorious Alexander summoned to his presence the defeated Indian king Paurava, and enquired of him how he should be treated. The Indian king replied, 'Act as a king'. The victor not only confirmed the vanquished prince in the government of his ancestral territory, but added to it other lands of still greater extent, and by this method secured a grateful and faithful friend.

Thus the first essential characteristic of the concept of the law of nations in ancient India was its universality of appliction irrespective of limitations of religion or civilization. To the State in ancient India, Islamdom, Christendom, Greekdom, or Aryandom would have made no difference as far as inter-State relationship was concerned, which is such an essential feature of the correct concept of the law of nations, whether we think of the world of today, yesterday, or tomorrow.

The contacts of ancient Indian civilization with States or political entities of a different civilization were many and well established. The institution of Rajduts [8]—that is the sending of ambassadors or envoys for *ad hoc* work or for short sojourns in the courts of other States (even if the modern concept of permanent embassies was not known then)—was not confined to States of Indian group, but was in vogue in relation to the Greek States that came into existence on the north-west border of India in the wake of Alexander's invasion of 326 BC. While both Christendom and Islamdom confined official inter-State relations within their sphere of belief, and no instances of any marked importance have come to light indicating exchange of ambassadors with countries outside their pale of civilization, India had not only such ambassadors accredited to foreign countries but received foreign envoys to Indian courts, as evidenced by

---

[7] Vincent Smith, *Early History of India, including Alexander's Campaigns* OUP, 1924), 125.

[8] The Code of Manu not only allots a distinct time in the programme of a monarch for discussions with foreign ambassadors and consideration of their reports, but describes in detail the qualifications of a good envoy and the functions he is required to perform. (*Manusmrti,* vii.63—6, 153).

Megasthenes, who came to the court of Chandragupta Maurya in 303 BC representing the kingdom of Seleukos Nikator.[9]

Lex as Rex and Pacta Sunt Servanda

The second distinguishing characteristic of ancient India is the supremacy of *dharma*, or law, so vital for the well-being of the community of States. In fact, the supremacy of law and the sanctity of treaties constitute the two basic principles which remain a *sine qua non* for the growth of law among States. If the conditions necessary for the origin and development of international law are examined, it will be found that, first, separate political units must exist, however loose-knit they may be, whether tribal or confederal, so long as they (a) are independent of each other and (b) have their own governmental machinery with an appropriate organ as a mouthpiece like the *Viçpati or the King, and that the rest* can be left to the human social instinct for developing inter-unit relations and the consequent need for their regulation. (This aspect is described subsequently when dealing with the concept of *Cakravartin*, cited as the fourth distinguishing characteristic of ancient India, which continued to dominate the entire course of Indian history, including the British period, right up to 1947.)

Second, but in no way less important than the first condition, is the basic need for an atmosphere of respect for law and a general feeling for due observance of agreements solemnly entered into, without which no amount of extensive or intensive inter-State relationship would give birth to a law of nations as such. It is this important aspect which needs elaboration and is discussed below.

The concept of *dharma*, or law, as identified with *danda*, or sanction, lies at the root of the origin of the State and society, as Manu holds that the Lord (creator) gave birth to his own son—*danda*, the protector of all creatures, an incarnation of the law itself, forged out of the glory of Brahma himself.[10] Thus *danda*, which in its crude aspect is the basis of the theory of force, is admitted only in its highly elevated legal concept of *dharma*, implying sovereignty and linking itself with the moral order not merely of human society, but of the entire universe. Thus naked force no longer remains the *ultima ratio* of kings, but a weapon for the implementation of *dharma*, or law. Sukraniti points out that *dharma* is enforced through *danda*, and both combined become the embodiment of the highest virtue in preventing aggression.[11] Thus Manu's equatation of *danda* with

---

[9] Vincent Smith, *Early History of Inndia Including Alexander's Campaigns* OUP, 1924), 124–5. It is clear that in 312 BC Seleukos recovered possession of Babylon, and that a few years later he assumed the regal style and title. He has been conventionally described as king of Syria and was the Lord of Western and Central Asia. This Megasthenes represented a separate, independent kingdom. See also Bevan, *The House of Seleukos*.

[10] *Manusmrt*, vii. 14. [11] Sukraniti, iv. 48.

dharma (dandam dharmam vidurbudhah) means the supremacy of *dharma* or law which has the highest sanction of *danda* behind it. The king and the entire political order under him have to serve *dharma* and bow to law at all times. Again, *danda* divorced from *dharma* could no longer be a weapon in the hands of the king, which meant that *dharma* alone was sovereign. Dr. Mukherji has aptly described this position as follows: 'The true sovereign of the Hundu state is dharma, the law and constitution, which is upheld and enforced by the king or supreme executive as danda.'[12] Dr. Kane has also come to the same conclusion after a very careful study of the ancient text. He summarizes the position thus: 'The Dharmasastra authors hold the dharma was the supreme power in the state and was above the king who was only the instrument to realise the role of dharma.'[13] Thus in both political and legal theory, the supremacy or sovereignty of law was well establìshed and recognized as such. It is difficult to talk of political practice, which may quite often have deviated from theory, but that does not cast any reflection on the theory as such, which is so well enunciated and clearly recognised by Srutis and *the* Smrtis, the two main sources of Hindu law.

If the theory of brute force based on Machiavellian tactics has been advocated in Arthasastra by writers like Kautilya, its position in strict law has to be examined in relation to the principles of Dharmasastra. As already mentioned, several authorities, including Yajnavalkya, can be quoted to establish that in the case of a conflict between Arthasastra and Dharmasastra, the latter was to prevail over the former. In fact, the supremacy of Dharmasastra was so well established that all-important literature on Arthasastra itself recognized *dharma* or law as the highest objective. Thus *Kamasutra* states that *dharma* is the highest goal, and Kama the lowest of the three Purasharthas.[14] Even Kautilya's Arthasastra categorically states that 'in any matter where there is a conflict between Dharmasastra and practice or between the Dharmasastra and any secular transaction, the King should decide the matter by relying on dharma alone.[15] Similarily, Yajnavalkya Smrti and Narda in *Vyavahar matrka* state that Dharmasastra rules are to be preferred to the dictates of Arthasastra.[16] As the word 'Arthasastra' connotes all literature on the science of policy and statecraft, the subordination of all State policies to *dharma,* or law, is of the highest importance for a correct appreciation of the legal situation in ancient India. The legal theorists who interpreted the sacred law in ancient India realized the deep-rooted conflict between the

---

[12] Presidential address given by Dr. R. K. Mukherji at the 25th Session of the Indian History of Congress, Gwalior. See also id., *Chandragupta Maurya and his Times,* 49.

[13] P. V. Kane, *History of Dharmasastra,* (Poona, Oriental Research Institute, 1946), iii, 241.

[14] *Kamasutra,* i. 2. 14.   [15] Arthasastra, iii. 1.

[16] Yajnavalkya Smrti, i. 39.

dictates of *raison d'Etat* and *rationes legis*. Mitaksara goes so far as to give an illustration of how *lex* was to prevail over all political connsideration which the principles of Arthasastra could put forward. Thus, for example, a conflict may arise if Arthasastra, or the science of policy as such (not confined to Kautilya's work), declares that a king should endeavour to make friends with his subjects since the acquisition of friends is superior to the acquisition of gold and land, and the rule of Dharmasastra [17] says that a king must dispense justice among his subjects without anger and avarice, and in accordance with the dictates of law or *dharma*. In such circumstances, if an appeal comes before a king for decision, he must act according to *dharma*, even though he may lose the friendship of a person if his decision goes against him. This example should establish beyond doubt that where principles of Arthasastra or the science of policy prescribed Machiavelliann tactics and adoption of acts completely divorced from rules of fair play and morality, the latter could not prevail over the code of conduct prescribed by dharma. Even Kautilya distinguishes a *dharmavijaya*, which is just conquest, from *asuravijaya* or unrighteous conquest, and *lobhvijaya*, which is conquest undertaken for sheer greed.[18] Kautilya does not hide his complete disapproval of *asura*, or *lobhavijaya*, which fact is often forgotten by Western writers, who tend to see only the praise for the many acts of perfidy which Kautilya advocates to attain success in war and politics, and ignore the considerations of *dharma*, of which Kautilya was not completely devoid.

Lastly, we may examine the concept of the supremacy of law in relation to the ultimate end or objective of the state. In the *Brhaspatya Sutra*, the ultimate fruit of policy is described as the attainment of *dharma* first and foremost, and *artha* and *kama* second and third.[19] The *raison d'être* of the State in ancient India, therefore, was the upholding of law and the creation of conditions of peace, order, and happiness, for which Divinity had precribed *dharma* as the doctrine, the king as its executor, and *moksa* (salvation) *attained* by dharma as the ultimate goal of all.

Thus viewed from all angles and every viewpoint, *dharma*, or law, ranked supreme in ancient India, first in the context of the origin of the State, where *dharma* and *danda* are indentified, since law without sanction is meaningless, and if law is to be supreme, it must have the supreme sanction behind it, and there is no entity higher than law itself when the State and society are created. Second, when the State expands or in its inter-State relations wages wars guided by the principles of *artha*, there is a limitation imposed by *dharma* that only wars fought in a righteous cause are justified. The sanction given to undertake just wars, as against unjust, basically upholds the principle of the supremacy of *dharma* as against

[17] Arthasastra, trans. Shama Sastri, 461.
[18] Ibid.   [19] Ibid.

artha. Third, in the peaceful existence of the State when it maintains law and order and dispenses justice internally, the king as the sovereign power is subjected to Dharmasastra, and it is *lex* which is crowned *rex,* and not vise versa. Lastly, the end of the state itself is *dharma,* and not *artha* or *kama.* Thus from beginning to end, *dharma* alone prevails. This basic idea governs all the theories of ancient India, though quite a number bring out prominently the concept of force and the administrative principle which led to the elaborate organization of defence, an essential limb of the State machine. Thus, whatever has been stated in the previous pages must necessarily be read in the context of the theory of the supremacy of law which was meant to regulate inter-State conduct as much as the internal governance of a State. The word 'law' could perhaps be used, in a loose sense at least, to indicate the governance of inter-State conduct, even if proper international law in the modern sense did not exist.[20]

The second principle essential for the growth of inter-State or international law is the observance of the rule *pacta sunt servanda.* When inter-State contact begins, according to ancient writers on polity, there is bound to be either indifference, agreement, or difference. Since in general differences have to be settled, whether by war or by peaceful methods such as negotiation, they often end in some sort of agreement reached amicably or otherwise. It is of the essence of law that such agreements, duly reached between States on the basis of accord or friendship or even after war, should be respected, or there would be a negation of law *ab initio*. There is abundance of authority in ancient India which attaches the highest importance to the maintenance of agreements reached either in writing or by word of mouth. Even Kautilya asserts that 'peace depending upon honesty or oath is immutable both in this and the next world.'[21] In this respect he goes a step further than his teacher in discarding the principle of obtaining hostages as a security to cement the binding nature of treaties. Kautilya remarks, 'It is for this world only that security or a hostage is required for strengthening the agreement.'[22]

In short, therefore, the existence of an atmosphere in which law is held to be supreme and agreements between States are regarded as inviolable must be said to furnish the necessary condition for the healthy development of international law, however rudimentary it may be beside the modern developed concepts of today.

In this connection, it is essential to examine further the first condition relating to the existence of independent political units, particularly because of concept of *Cakravartin* conflicts with the continuance of separate

---

[20] As the word 'nation' is used in a special sense in modern literature, it is perhaps safe to describe the regulation of the relationship between two independent States in ancient India as inter-State law rather than international law.

[21] Arthasastra, trans. Shama Sastri, 381.   [22] Ibid.

political entities and, therefore, appears, prima facie, to spell the eclipse of inter-State conduct.

The concept of Cakravartin *and the historical development of law among States in Ancient India.*

There are certain prerequisites for the origin and development of law among nations. First and foremost, there should be separate independent political units with their own governments, however primitive the latter may be, whether tribal, feudal, monarchical, republican, or oligarchical. Secondly, there must be the urge or need for intercourse among them. It is the growth of intercourse which requires regulation, and herein lies the *raison d'être* of international law. However, in order that such regulation may come to have the force of law, the third basic condition for the growth of international law would appear to depend upon the nature of the sanction developed in the sphere of governance of inter-State conduct.

In the socio-political order which existed about then dawn of human civilization, it would be premature to expect the existence of sovereign independent States in the modern sense described by jurists today as 'international persons'. It is true that intercourse among non-sovereign States cannot ever be said to be governed by international law. However, in the early growth of the law itself, which was bound to be associated with the growth of political units, the regulation of intercourse among States would appear to fall within the purview of international law, provided always that there was legal equality among those units that the essential feature of their independence was not lacking. As intercourse is between the governments of separate political entities, emphasis must be placed on the need for the existence of a governmental organ, even though the general structure of the State may be loose, being tribal or feudal, provided that the government functioned as that of an independent unit. The latter aspect is important, because if a unit existed and developed intercourse on a subordinate basis with another unit, the relationship would be as between a vassal and a suzerain, and hence not the inter-State or international plane. Thus the existence of a tribal society in Vedic times, and the concept of *Cakravartin,* or a paramount ruler of a world State in the age of the epic wars, as described in the Puranic literature, appear to disturb the conditions necessary for the development of international law. However, on closer scrutiny it could be demonstrated that the tribal set-up of Rig-Vedic society would be no hindrance to the development of a law among States, since several tribal units existed independently of one another and had a governmental organ in the form of a king. Similarly, the concept of *Cakravatrin* in the later era did not prevent the existence of units on the basis of legal equality, and, in any case, during the stage of attainment of the ideal of *Cakravartin*, there was bound to be inter-State conflict furthering the process of development of law among States. As international law in its earliest form can trace its existence to the origin of the State itself, the development of the concept of the political State is linked with the history of the development of international law. A brief historical sketch therefore, would not be out of place, if it could indicate the different conditions which governed the various stages in the development of law among States and nations.

(i) The Vedic Age (4000–1000 BC)[23]

According to Keith and Rapson, 'the earliest documents which throw light upon the history of India are the hymns of the *Rig-Veda*.'[24] From the scanty information provided by Vedic literature on the political organization then prevailing, it appears that there were separate tribes in existence which had their own governmental organ in the shape of the king, and there was intercourse between them, often giving rise to strained relations leading to warfare. Thus the distinguishing feature of the Vedic age was the growth of inter-tribal relationships.

Thus the broad prerequisites for the growth of inter-State law were present in the Vedic age. It was the existence of the governmental organ of the 'Rajan', or king, which by its very nature gave equality of status to the competing political units and fostered intercourse among them. However tribal a society may be in the age of the *Rig-Veda*, there is no dispute that the tribes were 'certainly under kingly rule'. As Keith mentions,

'there is no passage in the *Rig-Veda* which suggests any other form of government, while the king under the style 'Rajan' is a frequent figure. This is only what might be expected in a community which was not merely patriarchial—a fact whence the king drew his occasional style of *viçpati*, 'Head of the vic'—but also engaged in constant warfare against both Aryan and aboriginal foes.[25]

The functions of the sovereign on which most stress was laid related to his duty of protecting the subjects, and 'even the *Rig-Veda* despite its sacerdotal characters allows us to catch some glimpses of the warlike deeds of such men as Divodasa, Sudas and Trasadasyu.'[26] As it appears that the tribal set-up led to frequent warfare, the king was duly assisted by a hierarchy of officials, including a regular Senani, the commander-in-chief of the army. Again, the rules of warfare provided the first subject needing attention, since bitter experience had taught that wars fought without any regulations were likely to prove most damaging to both belligerents. Thus, as a matter of necessity and in the interests of all concerned, the regulation

---

[23] The dates adopted for the purpose of this chapter are those accepted by P. V. Kane, in 'History of Dharmasastra'.

[24] *Cambridge History of India*, i, 77.

[25] Ibid. [26] Ibid.

of warfare appears to have emerged as the starting-point of a law destined to govern several other spheres of inter-Sate relationship. The one great historical event described in the Samhita of the *Rig-Veda* is the contest known as the Battle of the Ten Kings. This conflict was perhaps between the Bharat king Sudas, who was lord of the country later known as Brahmavarta, and the tribes of the north-west. The account of Sudas's victory at Parushni records that kings Anu and Druhyu fell on the battlefield, but that there was no conquest of territory, since Sudas was compelled to return to the east of his kingdom to fight King Bheda, who was assisted by three tribal kings constituting a grand military alliance against King Sudas. These and other incidents indicate beyond doubt that the basic conditions needed for the development of international law existed even in the Vedic age in so far as there were independent political units with the institution of the king, furnishing the necessary governmental organ for communication. It is difficult to state with certainty whether the political units were fully sovereign in the modern sense, but there is ample evidence that the king in ancient India was always regarded as the personification of the sovereignty of the people. Thus when a king entered into a transaction with another king, it involved a relationship between two States, not two individuals. It would perhaps not be inappropriate to conclude that the king represented his people annd the organization which governed them. The petty tribal principalities so often mentioned in the *Rig-Veda* would thus appear to be externally fully sovereign so far as their relationship with other similar units was concerned. That there was legal equality among them can hardly be doubted, and this by itself satisfies the first essential condition for the origin and growth of a law of nations.[27]

(ii) *The Period of the Epic War (1900–1000 BC)* [28]
The law of war received added impetus during this period and, from the epic *Mahabharata,* it can be stated that the rules on the subject not only became crystallized and properly formulated, but the necessary halo of sanctity developed around them in regard to their observance. This is apparent from both *Ramayana* and *Mahabharata,* since even in the midst of the struggle, Bhisma and Karna referred to the sacred principles of warfare now given the distinct title of 'Yudha-Dharma'. Another important feature of this age was the concept of *Cakravartin* developed on the basis of religious ceremonies like the Ashvamedha, the Rajasuya, and the Vajapeya sacrifices. The one who was able to perform these sacrifices could best be described as an emperor having under him a number of vassal kingdoms which owed allegiance, however nominal it might be, to the

---

[27] According to Dr Beni Prasad, *The State in Ancient India* (1904), 23, it was only after the 6th century BC that the concept of territorial sovereignty superseded the tribal concept of State in ancient India. [28] Kane, *History of Dharmasastra,* 900.

imprerial person. Thus there were several grades of rulers in ancient India. the word 'Rajan' occurs at numerous places in the *Rig-Veda* and may be said to stand for an ordinary king. However, the word 'samrajya', which is used in an epithet of Varuna and of Indra, may be said to connote the idea of an emperor having suzerainty over several kings. In the *Satapatha Brahmana* a clear distinction is made between a king ('Rahjan') and an emperor. It is said that by 'offering the Rajasuya he becomes king and by the Vajapeya he becomes emperor; and the office of king is the lower and that of emperor higher'.[29] This concept of *Cakravartin,* or *Samarajya,* or *Ekarat,* was fully developed by the time of the composition of Aitareya and Satapatha Brahmanas. For example, the former mentions as many as twelve emperors of ancient India, the latter thirteen. Again, Panini defines 'sarvabhauma' as the lord of the whole earth. The famous Sanskrit dictionary *Amarakosa* states 'that a king before whom all feudatories humble themselves is styled "adhisvara' or "cakravartin" or "sarvabhauma", the last three words being synonyms'. Thus, ultimately, all things considered, the word 'Cakravartin' stands for one who wields lordship over a circle of kings, but not necessarily over all kings of the land. The fact remains that there were several *Cakravartins,* and the *Maitri Upanishad* mentions as many as fifteen of them. It is therefore, submitted that there was perhaps ample opportunity for the development of international law between these imperial units which were coequal in status. It is true that if there had been only one *Cakravartin* in the whole country, the relationship would not have been inter-Statel but confined to that of vassals to the suzerain, which is certainly derogatory to the conditions required for the development of law among equal political units. However, that was not the position in a law where *Cakravartins* apparently abounded.

Thus if the concept of *Cakravartin* did not conflict with the development of international law in ancient India, there is ample evidence to indicate that it gave considerable impetus to the development of the laws of war. It may be true, as Derrett puts it, that the 'Cakravarti-mirage' teased all rulers and, in practice posed an ideal before ambitious monarchs which resulted in constant warfare. However, in theory, the concept of 'Cakravartin was perhaps meant to provide lasting peace inasmuch as, in principle at least, it aimed at striving for one world government, taking in the geographical area from the Himalayas to Cape Comorin as the Cakravarti Kshetram. The petty chieftains who accepted the allegiance of the *Cakravartinn* did not thereby lose their independence, except for loss of control over external relations. They became protectorates or members of a loose-knit confederal empire in which they were internally sovereign.

[29] See also E. B. Havell, *A Short History of India,* 11, for the date of King Dushratha or Dasarathe. Kane, *History of Dharmasastra,* iii, 65.

Thus the discipline imposed by the concept of *Cakravartin* ruled out perpetual petty warfare amongst the innumerable chieftains who exercised authority in the plains of ancient India. It is true, however, that the theory remained far away from the practice, inasmuch as no single *Cakravartin* rose to the position of establishing a world (country-wide) government. On the other hand, several *Cakravartins* grew up, and the *Mahabharata* mentions as many as five empires of old with an ever-lasting rivalry amongst them leading to frequent warfare, which, in turn, necessitated enunciation of correct principles for regulating warfare and keeping it at the very highest level, so as to prevent a fall of humanity from chivalrous conduct. Thus proper restraints were placed on the inhumanity that a conqueror could resort to in the hour of victory. *Yajnavalkya* prescribes that it was the duty of the conqueror to protect the conquered territory in the same way as he would his own country, and the conqueror was at all times to respect the customs, laws, and usages of the conquered country. Again, *Vishnu Dharma Sutra* and *Agnipurana* also prescribe similar rules. Above all, however, is the celebrated verse of Katyayna in the *Rajniti Prakasa* laying down that even when the vanquished king is at fault, the conqueror has no right to molest the country, since the vanquished king cannot have resorted to his unlawful acts with the consent of all his subjects.

Thus, on the whole, the distinct contribution of this period was the formulation of the laws of war more than a thousand years before the birth of Christ. Their proper codification may be said to take place in *Manusmtri* 200 BC, when they were elevated to the sacred laws of Dnarmasastra. However, even prior to this date, there can be little doubt that the laws of war were well defined and recognized as Yuddha-Dharma.

Thus the existence of wars between one Cakravartin and another or between an aspiring *Cakravartin* and petty chieftains brought about the necessary conditions for the development of international law, particularly in the sphere of laws of war. Quite apart from the age of the epic wars (1900–1000 BC), there can be little doubt of the existence much later of a comity of States, if not of nations, since Rhys Davids[30] enumerates as many as sixteen republics and several independent monarchies (many more than republics in number) flourished even in the sixth century BC. *Ubi Societas ibi est Jus* and for the existence of the comity of States with their constant contacts, for which there is ample evidence, fostered the development of rules to govern their inter-State relations.

(iii) *Alexander's Invasion and the Growth of International Law concepts (326 BC and after)*

In the history of the development of concept of international law in ancient

[30] Rhys Davids, *Buddhist India* (1911), 23.

India, the invasion of Alexander the Great may be said to mark the beginning of a new age inasmuch as political and diplomatic relations came to be established beyond the frontiers of India. The establishment of inter-State relationships based on contact with Yavana states was the direct outcome of Alexander's invasion, since the kingdoms which he left behind him on the frontiers of India continued to exist long after he had departed from Greece. This period may, therefore, be regarded as remarkable in the growth of a new kind of inter-State relationship both in peace and in war. With Megasthenes in Chandragupta's court and political relations with Seleukos, who became the king of Babylon, and Syria developing across the frontiers of India, the institution of ambassadors, the legal formality and procedure of concluding treaties and their enforcement on a truly international plane, and the observance of rules of warfare when the enemy hailed from a quite different civilization were some of the important elements which obtained recognition. An entire book could be devoted to describing interesting episodes bearing on international practice, but suffice it to say here that the Greek invasion followed by the establishment of Greek kingdoms developed concepts and codes in more spheres than one to regulate inter-state conduct.

Alexander may be said to fill the role of *Cakravartin* more appropriately than ever before, both in regard to autonomous vassals he created, including Poros, whom he reinstated, and the extensive conquests he undertook. However, he was a foreign *Cakravartin*, as he failed to penetrate the heart of Aryavarta.

(iv) *The impact of Buddhism and Jainism (600–350 BC)*
Again, although chronologically the birth of Buddha (563 BC) and his death (483 BC) had taken place well before Alexander's invasion (326 BC), the impact of Buddhism, as far as inter-State relationships were concerned, was felt more in the reign of Asoka (274–237 BC) than ever before. The greatest contribution of Buddhism, as far as we are here concerned, was the renunciation of war based on the principle of shunning violence at all stages and at all events.

Asoka took upon himself responsibility for the spread of Buddhism beyond the Indian frontiers, and in doing so established deep-rooted inter-State relationships not only with neighbouring countries such as Ceylon, but also with countries in Asia and Europe. Exchange of ambassadors and envoys did much to develop the legal concept of this institution, which may not have been a permanent one as ambassadors are known today, but there is no doubt that they existed in full bloom, and were fully utilized in ancient India to propogate national or State viewpoints, whether religious or political, since envoys are known to have stayed for months and even years in the courts of other countries for this purpose. If the *Cakravartin* concept is to be regarded as persisting in Indian history, Asoka may be accepted as the first *Cakravartin* and the one and only of his kind. His greatness lay in his becoming a *Cakravartin* after imposing on himself a self-denying ordinance–namely, the renunciation of war in all inter-State dealings.[31]

He built and extended his empire of peace on the basis of the sacred law of *dhamma vijaya*. His domain, therefore, comprised a loose confederation of indendent units, States or vassals which accepted Asoka as the politico-religious head and in turn renounced their right of war in their relationship with each other. Externally, too, the empire was wedded to peace, and, as stated before, all inter-State relations were developed on that basis alone.

The end of the Ancient World and the beginning of the Middle Ages

(a) To AD 648 and after; the Rajput period

The rest of the period of ancient history could be divided into broad categories. The first would cover the period beginning with the fall of the imperial Guptas to the death of Harsa AD 647). The second would relate to the Rajput period of Indian history, beginning in AD 647 and going up to the conquest of India by Sultan Mahmud of Ghazni in the eleventh century AD. This is no place to give a chronological account of the Gupta emperors or of their great conquests or court splendours. In the pursuit of imperial expansion they came in contact with several States on the basis of both peace and war. The concept of *Cakravartin* was revived again, and both Samudragupta and Chandragupta Vikramaditya performed Asvamedha sacrifices. War again came to govern inter-State relationships after the interlude of peace, as the basis of State conduct furnished by Asoka. Samudragupta maintained diplomatic relations with the foreign Kushan princes of the north-west, as well as with Ceylon King Meghavarna (AD 352–79), desirous of founding a monastery in India for his nationals, sent a mission to Samudragupta offering presents of gems and seeking permission to build a monastery on Indian soil. The required permission was given and King Meghavarna built a three-storeyed monastery, which Hiuen-Tsang saw in flourishing condition in giving hospitality to pilgrims from Ceylon. Chandragupta Vikramaditya was also responsible for extensive conquests in pursuit of the Cakravartin ideal. Again, Harsa (AD 606–647), the last of the great emperors of ancient India, maintained diplomatic intercourse with the Chinese emperors. An incident which dates back to AD 647 immediately after the death of the king, deserves to be mentioned, as it involved violation of the principle of diplomatic immunity and its restoration with due apologies. King Harsa had sent an envoy in 641 to the emperor of China, and the latter had reciprocated by a Chinese mission

---

[31] See the 13th Rock Edict of Emperor Asoka, trans. Vincent Smith in *Ashoka, the Buddhist Emperor of India,* 24. The edict declares: 'Directly after the Kalingas had been annexed began His Sacred Majesty's zealous protection of the law of piety (Dhamma Vijaya), his love of that law and his inculcation of that law. Thence arises the remorse of His Sacred Majesty for having conquered the Kalingas, because the conquest of a country previously unconquered involves slaughter, death and carrying away captives of the people.' The great king never waged war thereafter.

which came to the court of Harsa and stayed for a considerable time. When it did go back to China in 645, another diplomatic mission returned the following year, with Wang Hiuen Tse as the Head of the new Mission with an escort of thirty horsemen. However, immediately after Harsa's death, the country was plunged into anarchy, and one of his ministers, Arjun, usurped power and attacked the Chinese mission. It is reported that members of the mission were taken prisoner or killed, and that the property of the Mission was plundered. However, Wang Hiuen Tse managed to escape to Nepal, and the succeeding year, with the help of the king of Tibet who had married a Chinese princess, descended to the plains and laid siege to the city of Tirhut. The usurper Arjun fled after fighting two battles in quick succession. On hearing this, Kumara, the King of Eastern India, who used to attend the religious assemblies of Harsa, while appreciating the violation of an important principle of law in molesting a foreign mission, apologized for this gross misconduct and sent Wang Hiuen Tse gifts and abundant supplies of cattle, which were accepted. It appears that Tirhut remained for some time subject to Tibet's control which at that time was a powerful State and, Vincent Smith records, was strong enough to defy even the Chinese Empire. It may be reiterated that diplomatic immunity of ambassadors was well established and duly recognized in ancient India. According to Valmiki, Hanuman was sent to Rama's ambassador and the doctrine of immuity from arrest and non-subjection to territorial laws was elucidated by Vibhisana, so clearly recorded in a passage in the *Sundara Kanda* of the *Ramayana*. Vibhisana states emphatically that, according to the Smrtis, ambassadors could not be injured or killed, and that Ravana had no rights to molest Hanuman. Again, the *Udyog Parva* of Mahabharata describes in some detail the embassy sent on behalf of the Pandavas by Drupata. Sanjaya, who was chosen as an ambassador by Dhritarashtra, was told by Krsna that, 'though the Pandavas were ready to fight, they were always willing for peace'. Later on, when Krsna went to see Duryodhana on behalf of the Pandavas, Duryodhana had an evil design to make him a captive. Dhritarashtra opposed this course, stating emphatically that it would be a violation of Dharmasastra to make an ambassador a captive. Moreover, in the *Santi Parva* there is a description in the *Rajdharma Kanda* of the sacredness of the protection to be afforded an ambassador.

(*b*) *The Rajput period (eighth to eleventh centuries AD)*
With the death of Harsa, the ancient world may be said to come to an end, as by 712 the armies of Khalif Walid under the command of Mohammad Bin Kassem had entered Sind. The whole of Northern India had been divided into petty Rajput principalities which were often at war with each other, and a new concept of inter-State relationships was to develop with the onslaught of Islam. However, when warfare became common both within and through attacks from without, it is to be said to the credit, the Rajput kingdoms did not depart from the principles of humanity and chivalry which had regulated warfare in ancient India. Thus, when for the

first time the Rajput states came into contact with the Central Asian invader professing a differennt faith, it was the Rajput who was still adhering to the laws of war as he had inherited them from the Srutis and the Smrtis. This is amply demonstrated by the two battles fought in 1191 and 1192 by Prithvuraj Chauhan of Ajmer against Mohammad Ghori.

With the advent of Islam in India, beginning in the ninth century, came one of the marvels of world history, namely the Islamic expansion, and with it the end of the practice of ancient Indian legal concepts. This was the beginning of the Middle Ages, with their own tale to tell. New principles were to evolve, and the history of the development of the law of nations was destined to face many difficulties. However, universality in the application of this branch of law was never totally eclipsed; and although that aspect did have its ups and downs, it triumphed in the end.

The basic modern concept of the law of nations today is indeed its unversality, and the ILA with its right-minded jurists like its chairman, Lord Wilberforce has rendered great service to humanity by helping to establish a *lex* which glories in its universality, quite unlike national laws, which must necessarily differ from nation to nation.

PART III
Arbitration and Commercial Law

9

Commercial Dispute Resolution: The Changing Scene

by THE RT. HON. LORD JUSTICE KERR

INTRODUCTION

Throughout his distinguished career as a barrister, Richard Orme Wilberforce practised in Chancery. Inevitably, his chambers were in Lincoln's Inn, where the mere address of many practitioners (even, as in his case, originally called to the Bar by another Inn) still connotes specialization in the various technical topics of equity as opposed to the wider fields of the common law. A century's fusion of the two systems has not changed the high degree of specialisation between them, both among practitioners and on the Bench. When he was elevated to the High Court in 1961, it was equally inevitable that Lord Wilberforce should be assigned to the Chancery division; and during the next few years his judicial experience and reputation were bound to remain within this conspectus. Thus, it is unlikely that he would have had any familiarity with charter-parties, bills of lading, c.i.f. and f.o.b. contracts, insurance policies, negotiable instruments, commodity markets, commercial arbitration, or other aspects of international trade. Indeed, judging by the traditional pattern of judicial careers throughout our history, he would ordinarily have been destined always to remain associated with the Chancery side of the law. But today, a quarter of a century later, we can see that in his case this did not happen. Lord Wilberforce's outstanding judicial qualities and experience will be associated largely with our commercial law. This is all the more remarkable when it is remembered that in 1964—uniquely in recent history—he was promoted directly from the Chancery Division to the House of Lords, leap-frogging the Court of Appeal. The nine or ten Lords of Appeal in Ordinary, dealing each year with only about 70 appeals (civil and criminal) and about 130 petitions for leave to appeal, will normally have spent at least four or five years in the Court of Appeal, where the Lords Justices of Appeal (now twenty-one; formerly eighteen) have to deal annually with well over 1,500 civil appeals. The great majority of these including many from the Commercial Court in the Queen's Bench division never reach the House of Lords. Lord Wilberforce missed the enormously variegated experience of the Court of

Appeal, and arrived in the Lords wholly nurtured in Chancery. And yet, two decades later, his reputation stands as one of the great commercial judges of our time.

This is a rare phenomenon in the history of our jurisprudence, perhaps unique. To a large extent, of course, it is due to the man himself, a lawyer of outstanding calibre, similar to that of Lord Radcliffe, whom he succeeded. But it is not my purpose to discuss his exceptional qualities here. My object is to consider the other side of the equation; the events in the forensic scene during his time which produced this phenomenon. In effect, to give a discursive anthology of some of the immense changes which have taken place in recent years in the laws, practices, logistics, techniques—call them what you will—of the business (for that is what it now is) of resolving commercial disputes, in particular those with international ramifications. This business has been one of explosive growth, both in the United Kingdom and throughout the world. The working life of Lord Wilberforce has seen and reflected it all, both in the Appeals Committee of the House of Lords and in his activities connected with arbitration since his retirement in 1982.[1]

COMMERCIAL

This term has a specialized meaning to an English judge or barrister, different from what it would convey to most English solicitors or foreign lawyers. Their firms frequently have departments styled 'commercial' or 'company and commercial' which advise clients on setting up commercial ventures and transactions. In that context the term has a constructive implication, of creating commercial relations, doing business, and hoping to make money for all concerned. In the present context the sense is different, and clinical, rather than constructive. It concerns the resolution—the process of resolving disputes arising out of commercial contracts by litigation, arbitration, and occasionally less confrontational means. Moreover, in England there is a further distinction, even when 'commercial' is used only in the context of the resolution of disputes. Its technical connotation is the jurisdiction of the Commercial Court established within the Queen's Bench Division.[2] This 'includes any cause arising out of the

---

[1] I have made no attempt to concentrate on cases in which Lord Wilberforce was involved; merely to refer generally to some of the topics of historical interest in the present context. But if he happened to deliver one of the leading judgments, I have marked this by adding (W) to the reference. Moreover, in view of the great importance of the part in the history played by arbitration, I have added '(Arb)' where appeals to the House of Lords or Court of Appeal originated from arbitrations. Virtually all cases cited—including all marked 'Arb'—are appeals from the Commercial Court; a few originated from the Admiralty Court, which exercises a parallel jurisdiction; see n. 31.

[2] From being merely a 'List', it was established as a 'Court' by the Administration of Justice Act 1970, s. 3.

transactions of merchants and traders and . . . any cause relating to the construction of mercantile documents, the export or import of merchandise, affreightment [i.e. shipping], insurance, banking, mercantile agency, and mercantile usage'.[3] Although most of the litigants are foreign parties, many of whom submit their disputes to the Court because they choose to litigate in England,[4] it can be seen at once that this limited jurisdiction—by way of a self-denying ordinance—excludes many important kinds of commercial ventures. In particular, the direct jurisdiction[5] of the Commercial Court excludes the kinds of transactions which are of the greatest financial significance in the world today: international contracts, frequently amounting to large investments, in the fields of civil engineering, construction, and building projects, and joint ventures in all kinds of commercial enterprises, often between multinational companies on the one hand and governments or government agencies on the other. Such contracts do not fall within the jurisdiction of the Commercial Court, and are in any event normally governed by *ad hoc* international arbitration clauses. Disputes arising under such contracts—often referred to as 'one-off' contracts, to distinguish them from 'standard' contracts containing arbitration clauses[6]—are no more likely to be arbitrated in England than elsewhere. Indeed, as explained below, there is nowadays considerable international competition to provide arbitral venues for 'one-off' contracts, with far-reaching consequences for the development of international arbitration law and practice.

However, the Commercial Court is crucially—albeit indirectly—concerned with disputes arising from arbitration under standard forms of contract, for which England provides a particularly highly frequented forum. It is a fair estimate that before the Arbitration Act, 1979 (as discussed below), something approaching half of the work of the Commercial Court concerned disputes arising from arbitration. The reasons go back to the dominant trading position of this country in past centuries. Trade and the demand for the servicing of trade disputes go hand in hand. From the eighteenth century onwards, markets, exchanges, and trade associations evolved in this country for all major international trades, and operated by means of standard contracts. Their use became customary, and many of their modernized forms are nowadays still used world-wide, even when the transactions have no connection with this country. However, with the notable exception of the standard marine insurance policy first issued by Lloyds, the great majority have not only traditionally provided expressly

---

[3] Rules of the Supreme Court, Order 72, Rule 1.
[4] It has been estimated that in about 80 per cent of cases in the Commercial Court, at least one of the parties is foreign, and that in about 50%, and perhaps more, all parties are foreign.
[5] As opposed to jurisdiction arising indirectly from arbitrations, mentioned later.
[6] See Lord Diplock's speech in *Pioneer Shipping Co. Ltd.* v. *B. T. P. Tioxide Ltd (The 'Nema')* [1982] AC 724.

that the governing law was to be English, but also that any dispute was to be arbitrated in England. Important examples are charterparties negotiated on the Baltic Exchange and bills of lading incorporating their terms, arbitrated mostly by members of the London Maritime Arbitrators' Association (LMAA), and many kinds of commodity contracts, too numerous to mention, issued by organizations such as The Grain and Feed Association (GAFTA), the Metal Exchange, the Liverpool Cotton Association, etc. incorporating provisions for arbitration which often include an internal appeals procedure.[7] Many thousands of arbitrations under such contracts take place each year. Because of this and the unusual degree of control exercised by English courts over arbitrations conducted in England, and therefore procedurally governed by English law, an exceptionally large proportion of litigation and appeals to the highest courts in this country had their origin in arbitrations. In this regard the position in England has always been exceptional and wholly different from the much lesser role played by national courts in relation to arbitrations in all other countries. The vast body of English commercial law, developed over more than three centuries, owes an enormous debt to arbitrations. Thus, if one glances through the index of cases at the beginning of any major English text-book on the law of contract, something like 50 per cent of the modern leading decisions, even in the House of Lords, will be found to stem from 'special cases' (or 'cases stated') by arbitral tribunals. These were non-final awards stated for the 'opinion'—that is the final decision—of the judges on any issues of law raised in any arbitration, until this procedure was finally abolished by the 1979 Act.[8] The reasons which led to this profound change in our law form part of the history which this essay is seeking to trace.

Recent developments in the business of international commercial dispute resolution accordingly fall to be discussed by an English lawyer in two senses of the word 'commercial'. There is the technical English sense, the work of the Commercial Court, whether directly by way of litigation or indirectly arising out of arbitrations conducted in England, mostly under standard contracts, but to some extent also under 'one-off' contracts. Second, there is the international sense: arbitrations, generally under 'one-off' contracts, which may be conducted in any country, under various regimes or rules or systems of law, depending on the type of arbitration clause or the venue in question, to resolve disputes under all kinds of

---

[7] A list of 16 Commodity Markets and Associations is to be found in the Schedule to the Arbitration (Commodity Contracts) Order 1979. By virtue of s. 4 of the 1979 Act, contracts for goods regularly dealt with on one of these may not be made the subject of 'exclusion agreements' before the commencement of an arbitration; see below.

[8] Section 1(1) of the Arbitration Act 1979 ('the 1979 act') abolished the 'special case' or 'case stated' procedure by repealing s. 21 of the Arbitration Act 1950. This was a consolidating statute; the procedure itself has existed for centuries.

international commercial ('transnational', in the modern jargon) contracts which are proliferating all over the world.

THE SOURCES AND NATURE OF THE DISPUTES

The last twenty years or so have produced something like an explosion in the demand for resolution of international commercial disputes in both the senses mentioned above. It is this changed scene which I want to consider, primarily in the context of events in this country, but also internationally.

To what has it been due? Overall, no doubt, to the proliferation of international trade itself, in the sense of a vast increase in the number of commercial transactions all over the globe. Those concerned simply with anticipated movements in prices, such as commodity and currency dealings, have no doubt been multiplied many times by the immense acceleration in the speed of communications. But this must have played a large part in all types of transactions. The more opportunities for business, the more contracts, the more alleged breaches of contract and disputes, the more claims and calls for litigation or arbitration. The fragmentation of large parts of the globe into smaller national units, their wealth of natural resources, notably oil, and the corresponding calls for 'Western' expertise have generated funds for a world-wide network of construction, civil engineering, and building projects. These result in chains of contracts, starting with drawing-board designs in one place and ending in roads, plants, hospitals, and bricks and mortar of every description at the other end of the world, and many kinds of contract in between. Moreover, each underlying transaction in its turn may give rise to many ancillary contracts. To take but one group of related transactions, contracts of import and export produce letters of credit, charterparties, bills of lading, insurances, towage, stevedoring, warehousing, road haulage, etc. And every form of basic commercial activity in its turn tends to generate ancillary contracts with bankers, middlemen, brokers and agents of every description. *Quot contractus, tot contentiones, tot lites.*

In addition, of course, this recent frenzy—as it has sometimes appeared—of commercial activity has not taken place against the relatively stable economic and political background of pre-war times or during the early post-war years of exhaustion and slow recovery before consolidation and expansion began. International crises, some due to confrontations and armed conflicts between new nations or bitterly differing ideologies, resulting in blockades, boycotts, and 'black lists', have produced a succession of wide-ranging repurcussions in world trade and commercial disputes. Constant fluctuations in the prices of oil, metals, and commodities, and consequently in the freight market, have given rise to tens of thousands of disputes under sale contracts and charterparties. And the money payable under all forms of international contracts itself has become subject to a host of problems, which had no counterparts in intensity or frequency before the war. Exchange controls, devaluations, constant currency fluctuations, and universal inflation have played havoc with long-term contracts and future obligations generally. Liquidity and cash flow have become major problems in themselves, and have raised the stakes all round. Debtors have increasingly contested claims which they had previously tended to settle in order to avoid going to law. For instance, contested insurance claims were rarely taken to court in the fifties, and I cannot recollect a single litigated reinsurance battle before the seventies. Thereafter they became commonplace, and defences of misrepresentation and non-disclosure to insurance claims have abounded, even under policies with Lloyds. Moreover, with the rise in interest rates, the value of cash in hand has become far greater in all aspects of commerce than the cost of fighting losing cases, particularly since judgements and awards—if their payment could not be avoided altogether—have normally carried interest at far lower rates than the cost of borrowing in the interim. Dragging out disputed legal processes as long as possible has become a commercial objective in itself.

To identify individual trends or landmarks over the last thirty years or so is not so easy, and the recollective impressions of different practitioners will vary. A few reported decisions of the House of Lords and the Court of Appeal may be no more than the surviving visible tips of vast icebergs of particular areas or topics of commercial disputes, which produced years of work for commercial barristers and solicitors. I can only mention a few, more or less at random, by way of illustration. The closures of the Suez Canal in 1956 and again in 1967 led to hundreds of disputes under allegedly frustrated c.i.f. contracts and charterparties[9] and under hull and war risk policies on vessels trapped in the Canal alleged to have become constructive total losses.[10] In recent years the war between Iran and Iraq and the navigational perils of the Persian Gulf have produced a similar pattern—and probably an even greater number—of disputes, providing years of work for the succeeding generation of commercial lawyers.[11] Then, still in the realm of shipping, the perennial battles between

[9] See e.g. *Tsakiroglou & Co. Ltd.* v. *Noblee Thorl* [1962] AC 93 (HL) and *Ocean Tramp Tankers Corporation* v. *V/O Sovracht* [1964] 2 QB 226 (CA) Arb.).

[10] Notices of abandonment were given regularly, at about weekly intervals, on behalf of shipowners, and were equally regularly rejected on behalf of underwriters. In the end these Suez Canal cases were settled in the late sixties without reaching the courts.

[11] See e.g. *Kissavos Shipping Co. S.A.* v. *Empresa Cubana de Fletes* [1982] 2 LL. Rep. 211 (CA) Arb.); *International Sea Tankers* v. *Hemisphere Shipping Co. Ltd.* (No. 2) [1983] 1 LL. Rep. 400 (Com. Ct.) (arb.); *Finelvet A. G.* v. *Vinava Shipping Co. Ltd.* [1983] 1 WLR 1469 (Com. Ct.) (Arb.); *Kodros Shipping Corp.* v. *Empresa Cubana de Fletes* (No. 2) [1983] 1 AC 736 (HL) (Arb.).

shipowners and charterers have never been waged more fiercely than during recent decades. Voyage charter-parties hardly ever seem to be performed without disputes about laytime and demurrage, mostly due to strikes and congested ports, which have given rise to innumerable permutations of problems.[12] Less tedious, or at any rate more dramatic, were the endless disputes under long-term time-charters due to violent fluctuations of the freight market: when it rises sharply, usually due to some international crisis, shipowners seek to 'withdraw' their ships for the slightest delay in the payment of the monthly hire, in order to refix them at the higher market rates;[13] when it slumps, charterers seek grounds for alleging fundamental breach to recharter at lower rates.[14] A vast overestimate of the world demand for shipping, particularly tankers, produced numerous battles between shipyards and shipowners seeking to avoid delivery and acceptance,[15] and the freight market has been depressed for more than a decade by an excessive supply of tonnage, much of it laid up, giving charterers clear advantages over owners in negotiating fixtures. Similarly, buyers of goods and services in developing countries were able to 'shop around' among willing suppliers in the more highly industrialized markets. Although irrevocable letters of credit remained the standard requirement to ensure payment, buyers were often able to insist upon the converse banking device of 'performance bonds', exigible from the suppliers' bankers upon demand without proof of breach of contract, whose abuse has led to frequent disputes.[16]

Then, leaving international sales of goods and shipping, the devaluation of sterling and its continuing decline against the dollar and other currencies led to many problems,[17] and ultimately to the revolutionary change in English law permitting awards and judgements to be expressed in the appropriate foreign currency, freed from the sacred evaluation of all

---

[12] For 'arrived ship' disputes, see, e.g., *E. L. Oldendorff & CO.* v. *Tradax Export* [1974] AC 479 (HL) (Arb.) in which the House of Lords reversed its own decision 13 years earlier in *The Aello* [1961] AC 135 (HL), which had been applied in innumerable arbitration awards and settlements in the interim. The manifold interpretations of the phrase 'time lost waiting for berth' produced the suggestion that the answer was buried somewhere in Proust's *'A la recherche du temps perdu'*. The modern doctrine of fundamental breach of contract was dominated for years by the speeches in the House of Lords on a demurrage dispute; see *Suisse Atlantique* v. *N. V. Rotterdamsche Kolen* [1967] AC 361 (HL) (W) (Arb.).

[13] e.g. *The Laconia* [1977] AC 850 (HL) (W) (Arb.) and *The Scaptrade* [1983] 2 AC 694 (HL) (W).

[14] e.g. *Federal Commerce & Navigation Co. Ltd.* v. *Molena Alpha Inc.* [1979] AC 757 (HL) (W) (Arb.). The Commercial Judge was reversed 8–0 in the Court of Appeal and House of Lords. His only consolation was Lord Wilberforce's phrase at p. 779H: 'My lords, with *genuine* respect for the judgment of Kerr J . . .' (emphasis added)

[15] e.g. *Reardon Smith Line Ltd.* v. *Sanko Steamship Co.* [1976] 1 WLR 989 (HL) (W).

[16] See e.g. *Edward Owen Engineering Ltd.* v. *Barclays Bank International Ltd.* [1978] 1 QB 159 (CA).

[17] e.g. *Woodhouse A. C. Israel Cocoa Ltd.*, v. *Nigerian Produce Marketing Co. Ltd.* [1972] AC 741 (HL) (Arb.).

monetary obligations in terms of sterling.[18] Another development was the increasing relevance of what might be termed 'international public law' factors which came to enter into the resolution of private commercial disputes. The approach to the interpretation of international conventions became less insular and more cosmopolitan.[19] The effect of governmental involvement in trade fell to be considered in many ways.[20] Conflicts of jurisdiction and 'forum shopping' were rife and had to be considered against the increasingly relevant background of international comity.[21] But not all was comity; there was also much open confrontation. In particular, the 'long-arm' jurisdictions claimed by the courts and authorities in the United States over foreign companies produced something of a forensic rift with the United Kingdom, reflected in the reported cases,[22] legislation,[23] and governmental policy decisions.[24]

In parallel with the enormous increase in commercial work generally, there was an even more dramatic increase in interlocutory work in England during this period. 'Interlocutory' means 'pre-trial', but a great proportion of the summonses and applications issued in the Commercial Court owned their origin to purely tactical considerations designed to put pressure on the opposing parties, usually the defendants, and often without any real expectation that the case would ever go to trial. Countless writs were issued solely for the purpose of obtaining some immediate tactical relief. Injunctions, particularly interlocutory orders with the attendant sanction of punishment for contempt of court in the event of a breach, have always been a particularly useful and flexible weapon in the English forensic armoury, and one could easily write a large book on the jurisprudence

---

[18] *Jugoslavenska Oceaneska Plovidba* v. *Castle Investment Co. Inc.* [1974] QB 292 (CA) (Arb.); *Miliangos* v. *George Frank (Textiles) Ltd.* [1976] AC 443 (HL) (W), not following the earlier House of Lords decision in *Re United Railways of Havana* [1961] AC 1007 and *The 'Despina R'* [1979] AC 685 (HL) (W).

[19] See e.g. *James Buchanan & Co. Ltd.* v. *Babco Forwarding & Shipping (UK) Ltd.* [1978] AC 141 (HL) (W) and *Fothergill* v. *Monarch Airlines Ltd.* [1981] AC 251 (HL) (W).

[20] e.g. *The Philippine Admiral* [1975] AC 373 (PC) and *I Congreso del Partido* [1983] AC 244 (HL) (W) in relation to State immunity, and *C. Czarnikow Ltd.* v. *Rolimpex* [1979] AC 351 (HL) (W) (Arb.) in relation to a defence of *force majeure* by a State trading organization based on a decree of its own government.

[21] See e.g. *The 'Atlantic Star'* [1974] AC 436 (HL) (W) *MacShannon* v. *Rockware Glass Ltd.* [1978] AC 795, *Castanho* v. *Brown & Root (UK) Ltd.* [1981] AC 557 (HL) (W) abd *The 'Sennar'* (No. 2) [1985] 1 WLR 490 (HL).

[22] See e.g. *Rio Tinto Zinc Corporation* v. *Westinghouse* [1978] AC 547 (HL) (W) and *British Airways* v. *Laker Airways* [1985] AC 58 (HL).

[23] *Shipping Contracts and Commercial Documents Act 1964,* superseded and repealed by the *Protection of Trading Interests Act 1980.*

[24] The disagreements reflected in these cases and statutes led to the breakdown of negotiations for a Reciprocal Convention for the Enforcement of Judgments with the United States, as a counterpart to the European Judgments Convention enacted in the Civil Jurisdiction and Judgments Act 1982. The other reason was the widespread objection by British industry and the insurance market to the enforcement of exorbitant awards of damages by American juries, quite apart from similar problems with anti-trust proceedings.

concerning interlocutory injunctions alone.[25] The judicial inventions of *Mareva* injunctions and *Anton Piller* orders, both named in memory of their early victims,[26] were the direct consequences of changes in the pattern and volume of commercial disputes. They now stand as monuments to the adaptability of the common law in the face of perceived commercial requirements,[27] although commentators from other jurisdictions can rightly point out that the need for something in the nature of *saisie conservatoire* should have been appreciated much earlier. The enormous expansions of such pre-trial processes is shown by the fact that about 40 per cent of the work of the Commercial Court is now concerned with interlocutory matters.

THE CONSEQUENCES FOR DISPUTE-RESOLVING PROCESSES

This conspectus is inevitably no more than an indication, based in part on personal impressions and recollections, of some of the causes of the enormous expansion in contested commercial disputes which has undoubtedly been seen in this country in the last twenty years or so. Presumably similar trends have been experienced in other commercial centres throughout the world; and economists might find it interesting to compare the predominant topics of commercial litigation and arbitration in different countries. One visible consequence, at any rate in this country, has been the quite startling increase in the number and size of commercial

---

[25] The House of Lords purported to lay down guide-lines for the grant of interlocutory injunctions in *American Cyanamid Co.* v. *Ethicon* [1975] AC 396 (HL) in a single speech delivered by Lord Diplock. (Lord Wilberforce was not sitting.) The indexes to the Law Reports refer to no less than 21 reported cases in which this decision has since been considered, but this is no more than a tiny fraction of the number of cases in which such orders are made each year.

[26] *Mareva Compania Naviera S.A.* v. *International Bulk Carriers S.A.* [1975] 2 LL Rep. 509 (CA) and *Anton Piller K.G.* v. *Manufacturing Processes Ltd.* [1976] Ch. 55. *Mareva* injunctions ensure the 'freezing' of assets of a defendant pending trial where there is a danger of their dispersal to avoid judgment. *Anton Piller* orders permit plaintiffs to enter and search premises for evidence (such as 'pirated' recordings) which might otherwise be destroyed. Both orders are normally made *ex parte* without the defendants' knowledge in the first instance. The indexes of the Law Reports include no less than 31 reported cases in which the *Mareva* jurisdiction has been discussed. But this is no more than a superficial indication of its frequency; many hundreds of *Mareva* and *Anton Piller* orders have no doubt been granted in the decade or so since their invention.

[27] The jurisdiction to grant such injunctions also extends to assistance in English arbitration proceedings, without any pending litigation, and is extensively exercised in the Commercial Court for this purpose; see Mustill and Boyd, *Commercial Arbitration,* p. 300. In *Siskina* v. *Distos Comp. Nav. S.A.* [1979] AC 210 the House of Lords rejected the view that a *Mareva* injunction could be granted in aid of purely foreign proceedings. But this was reversed by legislation in relation to proceedings in the courts of other EEC countries; see Civil Jurisdiction and Judgments Act, 1982, s. 25(1). By s. 25(2) there is power by Order in Council to extend this jurisdiction to grant interim relief in aid of foreign proceedings generally, as well as arbitration proceedings abroad. But no such Order has yet been made.

firms of solicitors and the great demand for commercial lawyers generally. Another is the widespread practice of leading commercial firms of lawyers of opening branches in other countries or entering into close association with foreign firms.[28] There appears to have been something of an explosion in the number of commercial lawyers throughout the world. In the main this is no doubt a consequence of the need to meet the demands of actual or potential clients. But it is more than a consequence; it is also a *cause*, which itself generates disputes and the need for machinery to revolve them. *Quot jurisconsulti, tot contestationes, tot lites.*[29] More commercial judges have been needed, at any rate in England, though the number of High Court judges is still remarkably low.[30] As regards lawyers and laymen in other professions who frequently act as arbitrators, many are finding that this work is being transformed from a part-time vocation into a full-time professional business. Furthermore, viewed nationally and sometimes chauvinistically, the availability of facilities for the resolution of commercial disputes has become something akin to a service industry, which is regarded by governments as ancillary to commerce itself. In the same way as commerce, the provision of dispute-resolving services—principally by means of arbitration—has become increasingly competitive. International commercial arbitration appears to be eclipsing litigation in national courts in many parts of the world. But, at any rate in England, international commercial litigation has equally been faced with something like an explosion in demand over recent years, and this is still increasing.

The consequences of the trends summarized in the foregoing section are reflected in the recent history of the Commercial Court. They have led to immense jurisprudential reforms in English arbitration law; and they are in the process of transforming international arbitration logistically and jurisprudentially. In all three aspects one can see how the administration of justice, and ultimately the substantive law itself, have been forced to adapt themselves to the needs of the dispute-resolving processes in international commerce, and even to the market forces operating within this new forensic industry itself.

---

[28] Many leading American and English firms now have offices in the major commercial centres of Europe and the Middle and Far East. As explained later, one historical aspect of this trend is that the perceived need for what became the Arbitration Act 1979 can to a large extent be traced back to the desire of a lobby of American firms of lawyers to conduct commercial arbitrations in London.

[29] The former Chief Justice of the United States, Warren Burger, often told of the small American town in which the one and only lawyer could hardly make ends meet, when—to his consternation—another lawyer put up his brass plate in competition. But within six months both were overworked, had heart attacks, and were advertising for assistants.

[30] There are only about 80 judges in the 3 divisions of the High Court; Queen's Bench, Chancery, and Family.

THE COMMERCIAL COURT

The Commercial Court provides an admirable statistical yardstick of recent developments in this country, as well as a clear illustration of the adaptation of the process of dispute resolution to meet the changing needs of the 'customers'.[31]

The court originated in the 1890s as a list of cases to be heard by judges whose practice at the Bar involved commercial work. Its main objectives were expertise, speed, and informality, and a special feature was that the judges themselves, not masters or registrars, dealt with all interlocutory matters. One, and later two, Queen's Bench judges used to devote a small part of their time to this list as and when necessary. Lord Devlin recently said that, when he was in charge of it in the fifties, he spent on it an average of only a few days each month. But with a vast increase in commercial disputes and the need to service them by quicker and more effective decisions, the picture changed dramatically. In 1960 a Commercial Court Users Conference was set up by the Lord Chancellor at the users' request, to deal with calls for greater efficiency; it issued a report in 1962. Numerous further procedural simplifications for commercial cases were introduced in the following years, and in 1970 the Commercial Court was formally set up by statute,[32] staffed by specialized judges appointed by the Lord Chancellor. There were only a few to begin with, but now there are ten, a fifth of the entire Queen's Bench division. Five of them sit in London every working day with the full-time assistance of a Clerk of the List and backed by a standing Commercial Court Committee composed of judges, practitioners, and representatives of the various trading communities. The vast majority of the litigants are neither resident nor incorporated in this country. The enormous expansion of the work of the court can be seen from a few figures. There were 8 commercial cases in 1947, 15 in 1957, and 21 in 1958.[33] There were then no official statistics until 1974, when the number of actions was still only 69.[34] But in 1978, 339 cases were listed for trial and 1,180 summonses were heard. By 1984/5 these figures rose to 446

---

[31] Although far less busy than the Commercial Court, with only one regular judge, the Admiralty Court should not be overlooked in the present context. Many of its cases arise from the physical—as opposed to the commercial—incidents of shipping, such as collisions, wrecks, and occasionally salvage disputes, though the vast majority of these are arbitrated in London under 'Lloyds Form'. But a substantial number of the cases cited in the foregoing section originated in the Admiralty Court, and it is frequently concerned with international jurisdictional disputes and allegations of 'forum shopping' or the wrongful arrest of ships as security for claims.

[32] See n. 2. By s. 4 of the 1970 Act of Commercial Judges can sit as arbitrators or umpires in commercial disputes, at low fees which are paid into central funds. But the system is little used, since the cases have to take their normal turn in the list.

[33] Colman *Practice and Procedure of the Commercial Court* (1983), 10.

[34] See 'Yearly Judicial Statistics' issued by the Lord Chancellor's Department, and in recent years the annual reports of the Commercial Court Committee.

and 2296 including over 337 applications for injunctions. In addition, more than 1429 documentary applications were made *ex parte* and dealt with by the judges in their rooms outside court hours. The 8 commercial cases heard in 1947 occupied 22 days. In 1984/5 the court sat on 934 judge-days, equivalent to about 93 per cent of the available judicial time. The overall increase in the work of the court in the last decade must be something of the order of 800 per cent and it is continuing to grow so much that there are now again unacceptable delays in getting dates for trials. Although cases can be expedited, and urgent applications are heard in a matter of days or even hours, ordinary actions estimated at about 3 to 4 days are having to be listed as much as 2 years ahead.

So for the second time since the war, the Commercial Court is in a state of crisis, despite its enormous expansion. The problem is that it is too popular. The obvious remedy—more judges—is said to be precluded by financial constraints. To ask the litigants—mainly foreign companies—to pay higher court fees[35] to provide the cost of more judges has so far been ruled out on constitutional grounds.[36] But reforms are constantly under consideration to cope with the continuously rising demands for court time.[37] Their invariable objective is to speed up, simplify, and shorten all hearings. Quantity, not quality, is the clear priority in the changing scene of dispute resolution processes, even in the Commercial Court.

THE TRANSFORMATION OF ENGLISH ARBITRATION

For arbitration, the changes have not been merely logistic, but fundamental. The exceptional degree of control traditionally exercised by the English courts over arbitrations conducted in England has already been mentioned and is indeed notorious. It enshrined what was until recently regarded as a fundamental principle of English law that the judges must be the final arbiters on all contested issues of law. For instance, when a reference to arbitration was challenged in a technical claim based on alleged breaches of contract, the Master of the Rolls said in 1912 in *Rowe Bros. v. Crossley Bros.*[38] that there was no doubt considerable force in the

---

[35] The cost of litigation in England (ignoring lawyers' fees!) is astonishingly low. The charge for the issue of a writ is £60, for a summons or other application £15, and £100 when a case is set down for trial. No more is payable, whether the case lasts one hour or months, and whether it involves a trifle or hundreds of millions of dollars, as some commercial cases nowadays do.

[36] Ch. 29 of Magna Carta, 1215, provides: 'We will sell to no man, we will deny or defer to any man either justice or right.'

[37] The 'Civil Justice Review' instituted by the Lord Chancellor will include the Commercial Court. The Commercial Court Committee has also recently adopted a report designed to simplify and streamline many procedures; in particular, to shorten counsel's speeches and oral testimony.

[38] [1913] 108 LT 11 (CA) (Arb.), 14, per Lord Cozens-Hardy, MR.

comment that 'there cannot be anything more absurd than to refer to a civil engineer difficult questions arising under the law of contract'. Admittedly, the arbitration clause was ultimately upheld, but only because any error of law by the arbitrators would in due course be corrected by the court under the 'case stated' procedure. And in the famous decision of a great Court of Appeal in 1922, *Czarnikow* v. *Roth, Schmidt & Co.*,[39] a commercial contract providing that neither party would resort to this procedure was held to be 'contrary to public policy'—a concept which has virtually no place in our commercial law. Lord Justice Scrutton added: 'There must be no Alsatia in England where the king's writ does not run.'[40] Alsatia was not Alsace, but a cant name for the London district of Whitefriars (derived from the Carmelites) between the Temple and St Paul's, which had been a sanctuary for debtors and criminals from 1214 until 1623. What Scrutton meant by Alsatia was a lawless realm within the kingdom, a 'no-go' area ruled by people called 'arbitrators'. Such a state of affairs was regarded as inconceivable, nefarious, and dangerous; only the courts could give a binding decision whenever any issue of law arose in a legal dispute. And in this connection it must always be borne in mind that in English law the correct interpretation of any provision in a contract is a question of construction, and therefore a question of law.[41] As recently as 1973 the Court of Appeal, with Lord Denning, MR. presiding, reversed a decision of the Commercial Court whereby—as a matter of discretion—a judge had declined to order two experienced maritime arbitrators to state a case for the opinion of the court on the meaning of a 'one-off' typed clause in a charterparty.[42] It was held that there was virtually no discretion to refuse to order a 'special case' if the dispute involved a material point of law. The decision was perhaps the apogee of an esoteric, though fundamental, aspect of English jurisprudence. But it had grown to the size of a dinosaur which could not survive in a changed forensic climate.

This ancient corner-stone of our law of arbitration, and the principle of public policy which it enshrined, were simply swept away, and with

---

[39] [1922] 2 KB 478 (CA) (Arb.); per Bankes, Scrutton, and Atkin, LL J.

[40] Ibid. 488. In Scots law this principle of public policy has never existed. There was no 'special case' procedure until recently, and when it was introduced by the *The Administration of Justice (Scotland) Act 1972*, the right to demand it could be excluded by agreement: see ss. 3 and 5. This remains the position; the 1979 Act does not apply to Scotland or to Northern Ireland.

[41] See *'The Nema'* (*supra*, n. 6), 736.

[42] *Halfdan Grieg & Co. A/S* v. *Sterling Coal (The 'Lysland')* [1973] 1 QB 843. I was again the judge in error. But the subsequent history of the case was hardly a good advertisement for the 'special case' procedure. The arbitrators disagreed and appointed an umpire. His award was reversed by another Commercial Judge, Ackner J. (as he then was), whose decision was upheld, but only by a majority, in another Court of Appeal over two years later, with Lord Denning, MR, dissenting; see [1976] 1 LL Rep. 427. The dispute had arisen in 1964! Lord Denning said later that he regretted the original decision.

amazing speed,[43] by the Arbitration Act, 1979, a historic landmark in our jurisprudence. The reasons were purely logistical and commercial. The logistical factor was that the Commercial Court could no longer cope with the flood of 'special cases',[44] in part because the procedure had become increasingly abused by defendants as a means of delay which the Court was powerless to prevent. The commercial factor was the desire to attract international arbitrations to this country, in response to pressure from—in particular—American legal and commercial interests.[45] But they were no exception; virtually all foreign lawyers and their clients disliked the 'special case' procedure intensely. This was only in part because of its inherent delays. The main, though closely connected, reason was that while anxious to arbitrate here, they were unwilling to risk—or in complex cases to face the virtual certainty of—subjection to the English courts by way of appeal on issues of law from their chosen arbitral tribunals. *A fortiori* foreign governments and State trading agencies were unwilling to arbitrate here, and the International Chamber of Commerce (ICC), still the most powerful body of international arbitration in the world, hardly ever selected this country as the nominated venue under ICC arbitration clauses, unless of course the parties had already done so by agreement. The commercial objective of this important piece of law reform was frankly acknowledged at the time. When Lord Elwyn Jones, then Lord Chancellor, introduced the bill which became the 1979 Act into the House of Lords, he said: 'The purpose is to remove certain legal obstacles which at present stand in the way of London being used to its full potential as an international centre for arbitration.'[46]

This is not the place for a detailed examination of the 1979 Act;[47] it is

[43] The origins of the Act stem from Lord Diplock's 'Alexander Lecture' in Feb. 1978 (Arbitration, Apr. 1978), 107) and the 'Report on Arbitration' by the Commercial Court Committee chaired by Donaldson J. (as he then was) in July 1978, Cmnd. 7284. The Act came into force on 4 Apr. 1979.

[44] A notorious, though exceptional, illustration stems from a partial embargo imposed for three months in 1973 on the export of soya bean products from the United States. This turned into a catastrophe for the world futures market in this unexciting commodity. The rights and obligations under thousands of international string contracts were thrown into utter confusion. Nearly all had been concluded on a standard form of contract providing for English law and GAFTA arbitration in London. Many hundreds were contested, and well over a hundred special cases were drafted for submission to the courts. Despite attempts at test cases, of which one was taken all the way to the Lords (*Bremer Handelsgesellschaft* v. *Vanden Avenne Izegem P.V.S.A.* [1978] 2 LL. Rep. 109 (HL) (W) (Arb.)) and innumerable settlements, about 50 special cases went to the Commercial Court, and many reached the Court of Appeal, some as recently as 1985, 12 years after the dispute arose. The original demands for arbitration unfortunately all predated the 1979 Act.

[45] See the debate in the House of Lords 'International Arbitration: London', on 15 May 1978, Hansard, vol. 392 col. 90. The desirability of bringing more "one-off" international arbitrations to London was likened to an invisible export, and Lords Wilberforce, Diplock, and Scarman were among the speakers who supported repeal of the 'special case' procedure.

[46] See *Hansard*, 397 (12 Dec. 1978) col. 434.

[47] For an early commentary see Kerr, *Modern Law Review* 45. But the jurisprudence

merely necessary to note three of its principal implications in the present context. First, the Act is itself a purely pragmatic compromise. Designed to provide the most acceptable machinery for the resolution of commercial disputes by arbitration in this country, it seeks to do so by a skilful combination of checks and balances. The special case procedure is abolished,[48], but a highly restricted right of appeal is substituted,[49] though this can only be taken beyond the commercial Court in exceptional circumstances.[50] On the other hand, in all cases other than domestic arbitrations and disputes arising out of international contracts relating to shipping, insurance, and commodity transactions, the right of appeal to the courts can be wholly barred by so-called exclusion agreements which can be made at any time, even upon conclusion of the original contract.[51] So parties can agree 'London arbitration' under virtually all 'one-off' contracts without any fear of the English courts.

None of these measures was designed to improve the quality of arbitral awards or of the arbitral dispute-resolving process itself. Their sole aim was customer satisfaction. The only qualification of the purely logistical aims of the Act is the restriction imposed upon exclusion agreements, which was designed, rightly, to maintain some uniformity in the development of these three important aspects of our commercial law and in decisions on the interpretation of important standard contracts which are in world-wide use. On the other hand, as a balance to this check, or a check to this balance, the categories of cases in which exclusion agreements are barred can be modified by the Secretary of State for Trade and Industry by Order in Council, without the need for further primary legislation.[52]

The second point to note is the somewhat ironic fact that an act designed to streamline the arbitral process to satisfy its 'customers' subsequently had to be rescued from failure in its main objective by two decisions of the House of Lords.[53] There can be no more striking examples of the modern 'purposive' approach to statutory interpretation than the effect of these two cases upon the wording of the 1979 Act. They clearly went much further than the draftsmen intended or dared. The Act empowers the Court to give leave to appeal from an arbitrator's award (assuming no valid exclusion agreement) if 'the determination of the question of law concerned could substantially affect the rights of one or more of the parties'.[54] That would have left the position much the same as under the

---

governing the right of appeal has been transformed by two decisions of the House of Lords; see n. 53.   [48] See n. 8.   [49] Arbitration Act 1979, s. 1(2)—(6).
[50] Ibid., s. 1(7).   [51] Ibid., s. 4(1) and (2).   [52] Ibid., s. 4(3) and (4).
[53] *The 'Nema'* (*supra, n. 6*) and *Antaios Compania Naviera S.A v. Salem Rederierna A.B.* [1985] AC 191 (HL) (Arb.). Lord Wilberforce was not sitting on either appeal. In the latter case the Commercial Court judge had (rightly) refused leave to appeal from the decision of the arbitral tribunal, but then gave leave to appeal to the Court of Appeal on the question whether he should have granted leave to appeal from the arbitrators!   [54] s. 1(4)

old 'special case' procedure. But by a tortuous process of construction, with Lord Diplock as the main architect on both occasions, the House of Lords managed to produce a very different regime. In doing so, Lord Diplock went much further than his own interpretation of this provision during the debate on the Bill.[55] The power to give leave to appeal from an arbitrator to the Commercial Court is now restricted to cases where the judges conclude, virtually as a matter of first impression,[56] that the arbitrator was 'obviously wrong' in relation to 'one-off' clauses or situations, or 'prima facie . . . apparently wrong' in relation to 'standard' provisions.

The general view of commercial practitioners appears to be that these criteria have caused the pendulum to swing much too far in inhibiting appeals, and that their application by different commercial judges in different cases is producing random decisions and great uncertainty. It must be hoped that this unfortunate state of affairs will not persist for long. The test should be simpler and more consistent, and should involve much more reflection than an 'off-the-cuff' reaction. Given those classes of cases in which the power to give leave to appeal on issues of law has been deliberately retained by Parliament, and where it has not been deliberately excluded by agreement between the parties, the test should not be excessively restrictive. Arbitrators are bound to apply the law; and we should retain a balanced regime of 'judicial review' over them, as was the policy of the Act.[57] It should be open to the Court to grant leave to appeal whenever it is satisfied that the arbitral tribunal may have erred in law in a respect which has materially affected its award. The present piece of what can only be described as 'judicial legislation' goes much too far in its purely utilitarian approach to the process of resolving complex legal disputes.

Thirdly, however, apart from this important criticism, there appear to be no convincing arguments or representations against the concept of the 1979 Act. Openly contrived compromises—as the Act was—seldom have outspoken admirers, and it will no doubt still take some years before it will be possible to assess the extent to which the Act has succeeded in its primary purpose of 'London being used to its full potential as an

---

[55] *Hansard*, 397 (12 Dec. 1978), col. 449. He then said he was sure that leave to appeal would be given 'only in serious cases where there is a genuine point of law which is important to the rights of the parties to be decided'.

[56] See *The 'Nema'* (*supra*, n. 6), 742G–743G. Lord Diplock went so far as to say that no reasons should normally be given for a grant or refusal of leave; see *Antaios* (*supra*, n. 53), 205H–206A.

[57] See Kerr, 'Arbitration and the Courts: The UNCITRAL Model Law', (1985). 34. *Int. and Comp. Law Quarterly*, 1 at 15, 16. The Commercial Arbitration Act 1986 of British Columbia (applicable to domestic arbitrations) is an improvement on the 1979 Act. It permits leave to appeal (*inter alia*) in cases where 'the importance of the result of the arbitration to the parties justifies the intervention of the court and the determination of the point of law may prevent a miscarriage of justice'.

international centre for arbitration'.[58] But a substantial measure of success in this direction does not appear to be in doubt. While there are of course no statistics of the cases in which parties nowadays agree on arbitration in this country in their contracts, with or without exclusion agreements, the experience of the recently restructured London Court of International Arbitration (LCIA) in receiving requests for the appointment of arbitrators is highly encouraging.[59] There are also signs that more ICC arbitrations are nowadays directed to this country. Moreover, while exclusion agreements may well be fairly commonplace, one also hears surprisingly often that the parties prefer to preserve the possibility of a right of appeal.

Finally, and of particular interest in this connection, it seems clear that there is no real pressure from any quarter to restrict—let alone abolish—the surviving rights of appeal from arbitral tribunals on issues of law. In 1984 the Commercial Court Committee set up a 'Sub-Committee on Arbitration Law' whose task included a review of the working of the 1979 Act. It was chaired by Mustill J. (as he then was), and included commercial practitioners, lay arbitrators, and a representative from the Department of Trade and Industry. After wide consultation it reported in 1985 as follows:

As regards the right of appeal to the High Court on questions of law, there appears to be fairly general satisfaction with the balance struck by the 1979 Act. We received no representations to the effect that the position should be restored to what it was before the 1979 legislation, and we would not ourselves favour this. Conversely, although there was some support for the elimination of the special categories of transactions in respect of which the parties cannot contract out of the right of appeal, this was a minority view. Our own opinion is that these special categories should be maintained.[60]

In the upshot the 1979 Act has effected a profound change and a substantial measure of modernization in our law concerning court control over issues of law raised in international commercial arbitrations held in this country. It represents a strong move towards the *laissez-faire* position in civil law jurisdictions. But, by a typically English compromise, it has

---

[58] See *supra*, n. 46.

[59] The LCIA is a legal entity set up by a Joint Committee of Management of representatives of the Chartered Institute of Arbitrators, the Corporation of the City of London, and the London Chamber of Commerce and Industry. It has 24 members, 6 from the United Kingdom and the remainder from other countries, with an English president and 3 foreign vice-presidents. Its task is to apply and keep under review the LCIA Rules (at present, 1985 ed.) which can be used for arbitration anywhere in the world, not only in England. The administration of the LCIA by its registrar and deputy is carried out from the premises of the Chartered Institute, 75 Cannon Street, London.

[60] Commercial Court Committee, Sub committee on Arbitration Law, Final Report, 22 Oct. 1985, conclusion (4) and p. 5 and paras. 12–15.

retained a measure of court control by a restricted right of appeal, though in all cases other than disputes concerning shipping, insurance, and commodities—virtually all governed by standard forms of contracts—the 'customers' have the option of excluding any such right.[61] The weakness of the act is the complex and unsatisfactory jurisprudence governing the remaining restricted rights of appeal, when these have not been excluded by agreement.[62] And the ultimate objective—in the 1979 Act and the jurisprudence to which it gave rise—has again been productivity and quantity, not quality, in the processes of commercial dispute resolution.

THE INTERNATIONAL SCENE

Space precludes any detailed review of recent developments in the processes of commercial dispute resolution in the world at large. I can give only an indication of the general picture, which is in any event well known and abundantly documented. There appears to be a vast expansion in international arbitrations, particularly in the last decade. The business of resolving international commercial disputes by arbitration has become a new forensic and commercial industry in its own right.

That there is need for more arbitration—and therefore for more arbitrators, arbitral organizations, venues etc—cannot be doubted. The English experience of an enormous increase in international commercial disputes, as described in the foregoing sections, is obviously symptomatic of a similar trend world-wide. And although commercial litigation in other countries has no doubt also increased, perhaps even to the same extent as in the Commercial Court in London, the parties to international commercial disputes and their lawyers are traditionally averse to litigating in any national courts other than their own, which the other side will dislike most of all. A surge in international arbitrations generally is the only possible outcome and this is what we are witnessing now.

In its turn, this development has brought with it a number of by-products. Lawyers, as well as important 'customers' in expanding fields such as construction and civil engineering, have been deluged with

---

[61] The 1979 Act has not affected the jurisdiction of the courts to exercise control over the conduct—or 'misconduct'—of arbitrations, even during the course of the reference if necessary; see Arbitration Act 1950, s. 23(1). However, as pointed out in Mustill and Boyd, *Commercial Arbitration,* the exercise of these powers is very rarely considered before the completion of arbitration; see p. 22 n. 20, and p. 473.

[62] In order to 'appreciate' the full effect of the decisions of the House of Lords (mainly contained in two speeches by Lord Diplock) in *The Nema* and *Antaios* cases (*supra,* nn. 6, 53), one might consult the 16 cases in the Index to the Law Reports 1981-5 in which they have been considered. See also Mustill and Boyd, *Commercial Arbitrations,* 559–63.

publications, learned articles, seminars and conferences dealing with international arbitration.[63] Arbitral institutions and organizations are being set up or expanded all over the world, particularly in the form of so-called arbitration centres, which seek to create focal points for the promotion of arbitration within their territory, with varying degrees of success.[64] Their products range from information and the provision of premises and office facilities to the compilation of panels of arbitrators and rules for arbitrations conducted under their auspices.[65] But by themselves these activities will never succeed in diverting the mainstream of international arbitrations from their traditional venues.

The principal impetus must come from reforms designed to ensure the compatibility of local laws and practices with the requirements of the 'customers' and their legal advisers. And this is what is happening. New arbitration laws are being enacted in many parts of the world.[66] Their philosophies differ, particularly in the context of judicial control as against arbitral autonomy. In some cases these conflicts of jurisprudential policy have been resolved by enacting different legislation for domestic and international arbitrations respectively;[67] in others, such as the English 1979 Act, by the compromise of a single statute incorporating various alternatives. The greatest advance is likely to stem from the concept of UNCITRAL Model Law, a ready-made package designed for adoption or adaptation to international commercial arbitration anywhere in the world.

Countries with a tradition of a highly developed system of commercial and arbitral law are obviously less likely to adopt this model without

---

[63] A reconstruction of my diaries shows participation in no less than 19 conferences or seminars on arbitration from 1983 to 1986 of which 14 were 'international'. Lord Wilberforce's experience since his retirement in 1982 will have been even greater. In particular, when the Chartered Institute of Arbitrators was accorded 'Observer Status' by the United Nations Commission on International Trade Law (UNCITRAL) in relation to its evolvement of the 'Model Law on International Commercial Arbitration', he represented the Institute at the final sessions of the Working Group and when the final text was adopted by UNCITRAL in June 19854. He is of course also in great demand as an international sole arbitrator and umpire.

[64] Records at the LCIA list arbitral institutions, or 'centres', in 25 territories, with 18 more planned for the near future. There is also a World Arbitration Centre in New York, presumably for interplanetary disputes.

[65] As long ago as 1975, 'International Commercial Arbitration' (Oceana) listed 'a selection' of no less than 43 conventions, draft uniform laws, agreements, enactments, and arbitration rules dealing with the settlement of international commercial disputes. In the following edition this list had grown to 76, and may have reached three figures by now.

[66] In the Commonwealth, the English 1979 Act was largely followed, with adaptations by Hong Kong in 1982 and Australia in 1984, but only for domestic arbitrations in British Columbia and other parts of Canada in 1986, where legislation for international arbitration has been based on the UNCITRAL Model Law. On the continent, France (1981), Switzerland (1982), and the Netherlands (1986) have all introduced new legislation to promote arbitration.

[67] e.g. in France in 1981 and various Canadian provinces in 1986. The UNCITRAL Model Law envisages this by Article 1, but it could be used for any type of arbitration.

modification than others.[68] But whatever the form and content of the network of new or reformed legislation which is spreading across the world, the objective is invariably promotional: to encourage commercial arbitration as an alternative to litigation,[69] and above all to attract international commercial arbitrations to local venues away from foreign competition, in the same way as commerce itself.

The crowded history of the process of resolving commercial disputes in recent decades has been purely logistical and utilitarian. It has had little to do with jurisprudence as such, and virtually nothing with the objective of promoting judgements and awards in accordance with justice and law. But, from the point of view of the parties, the results achieved by litigation and arbitration depend on the quality of the judges and arbitrators and of the rules they are obliged to apply.[70] We are in great danger of allowing the pendulum of expediency to swing too far. In particular, the world is losing sight of the real purpose of commercial arbitration. It is treating it as though it were merely something in the nature of a competitive service industry. But unless the parties have opted to have their disputes decided *ex aequo et bono,* arbitration—like the highest levels of litigation—is a complex forensic process. Its outcome should be rationally predictable, and subsequently justifiable, according to legal principles. At present it is often too arbitrary in comparison with litigation, much more expensive, and no speedier. Nevertheless, the future of commercial dispute resolution lies with arbitration. In relation to international disputes, at any rate, more and more businessmen and their lawyers will say with Shakespeare: 'The end crowns all; and that old common arbitrator, time, will one day end it.' "So to him we leave it." '[71]

---

[68] In the United Kingdom the government has set up a committee to advise on adoption of the Model Law, but this appears unlikely without substantial modification. For a view on this question see *supra,* 57. It is also unlikely to be adopted in the forseeable future by countries which have recently legislated on arbitration, such as France, Switzerland, and the Netherlands. Enquiries made by the LCIA suggest that apart from Canada, early adoption might ensue in Hong Kong and Japan, but is highly unlikely in any of the above-mentioned countries or in the United States, West Germany, Austria, or Spain.

[69] There are already signs of alternatives to arbitration being sought as well: see e.g. Schmitthoff 'Extrajudicial Dispute Settlement,' Forum Internationale No. 6., May 1985.

[70] The Chartered Institute of Arbitrators in London is believed to be the only arbitral institution which organizes courses, pupillage, and examinations for applicants to Fellowship. The Centre for Commercial Law Studies at Queen Mary College, London University, now has a School of International Arbitration for postgraduate studies.

[71] *Troilus and Cressida,* IV, v. 222-3. Hector and Ulysses are discussing the uncertain and distant outcome of the Trojan war during an interlocutory truce, when all the gods had clearly shown themselves to be partial and unfit to arbitrate. But Ulysses did not leave it on this quasi-arbitral basis, as he had agreed. He devised the Trojan horse, in breach of all the rules of pleadings, discovery, and natural justice.

10

State Corporations in International Relations

by DR F. A. MANN, CBE, FBA

I

Not long ago it was said by the Supreme Court of the United States of America:

Increasingly during this century, governments throughout the world have established separately constituted legal entities to perform a variety of tasks. The organisation and control of these entities vary considerably, but many possess a number of common features. A typical government instrumentality, if one can be said to exist, is created by an enabling statute that prescribes the powers and duties of the instrumentality and specifies that it is to be managed by a board selected by the government in a manner consistent with the enabling law. The instrumentality is typically established as a separate juridicial entity, with the powers to hold and sell property and to sue and be sued. Except for appropriations to provide capital or to cover losses, the instrumentality is primarily responsible for its own finances. The instrumentality is run as a distinct economic enterprise; often it is not subject to the same budgetary and personnel requirements with which government agencies must comply.[1]

This description certainly fits conditions in the United Kingdom, where there exist such diverse corporations as the British Steel Corporation, the National Coal Board, the Independent Broadcasting Authority,[2] the Secretary of State for Defence (who is a corporation sole[3]), or the regional health authorities, the area health authorities, the Special Health Authority, and the Family Practitioners Committee, each of which is a body corporate.[4] The list could be considerably extended, but one of the cardinal questions always is whether, and in what respects, the corporation can be identified with, or is to be considered, a department or organ of government, or, on the contrary, is independent of, and distinct from, the

---

[1] *First National City Bank* v. *Banco Para El Comercio Exterior de Cuba,* 462 US 611, 624 (1983).

[2] It is a body corporate: s. 1(1) of the Broadcasting Act 1981; but by para 4(2) of Schedule 1 of the same Act it is, for purposes of privilege, not to be treated as a body exercising functions on behalf of the Crown.

[3] Defence (Transfer of Functions) Act 1964, s. 2.

[4] National Health Service Act 1977, Schedule 5, para. 8. On public corporations see, in particular, the illuminating survey by Sir William Wade, *Administrative Law,* 5th edn. (1982), 139–56.

Crown, or, as one should perhaps say more accurately,[5] the State. The problem of the immunity of the Crown and its emanations from proceedings in the United Kingdom is today of little or no importance,[6] but subjection to legislation or privilege in respect of discovery may be a matter of difficulty; thus the Secretary of State for Social Services is clearly entitled to privilege, although he is a corporation sole,[7] but the health authorities have by statute been deprived of it,[8] although they exercise their functions on behalf of the Crown. The Custodian of Enemy Property is,[9] but the British Transport Commission is not,[10] a servant or agent of the Crown or a government department, yet if the latter body cannot pay the loss falls on the Consolidated Fund.[11] The Independent Broadcasting Authority is a body corporate exercising functions on behalf of the Crown, but for purposes of privilege is excluded from privilege.[12] As regards the status of British State corporations in international relations, there does not seem to be any material except one rather curious incident.[13] In connection with American anti-trust proceedings, Mr Geoffrey Lloyd, then Minister of Fuel and Power, in October 1952 ordered the Anglo-Iranian Oil Company 'not to produce any documents which were not in the United States of America and which do not relate to business in the United States without in either case the authority of Her Majesty's Government'. In November 1952 Sir Anthony Eden, then Foreign Secretary, certified to the United States court that Mr Lloyd's letter was signed

in his capacity as Minister of Fuel and Power in Her Majesty's Government in the United Kimgdom and was issued with the official approval and under the full authority of Her Majesty's Government in the United Kingdom. This letter from the Minister of Fuel and Power embraced a claim of sovereignty in that it was addressed to British subjects and organisations by Her Majesty's Government in the exercise of their Governmental authority and in the British public interest including the economic, strategic and political interests of Her Majesty's Government.

In the light of this correspondence and of the fact that the British Government owned 35 per cent of the capital and the majority of the

---

[5] In *Town Investments Ltd.* v. *Department of the Environment* [1978] AC 359 Lord Diplock suggested (381) that it would be appropriate 'if instead of speaking of "the Crown" we were to speak of "the government" '. But it is submitted with great respect that the Government is the agent of the Crown which is synonymous with the State—i.e. the United Kingdom of Great Britain and Northern Ireland.

[6] This is due to the Crown Proceedings Act 1947.

[7] Halsbury, *Laws of England,* VIII, para. 1239.

[8] National Health Act 1977, Schedule 5, para. 15(2).

[9] *Bank voor Handel en Scheepvaart* v. *Administrator of Hungarian Property* [1954] AC 584.

[10] *Tamlin* v. *Hannaford* [1950] 1 KB 18.

[11] Ibid. 23, per Denning L J (as he then was), on behalf of the Court.

[12] Broadcasting Act 1981, s. 1(1) and Schedule 1, para. 4(2).

[13] See, generally, Mann, *Foreign Affairs in English Courts* (1986), 6, 7.

voting rights in the Anglo-Iranian Oil Company, the American court held that 'the corporation Anglo-Iranian Oil Company is indistinguishable from the Government of Great Britain.[14]

It would be wrong to draw any general conclusion from this isolated case, which may well have involved an excess of power on the part of Mr Lloyd.

The problems arising in international relations are much more richly illustrated by cases relating to the State corporations which in the Communist world (and this expression is intended to include Cuba) have been established to carry on foreign trade. As Professor Knapp of the University of Prague has described the position in some detail,[15] in pursuance of complete control of each country's entire economy, the Communist States have created foreign trade corporations which are legal persons, and which 'are as a rule exclusively, i.e. by virtue of a monopoly, entitled to export and import certain kinds of merchandise that are strictly defined or to carry on another foreign trade activity'. In order to prevent misunderstanding it should be added that State corporations having the monopoly of trading in certain goods also occur in some other than Communist countries; an important example coming from Franco Spain will have to be considered later.

In discussing the international problems of State corporations, it is important to give due weight to two characteristic aspects. On the one hand, it should never be overlooked that, whatever the formal position may be, it is always the State which owns the entity. Though, for instance, the Secretary of State for Social Services in the United Kingdom is a corporation sole in whom hospitals and other property are vested,[16] he holds them on behalf of the Crown,[17] just as he exercises his functions on behalf of the Crown.[18] In the United States of America sovereign immunity is enjoyed by an instrumentality of a foreign State which is a separate legal person and a majority of whose 'ownership interest' is owned by the State'[19] Yet an American judge of first instance arrived at the surprising conclusion that this condition was not fulfilled by a Yugoslav workers' organization founded for the purpose of constructing and operating nuclear power stations, for it was mere 'political theory' that in a

---

[14] *In re Investigation of World Arrangements relating to Petroleum*, 13 FRD 280, 291 (1952), in part also in *Int. LR* 19 (1952), 197.

[15] *Sources of the Law of International Trade*, ed. Schmitthoff (1964), 61.

[16] The original vesting occurred by virtue of s. 6 of the National Health Service Act 1946.

[17] This follows from the case mentioned in n. 5.

[18] In *Nottingham Area No. 1 Hospital Management Committee* v. *Owen* [1957] 3 All ER 358 it was held that since 1946 hospitals have been Crown property occupied for the public service of the Crown; and in *Pfizer* v. *Ministry of Health* [1965] AC 512 it was held that National Health Service authorities exercise their functions on behalf of the Crown.

[19] S. 1603(b) of the Foreign Sovereign Immunities Act 1976, the text of which is conveniently printed in *Int. LR* 63, 655.

Socialist state all property ultimately belongs to the State.[20] On the other hand, there are many State corporations which are limited companies of the familiar type; this applies to the German Salzgitter A.G.[21] and the Portuguese shipbuilding company known as Setenave.[22] For international purposes it would be desirable if it made no or little difference which formal structure the state has chosen to attribute to its corporations.[23]

However this may be, one legal conclusion is common to all forms of State corporations and, it seems, to all countries. The status assigned to the entity, in particular its corporate character, is universally recognized. To quote once again the Supreme Court of the United States:

Due respect for the actions taken by foreign sovereigns and for principles of comity between nations . . . leads us to conclude—as the courts of Great Britain have concluded in other circumstances—that government instrumentalities established as juridical entities distinct and independent from their sovereign should normally be treated as such.[24]

The same attitude has been adopted, for instance, by courts and authoritative writers of the Federal Republic of Germany,[25] where, in particular, it was emphasized that there was no room for denying the legal personality of State enterprises on the ground of *ordre public*.[26]

II

The principal problem created by the international activities of State corporations[27] used to arise from claims to sovereign immunity, though such a claim was rarely made by a State corporation in a Communist country, because the character as a legal entity was believed to exclude the 'danger that the foreign trade corporations would claim for themselves the immunities and prerogatives which belong to the state and its property'.[28] That problem, however, has for all practical purposes disappeared. Since the State itself, its government or its organs, such as, for instance, an officer comparable to Britain's Secretary of State for Defence, cannot

---

[20] *Eldow International Co.* v. *Nuklearna Elektrarna Krsko,* 441 F. Supp. 827 (1977); also *Int. LR* 63, 100.

[21] The whole of this commercial company's share capital belongs to the Federal Republic.

[22] It is the principal debtor referred to in *Settebello Ltd.* v. *Banco Totta* [1985] 1 WLR 1050.

[23] This point is emphasized by Böckstiegel, *Der Staat als Vertragspartner ausländischer Privatunternehmen* (1971) 49, 73.

[24] See *Supra,* (n. 1), 626–7.

[25] Ebenroth, in *Münchener Kommentar,* n. 440 after Article 10, with ref.

[26] Grossfeld, *Internationales Gesellschaftsrecht* (1981), in Staudinger, n. 133, 153.

[27] A most useful survey is provided by Fischer and von Hoffmann, *Staatsunternehmen im Völkerrecht und im internationalen Privatrecht,* Berichte der Deutschen Gesellschaft für Völkerrecht, 25 (1984).

[28] Knapp (*supra,* n. 15), 63.

State Corporations in International Relations 135

invoke immunity in relation to 'a commercial transaction' or, indeed, to any contract of any kind wholly or partly performable in Britain,[29] no separate entity, however closely connected with the State it may be, can make such a claim; nevertheless the legislator has made it clear that no entity which is distinct from the executive organs of the State and capable of suing or being sued is entitled to immunity, except in rare cases which presuppose, *inter alia*, that the entity has exercised sovereign authority.[30] For all practical purposes, therefore, foreign State corporations will in future not be entitled to claim immunity, and the cases in the past in which such immunity was allowed will in future have to be decided differently.[31] This applies, in particular, to *Krajina* v. *The Tass Agency*,[32] the case which led to the setting-up of the unproductive Inter-Departmental Committee in 1949.[33] Yet it must be noted with some surprise that in the United States the Tass Agency, as well as the Novosti Press Agency, were not only identified with the Soviet State,[34] but were also held not to carry on a commercial activity.[35]

In most other countries, too, the fact of the State corporation having a distinct legal personality and carrying on business will exclude any claim to

[29] See s. 3 of the State Immunity Act 1978.

[30] See s. 14 of the State Immunity Act 1978. Before the Act there was room for the unfortunate impression that it was not the nature of the transaction at issue, but the nature of the act constituting the breach which was decisive for the question of whether immunity was to be granted; if the latter event was a sovereign act, there was a tendency to deny immunity. see *I Congreso* [1983] 1 AC 244, particularly per Lord Wilberforce, and the discussion by Mann, 31 [1982] *ICLQ*, 573. See also the decision by Donaldson J. (as he then was) in *Uganda Co. (Holdings) Ltd.* v. *The Government of Uganda* [1979] 1 Ll. LR 481, where the learned Judge reached the conclusion that a guarantee given by a Ugandan company could not be enforced, because the company had been confiscated by the State of Uganda, which by decree succeeded to the liabilities of the guarantors. The question of enforcement was a purely procedural matter, which in an English court ought not to have arisen. But the Judge said (488) that 'the litigation would involve the Court in expressing an opinion upon the meaning and effect—and perhaps the propriety—of Ugandan legislation in a suit to which the government of that State would not be a party. I do not think that even the most enthusiastic supporter of the restrictive doctrine of sovereign immunity would hold that it extends thus far.' The learned Judge's thought was wrong. To consider the meaning, effect, and perhaps the propriety of foreign legislation in the absence of the foreign legislator is a matter of daily occurrence and necessity. The case was similar to, and as unfortunate as, the decision of the Swiss Federal Tribunal, BGE 102 Ia 574 (5 May 1976), on which see Pierre Lalive, *Zeitschrift für Schweizerisches Recht.* 97 (1978): 529; Delaume, *American Journal of International Law* (1981). 789; and Mann, *Festschrift für Zweigert* (1981), 280. The Swiss decision is universally regarded as wrong, but it had the advantage, at any rate, that immunity was never even considered as a possible defence. The same confusion between the cause of action (which is the exclusively relevant test) and the history of the defendant State's acquisition of title marks the decision of the Italian Corte di Cassazione, 17 Oct. 1956, *Rivista di diritto internazionale*, 40 (1957): 248, also Int. LR. 24 211.

[31] This also applies to *Mellenger* v. *New Brunswick Development Corporation* [1971] 1 WLR 604, a corporate body which was held to be a department of the Province of New Brunswick. For the reasons see Mann, *BYBIL 1979*, 49.

[32] [1949] 2 All ER 274. [33] See Mann (n. 31) 45 and 53.

[34] *Yessenin-Volpin* v. *Novosti Press Agency*, 443 F. Supp. 849 (1978), also Int. LR 63, 127.

[35] The decision will not, it is hoped, be followed in this country.

immunity. This is so, for instance, in Germany,[36] Holland,[37] and, in particular, France, where the law was clarified by a very recent decision of the Cour de Cassation.[38] The Algerian Société nationale de transport et de commercialisation des hydrocarbures, better known as Sonatrach, had a claim against the French organization Gaz de France. One of its creditors obtained a garnishee order in respect of that claim. The Cour de Cassation upheld its validity:

> à la différence des biens de l'Etat étranger, qui sont en principe insaisissables, sauf exceptions, . . . les biens des organismes publics, personnalisés ou non, distincts de l'Etat étranger, lorsqu' ils font partie d'un patrimoine que celui-ci a affecté à une activité principale relevant du droit privé, peuvent être saisis par tous les créanciers, quels qu'ils soient, de cet organisme . . . la Sonatrach ayant pour objet principal le transport et la commercialisation des hydrocarbures, activité relevant par sa nature du droit privé . . . .

Two points should be noted. The court speaks of a public organization which need not be a corporation, but which has its own property and which is distinct from the State. The idea that incorporation is not required to deprive the organization of immunity seems to be very sensible, since this is a purely superficial and fortuitous feature. Furthermore it is sufficient that the organization's principal activity relates by its nature to private law. It need not necessarily be a commercial activity. Nor is the degree of government control of any relevance.

On the other hand, if the State corporation is made liable for sovereign acts of the State owning it, the immunities to which the State is entitled enure to its benefit. This follows from a decision of the French Cour de Cassation[39] which, if read together with the decision of the *judex a quo*, the Cour d'Appel d'Aix-en-Provence,[40] may safely be described as so extremely astringent that it is almost impossible to unravel the facts and to understand the law.

A French shipping company, Marseille Fret, obtained from a Marseille court the attachment of *The Ghat,* a vessel which, according to the Court of

---

[36] Federal Supreme Court, 7 June 1955, BGHZ 18, 1 (9, 10); Federal Constitutional Court BVerfGE 64, 1, also Int. LR. 65, 215.

[37] *Cabolent* v. *National Iranian Oil Co.,* 28 Nov. 1968, Int. LR 47, 138.

[38] Cass Civ., 1 Oct. 1985, Semaine Juridique 1980 No. 20566 with note Synvet, (or Clunet 1986, 170, with note Oppetit; or Rev. Crit. 1986, 527, with note Audit). See also Cass. Civ., 19 May 1976; *Rev. Crit.* 1977, 359, and Int. LR 65: 63: in so far as the privately owned Bank of Japan exercises functions of an exchange control authority—i.e. sovereign functions—it is entitled to immunity.

[39] Cass. Civ., 4 Feb. 1986, Rev. Crit. 1986, 718 with note Pierre Mayer.

[40] 20 Nov. 1984, Rev. Crit. 1985, 358, note Remond-Gouilloud. The underlying facts are not repeated in the text, because they seem to be irrelevant in law, but they are politically of great interest. *The Astor,* a vessel belonging to Marseille Fret and chartered by Ras et Hilal, carried 10 Russian tanks and ammunition destined for Idi Amin in Uganda. There was no bill of lading, and the cargo was seized at Durban. The Libyan courts held Marseille Fret responsible for the absence of a bill of lading.

Appeal, belonged to General National Maritime Transport Company (GNMT), a Libyan corporation described by the Court of Appeal, as 'une émanation de l'Etat libyen et comme telle appelée à répondre sur son patrimoine de la créance invoquée contre celui-ci'. The object was to secure a sum of $7,300,000 allegedly due to Marseille Fret on account of the arbitrary retention of its vessel *The Rove,* which, on the application of the Libyan company Ras et Hilal, had been authorized by a Libyan court. Ras et Hilal was, according to the Court of Appeal, a 'simple intermédiaire' acting as a screen ('paravent') for the Republic of Libya and making its claim in the Libyan courts for the benefit of the latter. According to the Cour de Cassation the attachment had to be lifted, because 'les conditions nécessaires pour le jeu de l'immunité existant au profit d'un Etat étranger *ou d'un organisme agissant sur son ordre ou pour son compte* se trouvent remplies.' The reason was that the French shipowner's claim existed 'à l'encontre de l'Etat libyen', since it resulted 'du préjudice occasionné par un acte de puissance publique émanant de cet Etat'. What is not clear is whether the 'acte de puissance publique' was the judgement of the Libyan court or the detention by Ras et Hilal, and why the damage caused by the latter could not be recovered from GNMT since both corporations seem to have been emanations of the Republic of Libya.

III.

It is a much more serious question whether and in what circumstances a State corporation and the State owning or controlling it can be identified for the purpose of liability or, in other words, for the purpose of piercing the corporate veil. The rule, accepted by learned writers,[41] undoubtedly is that the very fact of incorporation isolates the corporation from the State. It is by no means only the law of the Socialist countries that justifies the general conclusion[42] that 'the state is not liable for the obligations of foreign trade corporations or for those of other enterprises and that the enterprises are not liable for the obligations of other enterprises or organizations or for those of the State.'

Thus, as long ago as 1934, the Soviet Arbitration Commission decided the much-discussed case of the British ship *King Edgar*.[43] The ship's cargo was lost in territorial waters of the Soviet Union. When a Soviet State enterprise made a claim for salvage charges, the British ship replied that the loss was due to the salvor—namely, the Soviet Union—which was

---

[41] Riad. Rec. 108 (1963, i), 646, an early and excellent contribution; Seidl-Hohenveldern, *Recht in Ost und West* (1966), 1; Wolfgang Friedmann, 'Government (Public) Enterprises', in *Encyclopedia of Comparative Law*, xiii. 43 ff.; von Hoffmann (*supra,* n. 27), 66 ff.
[42] Knapp (*supra,* n. 15) 63.
[43] Rec. des décisions de la Commission d'arbitrage maritime, 1934, 13.

responsible for the failure of signals and thus for the accident. The Arbitration Commission in Moscow held that Sovtorgflott, the salvor, was a separate corporate entity to which any negligence of another Soviet legal entity could not be attributed. A closely reasoned judgment of the Swiss Federal Tribunal[44] is to the same effect. A Swiss creditor of the Polish State attached the debt due by a Swiss bank to the Polish National Bank on the theory that the bank was identical with the State. It was held that, according to Polish law, the National Bank was distinct from the State and could not be held responsible for the latter's liabilities.

The question however, arises, here no less than in the case of a private limited company of the familiar type, whether there are exceptions to the rule.

The most radical solution, amounting almost to a rule rather than an exception, has been adopted by the French courts, at least for the case of confiscation. In a decision of 1978 the Cour de Cassation was confronted with the following set of facts: Sapvin, a French company at Marseille, had a subsidiary in Algiers which obtained credits from Crédit Populaire d'Algérie, a state-owned bank. The parent company guaranteed them. In 1971 Algiers confiscated all the assets of the subsidiary, so that Crédit Populaire could not obtain payment from its debtor. It therefore sued the guarantor in France. In its defence the guarantor invoked Article 2037 of the Code Civil according to which the guarantor is discharged if the subrogation 'ne peut plus, par le fait de ce créancier, s'opérer en faveur de la caution'. The Cour de Cassation accepted the Court of Appeal's holding that the Crédit Populaire 'était une émanation de telle sorte que les actes de puissance publique accomplis par ledit Etat, et non par le Crédit Populaire algérien lui-même, étaient opposables à ce dernier'. Without denying the separate legal personality of the Crédit Populaire, the French courts deduced from the circumstances, typical of State corporations in Socialist countries, which are summarized in the appeal and, in short, involved the complete ownership, control, and supervision by the Algerian State, that the bank was to such an extent identified with the State that the facts created by the latter and rendering the subrogation inoperative were to be attributed ('étaient opposables') to the former.[45] This goes far, but

[44] BGE 76 III 60.
[45] Cass. Civ., 14 Feb. 1978, Rev. Crit. 1980, 708, note Pierre Mayer. The result of this decision is highly satisfactory, but in countries which do not have a provision similar to Article 2037 it may not be easily achievable. It is to be feared that in England, in particular, the courts are likely to be governed by the fixed rules which have governed this subject for so long. The case of *Bank Saderat Iran* v. *S. H. Farshneshani,* which was decided by Nourse J. on 30 Mar. 1982 and is reported in [1982] Com. LR 111, does not inspire much hope. The plaintiff bank had made sterling loans to the defendant. They were secured by the deposit of 370 shares in the bank. Later the bank was nationalized in Iran, apparently by the confiscation of its shares. The bank was allowed to recover, although the shares (the certificates of which it was prepared to return) had become valueless as a result of the confiscation. The result may strike some as grossly inequitable.

the result is attractive and persuasive. The solution was perhaps even more radical in an earlier case decided by the Cour de Cassation.[46] The respondent, the Banque populaire et industrielle in Algiers, claimed from the appellant various sums of money advanced to him. The latter's property in Algiers had been confiscated, and the respondent had become an Algerian State bank, 'une émanation de l'Etat algérien'. This fact was considered capable of operating as a discharge of the appellant. The reasons are far from clear. Was he entitled to claim a violation of *ordre public* or to rely on *force majeure*? Or did he have a counter-claim against the State for compensation which he could pursue *vis-à-vis* the respondent? Professor Pierre Mayer thinks so: 'la mise en jeu de la responsabilité de l'Etat algérien . . . peut seule expliquer, par le biais d'une compensation, que l'on ait envisagé de libérer le rapatrié de sa dette envers l'émanation de l'Etat.'[47] It will have to be submitted below that this explanation, though it may be the only possible one, is in law untenable.

This brings us to the remarkable decision of the Supreme Court of the United States in *First National City Bank* v. *Banco para el Commercio Exterior de Cuba*,[48] the only American decision on the subject, which, in view of the great eminence of its authors, requires careful analysis. On 15 September 1960 the Cuban branches of the First National City Bank were nationalized by the Cuban Government. On 20 September 1960 Citibank credited the amount due under a letter of credit to the account of Banco Nacional de Cuba as assignee for collection of a letter of credit due to Banco para el Comercio Exterior de Cuba (Bancec), and 'applied the balance in Banco Nacional's account as a set-off against the value of its Cuban branches'—that is, the compensation claimed by it from the Cuban confiscator. Bancec had been established by law in April 1960 as the Cuban Government's exclusive agent in foreign trade. The Government owned all the shares, received all the profits, and nominated the governing board. On 23 February 1961 Bancec was dissolved. Its banking business was vested in Banco Nacional, and its trading business was transferred to another State corporation, Empress, which was subrogated in the rights and obligations of Bancec as regards commercial export business. In December 1961 Empress was dissolved, and its sugar business was transferred to Cubazucar, also a State trading corporation. In 1980 the District Court gave judgment for Citibank; the Court of Appeals, Second Circuit, reversed but the Supreme Court restored the District Court's judgment. In the course of its reasoning three questions were (or ought to have been) discussed.

In the first place the court had to decide 'which body of law determines the effect to be given to Bancec's separate judicial status'.[49] The Supreme

---
[46] Cass. Civ., 9 Mar. 1971, Bull. I, No. 75.
[47] Rev. Crit. 1980, 714, 715, and Clunet 1986, 15, 16. [48] *Supra*, n. 1. [49] Ibid. 621.

Court rejected the view that the law of the State of incorporation determines not only issues relating to the internal affairs of a corporation but also the rights of third parties external to it. It is much more difficult to say which legal system was affirmatively held to be applicable. Without deciding the general question, the Supreme Court, in a somewhat puzzling passage, seems to have held[50] that 'the principles governing this case are common to both international law and federal common law which in these circumstances is necessarily informed both by international law principles and by articulated congressional policies.' It is difficult to interpret these words, for neither international law nor any branch of law of the United States can define the extent of a Cuban corporation's corporate existence. It would seem that the Court invoked American public policy as derived from 'international law principles and . . . articulated congressional *policies*'. No other solution of the conflict of laws problem can be inferred from the Court's phraseology. In fact, it may be that no other solution was available, for the only real and strongly supported contender,[51] the law of the corporation whose veil was to be pierced, was Cuban law, which in no circumstances would have permitted the disregard of one of its State corporation's corporate status.

The impression that the Court relied upon *ordre public* to solve the conflict problem is strengthened by the manner in which the Court dealt with the substantive problem of whether Bancec could be held liable for the compensation due from the Cuban Government so as to create the identity of parties, which was the pre-condition of a set-off. On this point the Court started from a clear and definite recognition of the corporate status of State corporations and concluded 'that government instrumentalities established as juridical entities distinct and independent from their sovereign should normally be treated as such'.[52] Here, however, 'equitable principles' (which governed the problem of the corporate veil in American municipal law) had to be applied. Since 'the Cuban Government could not bring suit in a United States Court without also subjecting itself to its adversary's counterclaim', and since 'the Cuban Government and Banco Nacional . . . would be the only beneficiaries of any recovery', the Court declined 'to adhere blindly to the corporate form where doing so would cause such an injustice',[53]—namely the injustice 'that would result from

[50] Ibid. 623.

[51] In private international law it is the general view that the question whether the shareholder is personally liable for the company's debts is governed by the law governing the company's status, the *lex societatis*: *Bateman* v. *Service*, 6 App. Cas. (1881) 386, at 389 per Sir Richard Couch; Austrian Supreme Court, 12 June 1981, Juristische Blätter 1982, 257; German Federal Supreme Court, 5 Nov. 1980, BGHZ 78, 318, at 334.

[52] *Supra*, n. 1. 627. On this point the Court cited with approval *I Congreso* [1983] AC 244, 258 per Lord Wilberforce; *Trendtex Trading Corporation* v. *Central Bank of Nigeria* [1977] QB 529, 559, and *Czarnikow Ltd* v. *Rolimpex* [1979] AC 351, 364 per Lord Wilberforce.

[53] *Supra*, n. 1., 632.

permitting a foreign state to reap the benefits of our courts while avoiding the obligations of international law'.[54] In the result, therefore, the Court held Bancec (or Banco Nacional) to be identical with the Cuban Government. However, it confined this judgment to the very specific case in which a State corporation had succeeded in the American courts, but the State had failed to perform its obligations under international law. Even so, the result is surprising. It is difficult to see why obligations under international law, if repudiated by the foreign State, should have a different force from any other obligations. Is it not equally inequitable that a State corporation should recover its debts in the United States, while the State creating it or a sister State corporation are in default in respect of their commercial debts? And if this question is answered in the affirmative (as logic would seem to demand and equity, in the eyes of many, may permit), what then remains of the Court's wish to avoid a decision which 'would result in substantial uncertainty over whether an instrumentality's assets would be diverted to satisfy a claim against the sovereign and might thereby cause third parties to hesitate before extending credit to a governmental instrumentality without the government's guarantee'?[55] From a legal point of view the Court's reasoning is by no means compelling.

There remains however, a third point which the Court did not discuss at all (perhaps because it was not put forward by Cuba[56]), and which causes the greatest difficulty and surprise. It may safely be assumed, and is undoubtedly correct in law, that in respect of the confiscation of American property, Cuba is liable to pay compensation and has failed to do so. But was such a claim for compensation available to Citibank for set-off? On this point one does not think of the provisions which are frequently to be found and may exist in the United States and in Cuba limiting a set-off against State claims.[57] The real problem is that the claim to compensation arises under public international law and is vested in the State of the victim, in this case the United States of America, rather than the victim itself. Is it possible in law that an individual can set off a claim arising under

[54] Ibid. 634. [55] Ibid. 626.
[56] See *Banco Nacional de Cuba* v. *Chase Manhattan Bank,* 505 F. Supp. 412 (1980), at 429. In *First National City Bank* (*supra.* n. 1), 26, the Supreme Court refers to 478 F.2d 191 (1973) where the decisions holding the Cuban confiscations inconsistent with international law are mentioned (194). But in none of them did the question arise; nor was it considered by the court in whom the claim for compensation was vested. This is very odd.

[57] In England, Order 77, Rule 6, of the Rules of Supreme Court excludes a counter-claim or set-off where the claim or counter-claim is based on taxes, duties, or penalties and can be made with the leave of the court only where claim and counter-claim are made by or directed against different Government departments. This is probably a procedural rule, which before a foreign court or arbitrator would not be effective. In Germany s. 395 of the Civil Code permits set-off against a claim by the Republic, a *Land,* or a municipality if payment has to be made to the office which is liable to pay. This is a rule of substantive law, but in England it may possibly be classified as procedural.

international law against a debt resulting from a credit to a bank account? And is it possible for that individual to set off a claim which under international law only the national State can prosecute and dispose of? Perhaps the two questions merge into one. In any case it is more than likely that they require a negative answer.[58]

This is not to say that a debt due to a State corporation can never be subject to a set-off, with a claim against the State creating it. It should be possible where (to use the language of section 14 of the State Immunity Act, 1978) the entity is part of the executive organs of the government. In England 'the mere fact of incorporation which is only for administrative convenience does not make a Secretary of State or a minister or a ministry an entity separate from the Crown,'[59] so it seems possible that outside England a claim made by the Secretary of State for Social Security or even a regional health authority may be subject to a set-off with a claim against the Secretary of State for Defence. They are all the Crown (and, probably, for the purpose of Part 2 of the State Immunity Act 1978, the United Kingdom). There may be foreign countries in which the legal position is similar. In such cases the constitutional law of foreign countries may require very careful investigation.

It may well be that in the case decided by the Supreme Court of the United States, Bancec could have been considered an organ of the Cuban State. If so, a set-off with a trade debt properly vested in Citibank might well have been possible. No such point arose. But if one looks at the status of Servicio Nacional del Trigo, Spain's National Wheat Corporation, the example may be instructive. It had the monopoly of buying and selling wheat as a department of the Ministry of Agriculture.[60] It formed part of

---

[58] The most recent authority is embedded in the decisions of the European Court of Human Rights in the cases of *Lithgow* v. *United Kingdom* and *James* v. *United Kingdom*, where the reference in Article 1 of the First Protocol to the general principles of international law was explained by the legislator's wish to eliminate the rule according to which non-nationals 'would have to seek recourse to diplomatic channels or to other available means of dispute settlement' (para. 115 and/or para. 62).

[59] *Town Investments Ltd.* v. *Department of Environment* [1978] AC 359, at 399 per Lord Simon of Glaisdale; and see Parker L J (as he then was) in *Baccus S.R.L.* v. *Servicio Nacional del Trigo* [1957] 1 QB 438, at 472: 'Many Ministers are constituted corporations sole. Some, as in the case of the Minister of Transport, for all purposes; some, as in the case of the Minister of Health, for limited purposes; and I do not think anybody could say that under English law the Minister of Transport or the Minister of Health was not the Crown.' See also *Commissioners of Works* v. *Page* [1960] 2 QB 274, at 290 per Devlin L J (as he then was): 'It has been admitted that the Crown is one and indivisible and acted as much through the Commissioners of Works as through the Commissioners of Crown Lands.' The former were created by the Minister under the Minister of Works and Planning Act 1942; the latter were a body corporate constituted under the Crown Lands Acts 1829–1943 and were reconstituted by the Crown Estates Act 1956. The case of *Baccus* is an excellent example of a situation (in this case in Spain) in which a trading corporation is an organ or part of the executive, and is therefore under the common law entitled to immunity.

[60] See the case of *Baccus* (*supra*, n. 59), 441.

the governmental organization. That it was a corporation did not necessarily mean that it could not be part of the Spanish State organization, as the Court of Appeal in fact held by granting it State immunity. On this basis it was the State of Spain which was the party to the proceedings. No question of piercing the corporate veil arose. The single State was represented by its various organs, of which the Servicio Nacional del Trigo was one.

IV

The final and most serious difficulty in the law relating to State corporations involves the question whether, and in what circumstances, contracts concluded by State corporations may be discharged by legislation of the State which created and controls them. In searching for an answer it is necessary to make a familiar distinction.

1. If the contract is governed by the law of the corporation's country, this will have to be given effect and, accordingly, impossibility of performance created by such country's legislation will normally have to be recognized. In particular, this seems to be the law in the Socialist countries. Thus the Polish Chamber of Foreign Trade has held since 1958 that a State enterprise of the German Democratic Republic was without remedy, when as a result of a change in the export plan of the Polish Council of Ministers the quantity of coal to which it was contractually entitled was reduced by one-sixth.[61] In Bulgaria, it appears, the law was the same between 1956 and 1961, on the basis of the theory that the identification of State and State corporation had to be rejected, and that, therefore, new governmental directives could create impossibility of performance. But the law seems to have changed in 1964, since when it has been held that, *vis-à-vis* foreign parties, changes in the economic plan could not relieve the Bulgarian State corporation of its contractual duties.[62] The law of the Soviet Union seems to have been settled by the much discussed decisions of the Foreign Trade Arbitration Commission in Moscow in the matter of the Israel–Soviet Oil Arbitration.[63] Sojuzneftexport, a Soviet oil export corporation, agreed to sell quantities of oil to two Israeli companies. On account of the Suez Canal hostilities of 1956, the Soviet Ministry for Foreign Trade refused the export licences which the seller had to procure. The buyer's claim was

---

[61] Award of 11 Feb. 1958; see *Yearbook of Commercial Arbitration*, 5 (1981) 147.

[62] Kozucharov in D. Pfaff, *Die Aussenhandelsschiedsgerichtsbarkeit der sozialistischen Länder* (1973), 650–2. See, generally, Kemper–Strohbach–Wagner, *Die AL Bedingungen des RWG 1968 in der Spruchpraxis sozialistischer Aussenhandelsschiedsgerichte* (East Berlin, 1957), 273–7.

[63] *American Journal of International Law*, 1959, 800, or Int. LR 27, 631. See the discussion by Domke, ibid. 787; Berman, RabelsZ 1959, 449; Riad (*supra*, n. 41) 651; Böckstiegel (*supra*, n. 23). 72.

dismissed on the ground that the legal prohibition rendered performance impossible, the underlying theory being that the State and the State corporation were different entities.[64]

Where the law of a Socialist State applies, foreign courts cannot avoid this practice, unless public policy may be invoked. This may be possible in either of two situations. In the first, it may be possible to identify the seller with the Socialist State, a point to which it will be necessary to revert. Secondly the supervening legislation may be designed to cover one particular contract or to apply to one particular State corporation, so that it may be discriminatory in character and offend against accepted standards of State conduct; though even then there may be countervailing circumstances, such as an emergency or economic necessity, which justify a State in taking special and unusual measures to protect the national interest, a condition which in the case of the Soviet-Israeli deal may have been fulfilled. Such measures, it is true, may amount to expropriation entitling the victim or its national State to compensation, but this is by no means a universally available remedy.

As far as can be seen there is only one award by an arbitration tribunal sitting in Holland and consisting of Professor Brunner, Mr R. A. MacCrindle, QC and Professor Frank Vischer, which held that emergency legislation of a Western State encroaching upon the terms of a contract was contrary to *ordre public,* on the ground that the legislation in question was enacted for the sole purpose of striking at one particular contract. Since an appeal is pending, it would be wrong to discuss the case in detail. It is however, very necessary to observe the utmost caution in resorting to public policy in the present context, for it is plain that no country can, or can be expected to, forgo the right of legislation in the general interest and that such legislation may apply to the State's own contracts. As the Supreme Court of the United States has said,[65] 'the United States when sued as a contractor cannot be held liable for an obstruction in the performance of the particular contract resulting from its public and general acts as a sovereign.'[66] And the same applies to England[67] and (probably) Germany.[68]

2. If the contract is governed by the law of a country other than that to which the State corporation belongs, foreign legislation is material only if it

[64] The decision has been widely criticized, but on the basis mentioned in the text it is difficult to find fault with it. See Mann, *ICLQ* 9 (1960) 691.

[65] *Horowitz* v. *United States,* 267 US 458, at 460 (1925), and other cases referred to by Mann, *American Journal of International Law,* 1960, 584, 585.

[66] See, generally, Mann, *Studies of International Law,* 316 ff.

[67] *Commissioners of Crown Lands* v. *Page* [1960] 2 QB 274, at 292 per Devlin L J (as he then was): any promise made by the Crown 'must by necessary implication be read to exclude those measures affecting the nation as a whole which the Crown takes for the public good'.

[68] RGZ 25, 354; on the problem see J. A. Frowein, *Festschrift für Werner Flume* (1978), i, 301.

creates an impossibility within the meaning of the proper law, or if a *force majeure* clause is included in the contract. Such a case fell to be considered by arbitrators sitting in Switzerland. A contract was made with a Polish State corporation for the installation of a plant for the production of heating gas in January 1980. In December 1981 Poland's Council of Ministers prohibited the importation of this plant, as well as twenty-three others. An award of unusual diffuseness rejected the defence of *force majeure*, probably because the State corporation and Poland were held to be identical.

In a similar case Kerr J.[69] (as he then was), the Court of Appeal (Lord Denning, MR and Lane and Cumming-Bruce, L JJ),[69] and the House of Lords (Lords Wilberforce, Dilhorne, Salmon, Fraser of Tullybelton, and Keith of Kinkel)[70] rejected such a conclusion. This unanimous decision by nine English judges, with which, it seems, the Supreme Court of the United States agrees,[71] is undoubtedly at present the leading authority. Yet it has been subjected to much criticism by Western traders and their associations. The truth of the matter is that the decision is founded upon the arbitrators' findings of fact as the nine judges understood them,[72] while the legal principle was never in doubt. Lord Wilberforce, the eminent judge and jurist and friend to whom these pages are dedicated, stated it very clearly: 'Rolimpex cannot on the evidence be regarded as an organ of the Polish State.'[73] This means, on the one hand, that the question whether or no Rolimpex was an organ of State was decisive, and on the other, that, had the evidence shown Rolimpex to be an organ of State, the plea of *force majeure* would have failed. From the point of view of the law in general these are very important conclusions, with which one can only respectfully agree and which should guide the approach to cases which may arise in the future.

The problem in the *Rolimpex* case, therefore, is one of fact: did the arbitrators make adequate findings of fact, and did the courts correctly understand such findings as were made? An outsider cannot, of course, form a view on these questions, but Mr Lasok suggests some gaps.[74] It may indeed be doubtful whether the finding in paragraph 52(c)[75] that 'Rolimpex is an organisation of the Polish state' really meant 'no more than that it was set up by the Polish state and controlled by the Polish state', as Lord Wilberforce stated;[76] for Mr Lasok also draws attention to the much

---

[69] [1977] 2 Ll. LR 201.   [70] [1979] AC 351.   [71] *Supra*, n. 1.
[72] These included the fact that the contract was for *Polish* sugar f.o.b. *Polish* port. A purchase on the world market was therefore ruled out. Furthermore, the *force majeure* clause was invoked solely on account of the governmental decree, not on account of the failure of the crop, which was the motive for it. If the sellers had alleged impossibility on the ground that only a fraction of the expected quantity was available for export, entirely different questions would have arisen.   [73] *Supra*, n. 70, 364.
[74] 44 (1981) MLR 249   [75] *Supra*, n. 69, 204.   [76] *Supra*, n. 70, 364.

neglected paragraph 22 of the arbitrators' findings, according to which Rolimpex 'is in Polish law a unit or organisation of the socialist economy',[77] a conclusion which, so he suggests,[78] 'betrays its status as a sub-division of the State apparatus'. In view of Mr Lasok's explanations and of what is generally known about the State and the economy in Communist countries, it is indeed difficult to believe that Polish State corporations can be put on the same level as, say, the National Coal Board in England. When the arbitrators described Rolimpex as 'a unit or organisation of the socialist economy', did they not perhaps intend to attribute to it the character of an organ of State?

The attitude of the English courts towards a problem of this kind is even more vividly illustrated by the decision of the Court of Appeal in *The Playa Larga*,[79] which concerned our old friend the Cuban state corporation Cubazucar. On 27 September 1973 Cuba enacted legislation freezing all Chilean property. Consequently Cubazucar was precluded from performing a contract for the sale of sugar concluded with a Chilean corporation. The buyers contended that Cubazucar was the agent or servant of the Cuban State and could therefore not rely upon the impossibility brought about by its principal or master. It was accepted.

that Cubazucar was not a department of the Cuban State. Its senior management was appointed by the Minister of Foreign Trade and it derived its working capital in the form of interest-free finance from the National Bank of Cuba, Cuba's central bank. Any profits returned, in one form or another, to the Cuban State. At all material times Cubazucar acted as the instrumentality through which the State of Cuba conducted its export trade in Cuban sugar. It purchased its sugar from provincial sugar manufacturers, state trading enterprises operating under the aegis of the Minister of Sugar. Each year a national plan for the use, allocation and sale of Cuban sugar is drawn up through the National Planning Board and enacted into law. This plan determines how much sugar is to be allocated for home consumption and how much for export.[80]

In these circumstances it is perhaps not fanciful to suggest that if and in so far as, in the realm of public law, such conceptions as agent or servant are appropriate at all,[81] Cubazucar was an instrumentality and, therefore, an agent of the State. However, the Court of Appeal tells us that the Chileans did 'not contend that Cubazucar were the agents or servants of the Cuban government'.[82] What they did argue is not stated. The Court of Appeal simply relied on its impression that they could not see 'any crucial differences between Rolimpex and Cubazucar'. Perhaps it is sufficient to

---

[77] *Supra*, n. 69, 203.   [78] Ibid. 255.   [79] [1983] Ll. LR 171.   [80] Ibid. 174.

[81] We know from the case of *Town Investments Ltd.* (*supra*, n. 59) that in England they would be inappropriate; and it is most likely that the same applies to the law of the Communist countries.

[82] *Supra*, n. 79, 192.

suggest that in *Rolimpex* the agency point does not seem to have been taken.

However this may be, it is submitted with respect that in construing a *force majeure* clause,[83] arbitrators and courts should take a much more realistic view of the character and function of State corporations in Socialist countries. They may enjoy a measure of independence. They may not come within the strict definition of an agent. But they admittedly are 'the instrumentality through which the State' conducts its trade. To use the language of Lord Simon of Glaisdale, in England they would be 'aspects of the Crown'.[84] Or to use the language of Professor Riad of Cairo University, in the eyes of the law of many Continental countries they constitute 'un service de l'Etat'.[85] Are they not in England to be seen as organs of the Commmunist State?

v.

At this point we reach the crucial general problem which touches on many subjects not discussed in the preceding pages, a problem which the judiciary of the Western world will have to solve and to which French scholars, stimulated by their rich judicial practice, have devoted much attention.[86] Should we decide to identify the State corporations of Socialist States with the State itself? In practice it would not make much difference if we asked the question suggested by a well-known writer[87] whether there should be a readily rebuttable presumption in favour of identification. An affirmative answer would have far-reaching consequences, but may be required by a realistic assessment of the specific policy of the Socialist State. There is no validity in suggesting that if in the capitalist State parent and subsidiary companies are not normally so identified, the same should apply to State and State corporations in Socialist States. In the usual capitalist case the subsidiary company carries on an independent activity, and is by law expected to do so; the parent exercises its rights as a shareholder, and it if exceeds the limits so drawn, it runs the risk of being identified with the subsidiary. In the Socialist State the structure is totally different. The degree and manner of control in a given case will, of course, have to be proved, but no court should close its eyes to what is general knowledge: it is more than likely that in a totalitarian State (and a Socialist

---

[83] A detailed discussion of a *force majeure* clause is outside the scope of this paper. A helpful German paper on the subject discussed in the text here is Khadjavi-Gontord and Hausmann, *RIW* 1980, 533, with much further material, particularly relating to Iran.

[84] *Supra*, n. 81, 400. [85] *Supra*, n. 41, 651, 652.

[86] See, in particular Paul Lagarde, *Études Colliard* (1982), 539; Pierre Mayer, Clunet 1986, 5 at 15, 16, with further references.

[87] Böckstiegel, (*supra*, n. 23), 55–75.

State is totalitarian—who would deny it?) the control of the State is all-pervasive. We should not hesitate to draw the appropriate conclusions. We should not pretend that a State corporation, whether we call it an 'emanation' or an instrumentality or an *alter ego,* has any degree of independence except, possibly, in matters of mere routine, or that the State has no other function or influence than as a majority shareholder.

Nor should English courts and arbitrators be more diffident than their French colleagues; if one compares the facts found by the Cour d'appel at Aix-en-Provence[88] and those found by the arbitrators in *Rolimpex,* they are so similar that it is odd that the former led to affirmation and the latter to denial of the corporation being an 'emanation' of the State.

The idea that the State corporation of the Socialist State will, as a result of identification, be liable for the debts of the State itself may come as a surprise, and perhaps as a disappointment, to some of the corporation's creditors. But there will be others who will welcome the State's liability for the debts of its corporations. Such arguments cut both ways and are, therefore, not decisive. We should search for the principle, a principle founded on reality rather than make-believe.[89]

---

[88] They appear from the 'moyen unique de cassation' printed with the report of Cass. Civ., 14 Feb. 1978, Rev. Crit. 1980, 707.

[89] There may be some arbitrators who will prefer to solve the problems discussed in the text by substituting discretion for law, and describe their decision so arrived at as being based on transnational law or *lex mercatoria* or general principles of law such as *pacta sunt servanda* or good faith. The courts should firmly disapprove such methods which, in substance, lead to decisions *ex aequo et bono.* They are rarely authorized by the parties.

11

The New *Lex Mercatoria*: The First Twenty-five Years

by THE RT. HON. LORD JUSTICE MUSTILL

Few readers are likely to welcome an article on the *lex mercatoria* by an English lawyer. The common lawyer will not look kindly on an addition to the extensive literature on what he may be tempted to regard as a non-subject, having no contact with reality save through the medium of a handful of awards which could well have been rationalized more convincingly in terms of established legal principles. Conversely, a scholar nurtured in other disciplines may well anticipate yet another reactionary response to any doctrine lying outside the tradition of Anglo-Saxon jurisprudence. Perhaps there is a middle course. The auspicious occasion which this volume is designed to commemorate deserves better than a reaction by rote or a routine polemic. The *lex mercatoria* has sufficient intellectual credentials to merit serious study, and yet is not so generally accepted as to escape the sceptical eye. It therefore seems appropriate to try a fresh approach. Commercial arbitration exists for one purpose only: to serve the commercial man. If it fails in this, it is unworthy of serious study. The commercial man in a conspicuous absentee from the writings on the *lex mercatoria,* and so indeed is his adviser. One may therefore approach the subject from an angle rather different from the one usually chosen. Imagine that a practical lawyer is retained to advise a client who has become involved in a dispute which may lead to an international arbitration. The lawyer knows enough about modern theory to have heard of the *lex mercatoria,* and can envisage the possibility that if the matter does come to arbitration, he may find that the arbitrators, whose identities are at present unknown, may at least consider the application of the *lex.* A conscientious practitioner, he recognizes the need to warn his client of this, and seeks to anticipate, and prepare himself to answer, the questions likely to asked by a businessman who encounters the doctrine for the first time. These are likely to be on the following lines. What is the *lex mercatoria?* What kind of law is it? When does it apply? Does it enable the arbitrator to decide in equity, according to his own inclinations? How does the *lex mercatoria* relate to natural law? What are its sources? How are its rules to be ascertained? What are the rules, when so ascertained?

We may follow the adviser in his search for answers to these questions, and conclude by asking—as he must surely ask himself—how the *Lex mercatoria* stands today, and what its prospects are for the future.

WHAT IS THE *lex mercatoria?*

Although the concept of a new *lex mercatoria* had been foreshadowed in earlier writings,[1] systematic discussion of the concept first began to flower in the early 1960s, under the stimulus of the London Conference on the Sources of International Trade in 1962:[2] hence the title of the present essay. There followed several important treatises, including influential discussions by Professor Berthold Goldman[3] and Professor C. M. Schmitthoff.[4] The proposals have not by any means passed unchallenged,[5]

[1] e.g. Professor Jessup, *Transnational Law* (1956), in which the word 'transnational' appears first to have been put into circulation.
[2] Proceedings collected and edited by C. M. Schmitthoff as *Sources of International Trade* (London, 1964).
[3] 'Frontiers du droit et "lex mercatoria" ', 9 *Archives de philosophie du droit* (1964), 177. (hereafter Goldman 'Frontiers'). The concepts and the problems to which it gives rise are here exposed with such moderation and felicity of expression that this study remains essential reading today, notwithstanding the wealth of writing which has succeeded it.
[4] Notably in *Sources of International Trade, supra,* n. 2, and 'Das neue Recht des Welthandels', 28 *Rabels Z.* 47 (1964). Among other significant contributions, mention must be made of Ph. Fouchard, *L'Arbitrage commercial international* (Paris, 1965), esp. Articles 604 ff. Ph. Kahn, in *Festschrift Schmitthoff* (Frankfurt, 1973), echoing earlier work in *La Vente commerciale internationale* (Paris, 1961); E. Loquin, *L'Amiable Composition en droit comparé et international* (1980); Goldman, 'La *Lex Mercatoria* dans les contrats et l'arbitrage internationaux: Réalité et perspectives', [1979]. *Clunet Journal du droit international,* 475 (hereafter Goldman, Réalité et perspectives'), and also in *Contemporary Problems in International Arbitration* (1983) (hereafter, *Contemporary Problems);* a series of commentaries by Y. Derains on International Chamber of Commerce arbitral awards, published in Clunet, from 1974 onwards, and also 'Le statut des usages du commerce international devant les juridictions arbitrales', [1973] *Rev. Arb.* 122; an interesting summary of unpublished awards in J. Lew, *Applicable Law in International Commercial Arbitrations* (New York, 1978), a seminal study of the topic in its relation to the conflicts of laws in P. Lalive, 'Les Règles de conflit de loi applicable au fond du litige', [1976] *Rev. Arb.* 155; Schmitthoff, in *Commercial Law in a Changing Economic Climate,* 2nd edn., (1981), 18 ff.; M. Bonnel, in *I UNIDROIT New Directions in International Trade Law* (1977). More recently, there have been studies by O. Lando, 'the *Lex Mercatoria* in International Commercial Arbitration', 34 *ICLQ* 747; B. M. Cremades and S. L. Plehn, 'The New *Lex Mercatoria* and the Harmonization of the Laws of International Commercial Transactions', [1984] *Boston Univ. ILJ* 317; W. Lorenz, *Festschrift für Karl H. Neumeier* (1986); E. Loquin, *Apport de la jurisprudence arbitrale: L'Application de règles anationales* (Paris, 1986); (hereafter Loquin, *Apport*) P. Lalive, *Transnational (or Truly International) Public Policy and International Arbitration: Proceedings of the I.C.C.A. New York Conference* (1986) (hereafter Lalive, *ICCA).* Indispensable to the enthusiast is the collection of essays in *Le Droit des relations économiques internationales: Études offerts a Berthold Goldman* (Paris 1982) (hereafter *Études Goldman).*
[5] Amongst the writers who have questioned the mercatorist position are F. A. Mann, P. Schlosser, F.-E. Klein, and P. Lange. Since the purpose of this essay is to examine that position, rather than attack it, I have not quoted extensively from the critics. They do, however, seem to me to have landed some powerful blows.

The New Lex Mercatoria

and a lively debate has continued to the present day.

A useful starting-point would be a definition. Unfortunately, there appears to be none which accommodates all opinions as to the nature of the doctrine. The same turn of phrase means different things to different scholars. The following may however serve to give the flavour;

A set of general principles, and customary rules spontaneously referred to or elaborated in the framework of international trade, without reference to a particular national system of law.[6]

A single autonomous body of law created by the international business community.[7]

This phenomenon of uniform rules serving uniform needs of international business and economic co-operation is today commonly labelled *lex mercatoria*.[8]

The customs of the business community may combine all general principles of law to create a principle of commercial self-determination.[9]

... un droit 'transnational', réceptacle des principes communs aux droits nationaux, mais creuset aussi des règles spécifiques qu'appelle le commerce international.[10]

Also, from a rather less enthusiatic hand:

... an anational *lex mercatoria* or ... a hybrid legal system finding its sources both in national and international law and in the vaguely defined region of general principles of law called 'Transnational Law'.[11]

Notwithstanding the absence of any definition commanding general acceptance which is at the same time sufficiently detailed to serve as the focus of examination, it is possible to state certain propositions which appear to reflect the majority of opinion.

In the first place, the *lex mercatoria* is 'anational'.[12] This concept has two facets. First, the rules governing an international commercial contract are not, at least in the absence of an express choice of law, directly derived from any one national body of substantive law. Second, the rules of the *lex mercatoria* have a normative value which is independent of any one national legal system.[13] The *lex mercatoria* constitutes an autonomous legal order.

---

[6] Goldman, *Contemporary Problems*, 116. [7] Cremades and Plehn (*supra*, n. 4), 324.

[8] N. Horn, Introduction to *The Transnational Law of International Commercial Transactions* (1984).

[9] W. L. Craig, W. Park, and J. Paulsson, *International Chamber of Commerce Arbitration* (Paris 1984), Article 35.02.

[10] Goldman, 'Frontiers', 1984

[11] H. A. Grigera Naón, *The Transnational Law of International Commercial Transactions* (*supra*, n. 8), 89.

[12] The term 'règles anationales' was, it is believed, coined by P. Fouchard in *L'Arbitrage* (*supra*, n. 4), passim.

[13] This is a paraphrase of principles stated by several authors, and may not be entirely accurate. Loquin *Apport*, expresses the second part of the principle by saying that the rules of the *lex mercatoria* 'echappent à l'emprise de tout ordre juridique étatique'.

A clear recognition of the anational character of the *lex mercatoria* enables a number of misconceptions to be avoided. Thus, the fostering of the *lex mercatoria* has nothing to do with the harmonization of international trade law. The aim of the latter is to minimize the differences between the laws of individual nations, so as to provide a stable and uniform basis for commerce. To the mercatorist the laws of individual states are irrelevant, save as a quarry from which to draw the raw materials for generalized rules.

Again, the *lex mercatoria* resembles in name alone the common body of doctrine the reception of which into various national laws has ensured that in matters of commerce there is a strong family resemblance between laws of developed trading States. Cross-fertilization between legal systems has been a powerful instrument for more than two centuries in the elaboration and refinement of national laws. So too has been the adoption of propositions and concepts advanced by influential commentators who command an international breadth of learning. Equally important has been the recognition of trade practices acknowledged as binding, regardless of national frontiers. But the national judge who draws upon this common reservoir of rules and notions does so for the purpose of better fitting his own law to the task in hand, not as a means of applying some other body of rules in preference to the governing national law.[14] Lord Mansfield, whose memory is not infrequently summoned to provide common-law credentials for the new doctrine,[15] did undoubtedly speak of the *lex mercatoria,* but I believe he would be astonished to learn that while availing himself of the experience of his special jury and the wisdom of the learned expositors, he was doing anything other than making sure that the English law which he applied to the contract was serviceable, up to date and intellectually sound. The idea that, sitting as he was in the court of King's Bench, it was his duty to set on one side the King's law, and to apply a law which was not the law of any nation, would have been quite foreign to his mind.[16]

It is convenient at this stage to mention another misconception: namely, that the *lex mercatoria* is in some way connected with, or a reflection of, the notion of transnational arbitration. The latter[17] posits that there exists a

---

[14] The point that when the old *lex mercatoria* was incorporated into the national laws of Europe it ceased to exist as an international system of law is very clearly made by C. M. Schmitthoff in *Commercial Law in a Changing Economic Climate* (*supra*, n. 4), 18 ff.

[15] As Holdsworth has pointed out (*History of English Law*, 119), the manner of development of English commercial law, and hence of the numerous common-law systems which have sprung from it, differed substantially from the contemporaneous evolution in the cities of Continental Europe. It is, I believe, unwise to found any generalization upon it or to draw any modern parallels.

[16] The great contribution of Mansfield was to bring a new depth of learning to the common law, which had hitherto been insular and uninformed.

[17] Some reflections by the present author on transnational arbitration may be found in *Current Legal Problems* (1984).

category of arbitration which is, or at least ought to be, detached from the procedural laws of the country where the arbitration takes place, or indeed of any other country, excepting only, in some limited degree, the law of the country where the award is sought to be executed. The subject-matter of the transnational doctrine is thus quite different from that of the *lex*. So too are its theoretical foundations. Not even the most enthusiastic transnationalist could claim that international commercial arbitration is now wholly distinct from national arbitration laws, or that it would be practical to sever all links with such laws, since the arbitral process does from time to time need the help of the courts. The proponents simply assert that the links should be no greater than are strictly necessary to ensure that, through the coercive powers of the courts, a party who wilfully fails to honour the letter and spirit of his agreement to arbitrate can be brought into line. The theory of transnational arbitration is essentially a statement of practical policy.

The concept of the *lex mercatoria* is quite different. It is not the positing of an ideal which all concerned should unite to bring about. Of course it is desirable that the *lex mercatoria* should be developed and promulgated. Nevertheless, independently of any such endeavour, the *lex mercatoria* simply exists. It springs up spontaneously, in the soil of international trade. It is a growth, not a creation.

Thus the debate on transnationalism is about whether it can and should be brought about. By contrast, the debate on the *lex mercatoria* is about whether it can and does exist as a viable system. A mercatorist need not be a transnationalist. There are, however, two possible points of contact. In the first place, the premise of the transnationalist theory is that, although an international commercial arbitration must in a physical sense take place somewhere, in the legal sense it takes place nowhere. It therefore cannot have a *lex fori,* and so cannot be the subject of any national system of conflicts of laws, such as would ordinarily be applied as part of the *lex fori.* This is an interesting idea, which may be said to be reflected in practice: for many practitioners would readily acknowledge that in the small minority of cases where it makes the least difference what law is applied to the substance of the dispute (for most disputes turn on the facts and on the words of the contract), the arbitrators frequently abstain from referring themselves explicity to the conflicts rules of the country in which they happen to be sitting, but rather proceed to an intuitive choice of the proper law. Whether this is because they are transnationalists at heart, I venture to doubt. I think it more probable that since the conflicts rules of most developed nations are much the same, so far as concerns the choice of proper law, it is not usually worth the trouble of deciding whether to follow one rather than the other.

A more testing question would be whether there is a body of

transnational conflicts law which governs matters such as status, capacity, consent, and rights *in rem*. But about this, the mercatorists can have nothing to say, since the function of the *lex mercatoria* is to expound the content of the rights and duties of the parties under a contract which is *ex hypothesi* valid as between them and them alone. Furthermore, in the present context the debate is academic, since the purpose of the conflict of laws is to enable the tribunal accurately to identify the national law which governs the contract. This is precisely antithetical to the premise of the *lex mercatoria*, which is that the arbitrator's first step is to reject any national law as the governing law.[18] Admittedly, it would be possible to have a specialist conflicts system with only one rule—namely, that all disputes concerning international trade should, when referred to arbitration, be regulated by the *lex mercatoria*. But this is not, I believe, the drift of the extensive literature on the topic.[19]

Another possible point of contact between the two theories lies in the fact that transnational law seeks to release the substantive content of an award from the control of a local court. If put into practice, this will, it is said, enable the arbitrator to make a free choice of norms, unfettered by any national law, and it will thus facilitate the development of the *lex mercatoria*. This scarcely seems a convincing ground for assimilating the doctrines. Absence of any method of demonstrating that the arbitrator has done wrong does not justify the inference that he has done right, and the release of judicial control is at least as likely to encourage the arbitrator to apply no law at all,[20] as to apply the *lex mercatoria*.[21]

One final misconception is that the application of the *lex mercatoria* is

---

[18] See Goldman, 'Réalité et perspectives' 492.

[19] This is not intended to be dismissive of what is an interesting and difficult practical problem. There is an extensive literature, led by Lalive, 'Les Règles de conflit (*supra*, n. 4). Some writers advocate a cumulative application of potentially relevant rules of conflicts. This will usually yield the 'closest connection' test or something like it. But the arbitrator may feel, when looking for the presumed intention of the parties, that this is not enough—for example, where one party is a sovereign State, and where the closest connection rule would yield the law of that State. The arbitrator might conclude that one party could not have intended that the other should have the power unilaterally to change the governing law. (See the arbitration *Sapphire* v. *NIOC* and note J.-F. Lalive, (1984) 13 ICCJ 987, 1011). But there is nothing transnational or mercatorist about this. A national judge might well take the same view. There are several relevant awards, including some made under the auspices of national rather than avowedly non-national institutions. These can be found in successive editions of *YBCA*. Among the ICC awards are some in which the arbitrators proceeded directly to a choice of law: e.g. 1717, Clunet (1974) 890; No. 2129, 2 *YBCA* 219 No. 2886, Clunet (1978) 991; No. 3380, Clunet (1983) 897; and a number of unreported awards in Derains, Clunet (1977) 949. In others, the arbitrators have gone through a more orthodox procedure: e.g. ICC No. 2735, Clunet (1977) 947; No. 1455 3 *YBCA* 215; *B.P.* v. *Libya* 5 *YBCA* 143; No. 1598 3 *YBCA* 216; No. 2637 2 *YBCA* 153. Sometimes again the arbitrators apply general principles, but check the result against the *lex fori* as in No. 2583, Clunet (1975) 950. On other occasions the arbitrators have decided that since the two competing laws are the same in all material respects, there is no need to make a choice: e.g. No. 2272, 2 *YBCA* (1977) 151. I suggest that this is an example of Occam's razor, not the *lex mercatoria*.

equivalent to a decision in 'equity' according to the arbitrator's own personal ideas of justice. This understanding of the doctrine may be at the root of the dismay with which it is still greeted in many circles not only in common law countries. It does, however seem clear from the writings that the classical mercatorist position is to regard the *lex mercatoria* as a system of law, and not as an expedient for deciding according to 'non-law'. I will return to this point later.

I now turn to the second of the general propositions which emerge from the literature: namely, that the prime sources of the *lex mercatoria* are the principles of law common to trading nations and the usages of international trade. These merit separate consideration.

Although the essence of the *lex mercatoria* is its detachment from national legal systems, it is quite clear from the literature that some, at least, of its rules are to be ascertained by a process of distilling several national laws. The intellectual justification for this process is nowhere clearly described, but it must, I believe, be found in the idea that the rules of the *lex mercatoria* exist *in gremio legis* as a complete, albeit inexplicit, and evolving whole; that they are received, at least in part, into individual national laws or are reflected by them; and that by careful analysis the dross of the rigidities, impracticabilities, and distinctions imposed by each individual national law can be purged away, leaving behind the pure gold of the underlying international legal order. This rationale seems neither more nor less convincing than an English jurisprudential theory to which it bears some resemblence: that the common law is revealed to and by the courts, rather than developed by them.[22] Quite apart from this, the concept of the *lex mercatoria* as being in part a distillation of national laws soon runs into serious practical difficulties. The proponents of the *lex mercatoria* claim it to be the law of the international business community: which must mean the law unanimously adopted by all countries engaged upon international commerce.[23] Such a claim would have been sustainable

---

[20] Loquin has suggested that the absence of a general requirement of reasoned awards in English law permits clandestine amiable composition (*L'Amiable Composition,* cited by Cremades and Plehn, (*supra*, n. 4) 333). Experience suggests that this occasionally happens, but it should not do so unless it accords with the wishes of the parties. A theory cannot gain credence from the fact that arbitrators may be able to act contrary to mandate without rebuke. (The question as to whether an award by an arbitrator who has purported to act as an *amiable compositeur* or to apply the *lex mercatoria* in the face of an express or implied agreement to the contrary will be susceptable to interference by the local court is a complex question of municipal law beyond the compass of this essay.)

[21] See Cremades and Plehn (*supra*, n. 4), 85.

[22] At first, it seems altogether more in accordance with real arbitral life to envisage the arbitrator as proceeding directly and often tacitly against an assumed background of general principles. See e.g. Goldman, 'Frontiers', 183. But in the end this surely means no more than that the arbitrator is intuitively generalizing from his own, possibly imperfect, experience of the major systems of commercial law.

[23] So stated, in relation to the principle in question, in ICC Award No. 3844, Clunet (1982) 978.

two centuries ago. But the international business community is now immeasurably enlarged. What principles of trade law, apart from those which are so general as to be useless, are common to the legal systems of the members of such a community? How could the arbitrators or the advocates who appear before them, amass the necessary materials on the laws of, say, Brazil, China, the Soviet Union, Australia, Nigeria, and Iraq? How could any tribunal, however cosmopolitan and polyglot, hope to understand the nuances of the multifarious legal systems[24]? In published awards the arbitrators occasionally make large claims aboaut the universality of principles, but these are rarely if ever substantiated by citation of sources. Equally if not more important is the question: How could any adviser hope to predict what a tribunal not yet constituted might make of such a task in the future?

Evidently oppressed by these difficulties, some proponents of the doctrine have somewhat drawn back from the concept of what may be termed a 'macro' *lex mercatoria,* and have suggested that the law may be one which is 'common to all *or most* of the states engaged in international trade'.[25] To some readers it may seem that this solution gets the worst of all worlds. It fatally comprises the appeal of the *lex mercatoria* as a *lex universalis.* It undermines the intellectual basis of the doctrine, so far at least as this is understood to lie in the presumed intent of the parties to the individual contract, for how can it plausibly be asserted that a party of nationality X has tacitly agreed to submit his relationship with a co-contractor to a generalized law which is inconsistent with the national law of state X? In practice, moreover, the idea seems quite unworkable. If there are two intellectually respectable and firmly established doctrines on a particular issue, one adopted by one group of legal systems and one by another—as does of course, quite often occur, even within the modest horizons of the Western European and common-law systems—how is the arbitrator to know which is adopted by the majority of States? Surely not by arithmetic. When the generality of trading nations enters into the calculation, it may verge on the absurd. There may be instances in which, if the data were meticulously examined, a number of solutions would be disclosed, all sustainable and none commanding a majority. True it is that one or two of the very few reported awards have claimed to apply rules of law adopted by the majority of States; but I suggest that in reality this

[24] In the literature, the use of legal encyclopaedias is sometimes advocated. I suggest that these are usually worse than useless for this particular purpose, unless the reader is guided by someone with direct knowledge: a little learning is indeed a dangerous thing. Anyone with practical experience of international disputes must acknowledge the difficulty of making an accurate assessment of the law of only one unfamiliar legal system, absent the kind of prolonged and expensive expert guidance which would be quite out of the question if dozens of different laws had to be assimilated.

[25] Lando, 'The *Lex Mercatoria*', (*supra,* n. 4). So also ICC Award No. 2583, Clunet (1977) 950 '. . . Admis communément de la plupart des pays'.

meant the majority of states with whose laws the tribunal was familiar. This cannot be the basis of a workman-like framework for the conduct of business relations.

Perhaps in response to these pressures, another concept has evolved. By contrast with the world-wide horizons of the orthodox doctrine, there has emerged the idea of what may be called a 'micro' *lex mercatoria.* This is a law merchant generated with specific reference to the individual contract. On this basis, the *lex mercatoria'* need not be the same all over the world. The arbitrator will tend to confine his investigations to those legal systems which are connected with the subject matter of the dispute.[26] Thus, the arbitrator will seek out 'au sein d'un petit groupe de systems juridiques', an individual solution to the problem under scrutiny thereby arriving at a partial internationalization of private law.[27] Looked at in terms of the individual dispute, this does provide the arbitrator and the adviser with a task which it is more practicable to fulfil. But what precisely is the nature of this variety of *lex*? Is it to be supposed that there exists a constellation of para-laws, Franco-Belgian, Anglo-Dutch, Italo-Hispano-Korean, and so on, from which the arbitrator chooses the one most appropriate to the individual dispute? The idea is surely fanciful. The only alternative[28] is that a law is newly minted by the arbitrator on each occasion, with every contract the subject of its own individual proper law. Whatever the merits of this concept, it appears to have no point of contact with the classical *lex mercatoria*, conceived as a universal and pervasive 'arrière-plan'[29] underlying every arbitral decision in the field of international commerce.

We may now turn to the second of the primary sources: namely, international trade usage. Here again, there is a risk of imprecision through the use of the same label to denote different concepts. At its widest, usage is simply a practice which is generally followed. So understood it cannot be a source of law or of individual legal rights. It can be such only if the practice is generally followed because commercial men regard themselves as bound to follow it in the absence of express stipulation to the contrary. Nobody could deny that usage in this sense can be an important element in the assessment by a tribunal of the rights and duties created by the contract, either because in a codified[30] or inexplicit form it is tacitly incorporated into the contract, or because it has been received into the relevant national law. But there is nothing special about international trade in this respect, nor anything special about arbitration.[31]

---

[26] Lando, 750 and also 766. [27] Fouchard, *L'Arbitrage*, (*supra*, n. 4), 424.

[28] An intermediate solution has been proposed whereby the *lex* is derived from the national laws of countries in various groupings, such as the EEC and Comecon: see Matrey, *Lis. Am. Sanders*, 244. Unfortunately, one has only to look at the diversity of laws within the EEC to see that even this is likely to be too ambitious—for the time being, at least.

[29] Goldman's expression in *Frontiers*, p. 183.

[30] As e.g. in the case of INCOTERMS.

Any worthwhile national court ought to be capable of taking usage into account, without the need to accord to usage the status of a prime element in self-contained system of law.

There is, however, a different form of usage to which some of the proponents have had recourse, namely, the practice of contracting within various trades, on standard forms of contract.[32] The mechanism whereby these terms become part of a standing body of law is rarely spelt out. One suggestion is that they express the sense of justice of those who draft and enter into them.[33] I confess to some reservations about this proposition. Often, one party to a standard form contract adopts it because the other party gives him no choice. More important, the form does not, it seems to me, reflect the ideas of anybody as to the justice of the transaction, if indeed this concept has any meaning in the field of commercial transactions negotiated between parties on an equal footing. Rather, the form is designed to serve as a convenient peg on which the parties can hang the specifically negotiated terms, without having to work out all the details of the transaction from scratch. Experienced traders are aware of the general financial balance of the transaction contemplated by the standard form, and know the way in which it distributes the commercial risks between the parties. With this in mind they can negotiate towards agreement on matters such as price, delivery date, insurance, demurrage, and so on. If the standard form is altered so as to throw more obligations or risks on to one of the parties, the negotiated terms will have to be adjusted to restore the balance. The second form will be neither more nor less 'just' than the first.[34] It simply calls for a different assessment of the price, in the widest sense of the term.[35]

Furthermore, there are serious practical objections to the use of standard forms as a source of law. Quite apart from the fact that a single institution within a single trade may publish a repertoire of different and

---

[31] Article 7(1) of the European convention, Article 33(3) of the Uncitral Rules, Article 13(5) of the ICC Rules, among several others, require trade usages to be taken into account. But the position would surely be just the same without them.

[32] A reading of Ph. Goldman's published works on the topic indicates that this scholar would attach particular importance to standard-form contracts.

[33] See e.g. R. David, 352.

[34] In the days when the shipping industry was more varied than at present, and the standard forms were more numerous, some forms were regarded as owner's forms, others as charterers forms, to reflect the way in which the risks were distributed. They simply called for different assessments of freight and other financial incidents. I doubt whether it crossed anybody's mind that one form was more 'fair' than another.

[35] This point often escapes those who, under the auspices of international agencies, have urged changes in international legislation to favour importing countries (or, sometimes, exporting countries). They overlook the fact that in the commercial world something is rarely had for nothing. For example, if carrier bears more of the risks, the freight charges ultimately borne by the importer will have to be increased to reflect the extra costs of the 'carrier's' liability insurance. One basis for the contract is no more fair than the other.

mutually inconsistent documents from which the contracting parties may choose the most suitable to reflect the balance of their bargain, there coexist in many trades a number of institutions, each offering its own standard form; and it is, of course, a commonplace that parties alter the standard forms to suit their own purposes. There is thus no guarantee of homogeneity even within a single trade. Moreover it may legitimately be asked why a participant in one trade should be supposed to have consented to have his contract governed by rules drawn from contract forms current in a quite different trade.[36]

Finally, it must be confessed that the mechanism whereby the use of standard forms becomes a source of law is nowhere clearly explained. The simple repetition of contracts on the same terms is as consistent with the exercise of freedom of contract as with subordination to a system of binding norms; indeed, far more so, since if the parties to a commodity transaction do not wish to bind themselves to, say, the GAFTA[37] Contract Form No. 100, there is no legal or other institution which can compel them to do so. Moreover, the repetition of transactions in the same form could at most create a group of norms peculiar to the individual trade, thereby creating a network of para-legal systems. This is quite inconsistent with the theoretical premises of the *lex mercatoria,* which is that it springs spontaneously from the structure of international commerce—which is quite plainly regarded as an indivisible whole.

WHAT KIND OF LAW IS THE *lex mercatoria*?

This question cannot fruitfully be debated without some sort of common ground about what is meant by a law, and what is meant by the *lex mercatoria.* Since philosophers of law cannot agree about the one, and students of international law cannot agree about the other, the discussion soon becomes clouded. Interesting as it is, the businessman would be unlikely to linger over the question, and lack of space compels the present author to follow suit.[38] As Jenks pointed out, the question whether the general principles of law, conceived as a system, can serve as the proper law of a contract depends, not on any preconceived notion of what constitutes a legal system, but on whether they can fulfil satisfactorily in

---

[36] This point is clearly made by P. Lagarde in *Études Goldman*, 136.

[37] The Graind and Feed Trade Association Limited of London, the successor to the London Corn Trade Association, whose standard forms have not infrequently been called up in the literature as exemplars of this particular source of the *lex mercatoria*.

[38] There is a wealth of literature on this subject. It was addressed at the very beginning by Goldman, in 'Frontiers', with conspicious moderation and realism. More recently, there have been penetrating analyses by J.-D. Bredin and P. Lagarde, in *Études Goldman*; and the present author has nothing useful to add to these.

practice the function of a proper law, and are in fact used for that purpose.[39] To this the present author would add the rider that the principles applied by the arbitrator must be such that they will be recognized by courts as founding a valid award, for an unenforceable award is not an instrument of law or of commerce. The reader must form his own opinion on the question, but even the most ardent supporter would hesitate to say that the *lex mercatoria* is yet ready to satisfy these criteria in full.

One facet of the problem might however interest the businessman and his adviser. If the transaction is governed by an international agreement or a standard form of rules which requires the arbitrator to choose the 'law' which he deems applicable to the substance of the dispute, is he thereby enabled to apply the *lex mercatoria* to the exclusion of any national law? For example, is the *lex* a permissible choice under Article 33(1) of the Uncitral Model Arbitration Rules or Article 13(3) of the ICC Arbitration Rules or Article 42 of the World Bank Convention or Article 7 of the Geneva Convention or Article 28(2) of the UNCITRAL Model Law? The point does not admit of much development, but I suggest that the answer must surely be no.[40] Again, although there is room for difference of opinion,[41] the same answer suggests itself where there is a reference to 'law' in the contract itself, or in the submission to arbitration.

The juridicial status of the *lex mercatoria* has another, more troubling aspect. Let it be assumed that whether or not the *lex* qualifies as a law, it has sufficient solidity to be capable in appropriate circumstances of controlling the rights of the parties; then the question must be asked, from where does its normative power arise? Here, I believe, there are two deep-rooted divisions of opinion among the proponents, quite distinct from the differences of emphasis already noted as to the respective weight to be given to custom and the common core of national laws.

The first concerns the method by which the *lex* comes to govern an individual transaction. One concept is that the *lex* is a standing body of legal norms, which automatically applies *ipso jure* to every transaction within its purview, unless expressly excluded. The other is that the *lex* provides, so to speak, a repertoire of rules available to those parties who, expressly or by implication, choose to incorporate them into their dealings, and who, by the same token, choose to detach their contracts from the national law to which they would otherwise be subject. There is really no common ground between these two perceptions of the *lex mercatoria*.[42]

---

[39] In the *Proper Law of International Organisations* (1962).

[40] As to the Geneva Convention, see L. Kopelmanas, *Revue trimestrielle de droit commercial* (1957), 895.

[41] As demonstrated by *Soc. Fougerolle* v. *Banque du Proche Orient* [1982] *Rev. Arb.* 183, the decision in which I would venture to question.

The second discontinuity in mercatorist theory concerns the role of arbitration and the arbitrator. One view is that the lex is a constant presence, applicable or not according to the circumstances of the individual transaction. If it applies at all, it does so from the inception of the bargain, and the sole function of the arbitrator is to uncover it and apply it to the dispute in hand. The alternative opinion is that the *lex mercatoria* reflects an economic order of which international arbitration is an indispensable element. In making his award, the arbitrator does not simply expound a *lex mercatoria* which is already there, albeit inchoate; but rather creates new rules, which he then applies retrospectively to the original bargain. Yet further away from the first concept is the notion that, in the absence of established norms, the arbitrator exercises a creative function, acting as a social engineer.[43]

It is plain that these appreciations of the *lex mercatoria* have little in common. This may be illustrated by assuming that an international arbitrator is faced with a previous award which decided precisely the question of law which is brought before him. If the arbitrator's function is simply that of an exponent, then the second arbitrator need do no more than pay appropriate respect to the reasons of his colleague, without being obliged to arrive at the same decision. If he thinks fit, he is at liberty to hold that his predecessor misunderstood the *lex mercatoria*. Again, at the other extreme, if the first arbitrator has exercised a creative function as a social engineer, his successor can fairly regard him as no more than a part of the self-regulating mechanism of the contract under which he acted, and can thus feel free to exercise the same function, in a different sense, under his own contract. But if the intermediate theory is correct, an award which enunciates a new rule thereby adds to the corpus; and since the *lex* is conceived to be a binding law, the subsequent arbitrator must apply it, whether he agrees with the conclusion or not.

These examples may serve to explain why the present author has been driven to the conslusion, after a study of the literature, that the theoretical foundation of the doctrine has not yet been made explicit. Thus far, the number of awards in which the arbitrator has set out to apply the *lex mercatoria* has been so small that the theoretical problems have been of little practical significance. But if the *lex mercatoria* is to assume the role in world which its proponents claim for it, there must be a clear consensus about what the label actually means; for otherwise there will be a risk of that inconsistency and uncertainty which is fatal to the efficient conduct of commerce.

---

[42] The dichotomy is clearly stated by Loquin, *Apport,* para. 20. The word 'spontane' is often used in relation to the first theory. e.g. Goldman 'Réalité et Perspectives', 476, ed *Contemporary Problems,* 114.

[43] The terminology is that of Lando (*supra,* n. 4), 110.

WHEN DOES THE *lex mercatoria* APPLY?

Given the weight of analysis to which the *lex mercatoria* has been subjected, it is surprising how little has been done to identify the criteria which distinguish those transactions which are governed by it from those which are not.

One matter is treated by commentators as axiomatic: namely, that an express agreement to apply the *lex mercatoria* will and must be honoured by the tribunal, as well as the parties, and that such an agreement may take the form of a reference to, say, the general principles of law recognized by civilized nations or to the usages of international commerce.[44]

In the absence of express consent, it is generally held[45] that the arbitrator should proceed by three stages, asking himself first whether the application of any national system is appropriate; then, if not, whether he should proceed by amiable composition or by the application of anational rules; and finally, if the latter, what anational rules exist and are relevant to the dispute. Various groups of factors have been regarded as relevant to this process.

The first group concerns the parties themselves. Clearly, the fact of their having different nationalities is important, and perhaps indispensable. Their character is also material, since it is easier to hold that the *lex mercatoria*, or that variant of it known as 'the general principles of law', is relevant if one of the parties is a sovereign State or an entity under immediate State control, especially in those cases where the proper law of the contract, according to the orthodox conflicts rules, would be the law of that State.[46] It is also said to be significant if one of the parties has a 'transnational' character, apparently because such parties are to be regarded as existing in free space, detached from national allegiances, and

---

[44] There seems to be no example of a reference to the *lex mercatoria* in so many words. Examples of formulae employed in practice may be found in P. Weil, in *Études Goldman*, p. 387 ff. Not all these formulas will serve to call up *lex*.

[45] Loquin, *Apport*, Article 13, and Goldman, 'Réalité et perspective', 480 ff. Y. Derains proceeds on the same assumption.

[46] Otherwise there is a real risk that the state may change its law adversely to the other party. Whether there is a real need for the *lex mercatoria* in such a case, or whether sufficient protection can be obtained from the *ordre public* of the *lex fori* is, perhaps, debatable. The mercatorists are certainly on their strongest ground here, but care must be taken not to place too much weight on cases, interesting as they are, such as *Sapphire International Petroleum* v. *NIOC* (1984) 12 *ICLQ* 987, note by J.-F. Lalive, and also at 1011; *Liamco* v. *Government of Libya* (1981) 6 *YBCA* 89; *Government of Kuwait* v. *Aminoil* (1982), *YBCA* 71; and *International Legal Materials* (1982), 976–1053, for the terms of the contracts or the submissions expressly opened up the possibility of looking beyond the national law. Moreover, there scarcely seems enough consistency of decision even within this small group of cases to create much confidence in the existence of universally accepted principles. (Note also the refusal in the last-mentioned case to apply a suggested *'lex petrolea'*.) The 'Pyramids' case, *SPP (Middle East)* v. *Arab Republic of Egypt*, ICC No. 3493, 9. *YBCA* 111, is however, closer to the mercatorists' r ıt.

hence especially apt for subjection to a system of law which is similarly detached.[47]

Other indicators relate to the nature of the transaction. It is said to be significant, and perhaps conclusive, if the transaction has an 'international character'. Apart from the obvious case where the parties are of different nationalities, it is not clear what this expression implies.[48] Is a contract between private parties of the same nationality for the carriage of goods from one country to another or for the performance of services abroad of an international character sufficient to make the *lex mercatoria* applicable in a case where, according to ordinary principles, the law of one of the two countries would be the governing law? The literature does not develop the question.

The subject-matter of the transaction may also be relevant. It is plain that many authors instinctively picture international arbitration as concerned with disputes under complex contracts, negotiated *ad hoc,* for the execution of major engineering or similar projects over a substantial period of time. This is perhaps natural, since the attention of mercatorists has tended to focus on awards springing from ICC arbitrations or from *ad hoc* arbitrations, of considerable size and duration. These arbitrations, which are not typical of international commercial arbitration as a whole, are more readily accommodated within the concept of an isolated autonomous legal system than the far more numerous arbitrations arising from everyday informal commercial transactions. Yet it seems that even the latter are regarded as being subject to the *lex*; for although the much discussed ICC Award No. 2291,[49] which concerned just such a transaction, has been described as particularly ambitious as regards the manner of reasoning,[50] there is no suggestion by the commentators that the tribunal should never have been thinking in terms of the *lex mercatoria* at all. This seems far removed from practical reality. Disputes concerning sale and transportation are being arbitrated by the thousand every year, and the present author has never heard of any instance in which it has even been suggested, let alone decided, in any such arbitration held in the common-law world that in the absence of express provision the dispute should be referred to an anational system of law.

---

[47] This is not the place to debate the concept that there exist types of corporation or group which can properly be assigned to a separate category labelled 'transnational', which deserve and automatically obtain the benefit of a special legal regime, more flexible and practical than ordinary national laws.

[48] Loquin, *Apport,* Article 5, quoting P. Kahn, speaks of relations 'internationales par nature, . . . parce que dès leur origine, en fonction de leur objet, elles ne situent pas dans un cadre étatique'.   [49] Clunet (1976) 989.

[50] Goldman, 'Réalités et Perspectives'. The attention given to this award does perhaps suggest a certain shortage of raw material in the mercatorist terrain. The case is rather economically reported, but it appears to be one which the arbitrators could have decided by reference to the terms of the contract, the facts, and some commercial common sense, without reference to any national law, still less the *lex mercatoria.*

Another group of indicators relates to the terms of a contract. This is certainly understandable in so far as the application of the *lex mercatoria* is taken to rest on express or implied consent; but it is less easy to comprehend when the law is said to apply because the transaction is effected within the matrix of the legal order constituted by international commerce, for the transaction either is, or is not, of a type falling into this category, and its terms as to jurisdiction and so on should be immaterial. Be that as it may, the presence of a clause of amiable composition is material, for reasons which will be mentioned below; it has also been suggested in the literature that the inclusion of an arbitration clause or the choice of an international tribunal[51] or of a clause referring disputes to an international arbitration centre[52] are pointers towards the *lex mercatoria*. If this is right, then international arbitrators have been mistaking their functions, day in, day out, for many years.

Again, it has been suggested[53] that the absence of a choice of law clause is an indication that the parties wish to apply an anational system, apparently because it shows that the parties could not agree about which systems should govern. This striking proposition ignores the possibility that the choice of a national law was so obvious as not to be worth mentioning, or that the parties never thought about the matter at all. Moreover, even if the parties had in fact disagreed, there seems no warrant for inferring unanimity in favour of ruling out all potentially relevant national systems and substituting an anational system of which only the smallest minority of businessmen can ever have heard.

These are the factors which are said to be material to an arbitrator's decision to set aside national law, to direct himself towards a system of law rather than a free equity, and to find that system in the *lex mercatoria*. Unfortunately, it is not explained in the literature how he is to perform this operation, and in particular, how much weight is to be attached to the individual factors. The mercatorists can fairly respond that there is no mechanical process for arriving, by way of the conventional conflicts of laws, at a choice of the governing law; and that indubitably a decision on

---

[51] Loquin, *Apport*, Article 19; Goldman, 'Réalité et Perspectives', 480 ff. Since few arbitration clauses nominate the arbitrators or specify the latters' nationality in advance, it is evidently assumed that where the parties are of different nationalities and each has the right to nominate an arbitrator, they will always choose someone of their own nationality, thus making the tribunal multi-national. This assumption is not justified, since in the great majority of commodity and shipping arbitrations, even conducted *ad hoc,* the nominated arbitrators are of the same nationality as each other.

[52] Loquin, *Apport,* Article 27, citing unreported ICC award No. 1569. These criteria are not the same, of course. It is not clear when an arbitration centre ranks as international for this purpose. Would the Society of Maritime Arbitrators or GAFTA whose clients are mostly foreign, come into this category?

[53] Loquin, *Apport,* Article 19; Goldman, 'Réalité et perspectives', 480 ff., citing ICC Nos. 1641, 2291, and 2583.

this issue may be finely balanced and susceptible to differing conclusions. Nevertheless, the general nature of the exercise to be performed is comprehended well enough. Looking for the 'closest connection', or some local variant, may be difficult to perform; but it is not difficult to understand. By contrast, the process for deciding when and when not to apply the *lex mercatoria* seems never to have been clearly spelt out.

Two more points are important. The first concerns the application of the *lex mercatoria* in cases where there is no arbitration clause and the dispute necessarily falls to be decided by a national court. It appears to be taken for granted that an express choice of the *lex mercatoria* would be effective in such a case. This may be over-optimistic, for it cannot be assumed that a national judge will be permitted by local law to enforce such a choice, or will even know how to do so. There appears to be little trace in the literature of attempts to apply the *lex* in national courts.

Of much greater theoretical importance is the question whether the national judge ought to apply the lex mercatoria to the exclusion of whatever national law would otherwise be regarded as the proper law, even in the absence of an express choice, in those instances where it would have been applicable if the contract had contained an arbitration clause. (By this I mean the *lex mercatoria* applied directly as a body of anational law, rather than a series of trade customs carried into a contract via the proper law.) It is disappointing that this problem has been so little addressed for it discloses the existence of a fundamental uncertainty about the theoretical underpinnings of the doctrine. If application of the *lex* to the individual contract is seen as a matter of implied consent, then the relative importance of the arbitration clause becomes crucial, for if it is conslusive or near conclusive evidence of a wish to apply the *lex,* then it might be said that its absence is equally significant; so that instances in which a national court should give effect to the *lex* must be non-existent or at best rare. Again, if the *lex* applies independently of consent to all transactions falling within its purview, one must ask whether a contract without an arbitration clause is within its purview. This in turn raises the question whether the *lex* is generated by, and is an integral and necessary part of, the societas mercatorium; or whether it is generated by, and is an integral and necessary part of, international commercial arbitration: two entirely different matters. These uncertainties will have to be resolved before the *lex* can present itself convincingly to the business community, which can hardly be expected to accept it as a substitute for the existing regime in the absence of an explicit formulation of precisely what it is.

Finally, it must be noted that the *lex mercatoria* has not yet laid claim to the whole territory of potential disputes arising from international commerce. Thus: (i) there appears to be no instance in which the *lex* has been invoked in a case of pure delict; (ii) the *lex* has rarely been applied where the issues are those of consent, fraud in the making of a contract, and so on; (iii) the *lex* has not, as far as the present author is aware, ever been credited in the literature with a power to create rights *in rem,* valid as against third parties—for example, by way of a transfer of title of corporeal assets, or pledge, or the creation of a monopoly such as patent or copyright. This is explicable, and indeed inevitable, if the *lex* is regarded as applicable only by express or implied consent, but is harder to understand if it is merely a reflection of the international commercial organism. Moreover, once it is accepted that the *lex* may on occasion have to be applied to some aspects of a dispute, whereas national law is applied to others, the practical attractions seem less apparent.

DOES THE *lex mercatoria* EMPOWER THE ARBITRATOR TO DECIDE IN EQUITY?

Much of the unease about the *lex mercatoria* stems from the idea that it frees the arbitrator to apply his own unfettered standards of justice to the individual case. The fact that this misconception is so widespread is due in part to the ambivalence in much of the literature about the relationship between the *lex mercatoria* and the concept of amiable composition,[54] a concept which is itself hard for the common lawyer to grasp.[55] Nevertheless, a misconception it undoubtedly is, at least by classical mercatorist standards.[56] The *lex mercatoria* is a *lex*, albeit not yet perfected. It creates norms which an arbitrator must seek out and obey in every case to which the *lex* applies. Whether the reason for its application is understood to be an express or implied agreement between the parties, or the concept that it forms the essential juridicial context of the bargain, there is no room here for the arbitrator to impose his own ideas, unless of course they happen to coincide with the rules of the *lex mercatoria*: for if he does so, he falsifies the transaction. Naturally, everyone hopes that the *lex mercatoria* will in every case yield a solution which will seem fair to all. But even if this expectation is disappointed, the *lex mercatoria* must still prevail; otherwise it would not be a law. Thus, since the prime maxim of the *lex mercatoria* is

[54] Y. Derains moderately observes that the relationship between the two concepts is not free from ambiguity; see Clunet (1980) 967.

[55] In involves no disrespect to Loquin's authoritative treatise—indeed quite the reverse—to say that, at the conclusion of his meticulous examination, a reader accustomed to other disciplines is left with the feeling that the concept of amiable composition has not yet, even on its own native heaths, been fully brought to hand. (A common lawyer may read with especial interest the three recent decisions of French Courts discussed in [1985] *Rev. Arb.* 199 ff. Some reflections on amiable composition, from an English point of view, may be found in Mustill and Boyd, *Commercial Arbitration* (London, 1982), 605 ff.

[56] See Derains, Clunet (1979) 996; goldman, 'Frontiers' 184–5, 187; id., *Contemporary Problems,* 117; id., Réalité et perspectives', 480; Lando, in *Contemporary Problems,* 110, and also 34 *ICLQ* 754. The difference between equity and rules of justice law was clearly stated in *Sapphire International Petroleum. NIDC, (supra,* n. 46), 1015.

that *pacta sunt servanda*; an arbitrator who smoothes the corners of a contract which seem to him too sharp is not complying with his mandate.[57]

More difficult is the reciprocal relationship between the two concepts. It has been said[58] that an agreement to make the arbitrator an amiable *compositeur* enables, even if it does not require, the arbitrator to take note of the *lex mercatoria*. To an outsider, this seems strange. The essence of amiable composition is to dispense the arbitrator from the duty of enforcing any system of law. Yet the *lex mercatoria* is a system of law. Why should an agreement to amiable composition summon up a reference to *lex mercatoria* any more than to any other developed system of commercial law? The literature gives no convincing answer.[59]

Another idea is that the repetition of decisions in equity will generate rules apt to be applied even by an arbitrator who is not authorized to act as an amiable *compositeur*.[60] In practice, this seems far distant, as scrutiny of the reported awards will disclose. But the theory is also difficult. How can decisions by arbitrators who *ex hypothesi* are released from the duty of applying the law ever yield a system of law which all arbitrators are bound by?

WHAT IS THE RELATION BETWEEN THE *lex mercatoria* AND NATIONAL LAW?

A hypothetical client is likely to ask how a conflict between the *lex mercatoria* and any national law which might otherwise have been relevant ought to be reconciled. His adviser would probably reply that the question has two aspects. First, what solution should the conscientious arbitrator adopt? Second, what is likely to be the attitude of the courts claiming jurisdiction over the matter—namely, the courts of the countries in which the arbitration takes place and the country in which enforcement of the award is sought?

On the first aspect, the bluntest question which the client may pose is this: If the contract expressly stipulates a choice of governing law, and if

---

[57] There is a particular risk in those instances in which the tribunal consists of one arbitrator nominated by each party together with a chairman. As P. Schlosser has pointed out (in *What is International in the Legal Basis of International Arbitration* (Japan, 1984), 101–2), when left a free hand, such tribunals tend to gravitate towards a compromise. This does not necessarily reflect the ideas of justice of any individual member, still less what the parties have actually agreed. Significantly, Loquin states that the clause of amiable composition authorizes the arbitrator to pronounce an award 'd'apaisement'.

[58] e.g. Loquin, *Apport*, Article 577, and Goldman, 'Réalité et perspectives', 480 ff.

[59] R. David suggests, in 'Arbitrage et Droit Comparé', [1959] *Rev. Int. dr. comparé*. 14, that two functions of amiable composition must be distinguished: first, where the parties look essentially for a solution by conciliation; and second, where they wish their disputes to be decided in conformity with law, but with a law which is not a national law. If so, some means must be found of deciding which of these antithetical solutions the parties to any given contract have actually chosen.

[60] See e.g., Y. Derains, Clunet (1975) 920.

the arbitrator is not an *amiable compositeur,* can the arbitrator properly apply the *lex meratoria* in preference to the chosen law? The answer must surely be an equally blunt no.[61] The arbitrator is mandated to decide the dispute in accordance with the contract; and the contract includes an agreement to abide by the denominated law. An arbitrator who decides according to some other law, whether anational or otherwise, presumes to rewrite the bargain. He has no right to do this. However good his motives, he does a disservice to the parties and to the institution of international arbitration.

Most complicated is the situation where the parties have expressly chosen to apply both a national law and some variety of 'general legal principles of law'.[62] This does happen on occasion, particularly where one party is a State enterprise. In practice, this rarely creates problems, because most often either the State law[63] or the *lex mercatoria*[64] are silent on the crucial question, or the answers given by the two laws happen to coincide.[65] Occasionally, however, a hierarchy must be established. Here, the literature offers no clear solution, and there appears to be no reported award where the arbitrators have been forced to make a choice.

There is a similar lack of authority in the converse situation, where the contract contains no express reference to a national law or to the *lex mercatoria*.[66] This is not surprising. Classical mercatorist doctrine requires the arbitrator to reject the choice of a national law before proceeding to choose the national law (see page 162 above). A conflict between the two should not arise. This theoretical conclusion appears to be reflected in

---

[61] It is possible to find passages within the literature which might be read as indicating a contrary view. But there is so much room for ambiguity in the expression *lex mercatoria* that it would be unsafe to assume that they can be read in such an extreme sense.

[62] Such a reference has, of course, nothing to do with the trade custom or common forms of contract.

[63] This was the case in relation to the concessions negotiated before and after the Second World War with states in the Middle East for the extraction of crude oil. The local law incorporated, in the shape of the Majallah, a most refined legal system. But it was one which had nothing to say about mineral rights and petroleum exploitation. There could thus be no conflict between the local law and the additional rules which, as everyone acknowledged, were necessary to make the concessions work. In theory, these rules might be regarded as anational. In practice they were conceived on both sides as having a shape remarkably similar to that of traditional Western European law. (Thus, it is not surprising that when Lord Asquith had recourse to general principles in his renowned Abu Dhabi award, these proved to rest on a few English decided cases). I suspect that it would have surprised the grantors as much as the concessionaires to learn that their contracts were governed by sources as heterogeneous as those called up by the literature on the *lex mercatoria*.

[64] As will very often be the case, except in so far as it consists of generalities which are unlikely to be in serious conflict with the relevant national laws.

[65] In which event the two laws can live in what Loquin, *Apport,* Article 16, has called 'peaceful coexistence'.

[66] The problem is touched on from time to time in the literature. See e.g. Lambert Matray, *Lib. Am. Sanders,* 241 ff. and Grigera Naón, *The Transnational Law of International Commercial Transactions,* (*supra,* n. 8).

practice. Those few awards in which the topic is touched upon seem to avoid discussion of conflicts between the *lex* and national laws, but rather tend to call up concordant national laws as reassurance that the rules of the anational laws have been correctly stated.[67]

There has, however, been some degree of discussion about the relationship between the *lex mercatoria* and national rules of *ordre public*[68] and between the *lex* and what has been called international *ordre public*.[69] Regrettably, space does not permit a discussion of this interesting and elusive topic.

The second questions concerns the likely reaction of national courts to an overtly anational award. A study of this question, which is difficult enough even when expressed in terms of a single national law, is far beyond the scope of the present essay, and indeed never appears to have been attempted. The question seems scarcely to have arisen in practice but if it had done so, the attention currently given to the world-wide claims of the *lex* would hardly have allowed it to be overlooked. It is, however, impossible to part from the subject without mentioning, much more brief than the author would have wished, three[70] awards where the issue has come to the surface.

The first was rendered in the arbitration *soc. Fougerolle v. Banque de Proche Orient*.[71] Arbitrators were authorized to decide what law was to be applied. Without the possibility being mentioned by or to the parties, the tribunal decided the dispute according to the principles generally applicable in international commerce. The Cour de Cassation in France rejected an attack on the award, but it is not clear from the economical reasons

---

[67] Thus, in the 'Pyramids' case (*supra*, n. 46) the tribunal proceeded by interpreting Egyptian law as conforming with the general principle exemplified in Article 42(1) of the ICSID convention, and then applying it in that sense. See also ICC No. 2478, Clunet (1976) 925, and No. 3540, Clunet (1981) 914 (amiable composition).

[68] Which laws are to be regarded as relevant for this purpose is nowhere clearly prescribed. If they include the putative proper law, then the arbitrator will have to carry out the conflicts exercise, the avoidance of which is claimed as one of the major benefits of the *lex mercatoria*. O. Lando suggests (*supra*, n. 4), 765) that the arbitrator must also give priority to the mandatory rules of countries closely connected with the contract and to the rules of the country in which the award is likely to be enforced (if the arbitrator can predict which country this will be, which is not always the case).

[69] The concept is developed in a number of interesting writings by P. Lalive, including *ICCA*. Recent treatises by the same author and by Y. Derains may be found in [1986] *Rev. Arb.* 329 and 375. It is important to note that international *ordre public* is not the same as the *lex mercatoria*. If the two conflict, as they may do, *ordre public* must prevail. See the illustration provided by the 'creole' case, cited in Lalive, *ICLA,* 113.

[70] Some authors would add a fourth in the shape of the decision of the Corte di Cassazione dated 8 Feb. 1982. Although the judgment certainly does contain an excursus of the *lex mercatoria*, in terms which quite clearly assume its existence, the present author cannot read this as forming a link in the chain of reasoning which led to the award being upheld. Moreover, the supposed rule related to procedure and not to substance, which is the true province of the *lex mercatoria*.

[71] 9 Dec. 1981, *Rev. Arb.* [1982] 183, and note thereon, G. Couchez at 187.

given by the court whether the decision was founded on the principles of contradition or on the *lex mercatoria* itself. As a commentator has suggested, it may be unsafe to draw too many conclusions from it.

The second instance is the much debated case of *Pabalk Ticaret* v. *Ugilor/Norsolor*. The arbitrators found it difficult to choose between two national laws, and therefore elected to choose neither, applying the rule of the *lex mercatoria* which requires the parties to act in good faith in the execution of the award.[72] Holding on the facts that one party has abused its position of strength in a manner which had led to the breakdown of the agreement, they awarded damages to the other.[73]

The award came under repeated scrutiny in the courts of two countries. In Austria, where the award had been made, the Oberster Gerichtshof confined itself to the question of whether the award should be annulled on one of the grounds set out exhaustively in ZPO, Article 595, of which only paragraphs 5 and 6 were relied upon. These dealt respectively with situations in which a tribunal had entered upon matters beyond those confided to it, and those in which an award violated mandatory provisions of law. As to the first, the court held that an award resulting from an unauthorized application of equity was not an award on matters outside the powers of the tribunal. As to the second, there was no evidence that the application of equity contradicted any statutory imperative of the two laws in question. Thus, it appears that the decision was not an endorsement of the *lex mercatoria* so much as a recognition of a court's limited powers where a tribunal's reasoning is under attack.[74]

In France the successful party sought *exequatur*. It was first granted, then denied, and later the denial was made the subject of cassation, each decision following the fortunes of the proceedings in the Austrian courts. The decision of the Cour de Cassation certainly does lend support to the mercatorists, to the extent that the court did not repudiate the notion of the *lex mercatoria*, which would have furnished a short answer to the problem. Whether it amounts to a vindication of the *lex*, as has been claimed, is an altogether different matter; and it may be noted that Professor Goldman, among others, has expressed the opinion that it does not go so far.[75]

The third decision, arising from a dispute between *Deutsche Schachtbau- und Tiefbohrgesellschaft mbH* and *The Government of Ras al Khaimal*, was

[72] The sum awarded was 800,000 French francs, arrived at ('en équité') without calculation. It is reasonable to speculate on how this sum compared with the costs involved in proceeds to the highest tribunal in the courts of two countries. If the arbitrators had chosen one national law or the other, rather than the *lex mercatoria*, the award would have been unassailable. Perhaps the victory of the *lex mercatoria*, if such it was, had its pyrrhic aspects.
[73] The award is reproduced in [1983] *Rev. Arb.* 525.
[74] On the Austrian aspects of this litigation, see W. Melis, 9 *YBIL* 163, and also B. Goldman [1983] *Rev. Arb.* 407–8.
[75] [1985] *Rev. arb.* 438.

delivered by the Court of Appeal in England just as the present article was going to press. It will be welcomed by mercatorists, and seems likely to be the subject of extensive academic discussion. The circumstances were as follows.

An agreement relating to exploration for oil and gas was made between a government and a government oil company on the one hand, and a consortium of companies registered in various countries on the other, upon terms which included an ICC arbitration clause providing for the arbitration to be held in Geneva. Subsequently the government and the oil company declined to continue performance of the agreement, contending that it had been induced by misrepresentation. The dispute which then arose was submitted to arbitration. The government side took no part. In due course terms of reference were formulated, stating a number of issues for decision. The second was: 'What body or bodies of substantive law should be applied by the arbitral tribunal?' Ultimately, the arbitration was decided on the facts, the arbitrators holding that the alleged misrepresentation was not established and that there was no other ground for holding that the agreement was invalid. As the arbitrators themselves said in their award (ICC No. 3572) 'the choice of the law to be applied to the agreement is of little significance, if any, under the prevailing circumstances'. In spite of this the arbitrators went on to express a choice, presumably because they felt obliged to do so by the terms of reference. Rejecting the law of the state where the agreement was to be performed they held that internationally accepted principles of law governing contractual relations were 'the proper law'.

Understandable as it was, the election to include in the award a reference to international principles which had no bearing on the outcome of the dispute proved to be unfortunate, since the oil company relied upon the choice of these principles as a ground for resisting enforcement of the award in England, thus postponing the time when the sums awarded would be recovered.

When it was discovered that the oil company might have assets in England various proceedings took place including in particular a summary application to the Commercial Court to enforce the award in the same manner as a judgment. This was granted. Subsequently there was an application to the same court to set the order aside on the ground that it would be contrary to public policy for the Court to grant enforcement, where the principles applied by the arbitrators were so uncertain. This application failed. The oil company appealed to the Court of Appeal, and failed again.

This is an important case for an English lawyer, as regards both the recognition by the Court of a doctrine of *competenz competenz* applicable under the *lex fori*, and also the application of a narrow view of English public policy. The significance so far as regards the *lex mercatoria* is, however, substantially less than might at first sight appear. The starting-point of the judgment was a decision that the agreement to arbitrate was governed by the law of Switzerland. Since the oil company did not participate in the arbitration, there had been no contest on the propriety of a choice of general principles under that law. The company had not sought to set the award aside in Switzerland, nor did it offer any evidence to contradict the expert evidence of Swiss law tendered by the claimants to the effect that the general principles were a valid choice under the ICC choice of law clause. Thus, the English court could accept that the decision to apply the general principles was a permissible performance of the arbitrators' mandate under the choice of law clause according to both the *lex fori* and the *lex causae*. Against this background there was nothing in English public policy to preclude enforcement of the award in England.

Thus far, the import of the decision is clear, and it must greatly hearten the mercatorists. The wider implications, so far as concerns English law, will require careful analysis. As an immediate reaction, the present author would venture the following very tentative observations, the more tentative since at the time of writing the possibilities of an onward appeal cannot be excluded:

(i) The case was not concerned with transnationalism. The claimants' evidence proceeded on the assumption that Swiss law was the *lex causae*. Nobody suggested that there was no national *lex causae*.

(ii) Although the judgment contains a discussion of two English decisions on the effect on a contract of including various types of 'general principles' clauses, this was probably *obiter*, since (a) there was no such clause in the contact, (b) English law was neither the *lex causae*, the *lex fori*, nor the 'putative proper law', and (c) the issue had not been debated at the hearing.

(iii) The judgment did not address the question whether, under English law, when a contract does not contain any explicit choice of the 'general principles' the arbitrators can validly purport to apply them. This extremely important question did not arise in the Court of Appeal, and could not have been decided without reference to certain reported cases, not cited in the judgement.

WHAT ARE THE SOURCES OF THE *lex mercatoria?*

It is, I believe, clear from a reading of the literature, that the proponents of the *lex mercatoria* do not wholly agree about the sources from which it is drawn, or about the relative importance of those sources which they regard as admissible. There is a wide gulf between those who look (for example) to sources such as standard form contracts and those who seek to distill the common features of national commercial law. Nevertheless, an adviser could not begin his task without first having an idea of the sources which the arbitrator might regard as relevant. For this purpose he could usefully have recourse to a list compiled by Professor O. Lando,[76] noting, however, the caution added by that author that it is not possible to provide an exhaustive list of all the elements of the law merchant.[77] Reduced to its bare headings, this list is as follows:

A. Public International Law.
B. Uniform Laws.
C. The General Principles of Law.
D. The Rules of International Organizations.
E. Customs and usages.
F. Standard Form Contracts.
G. Reporting of Arbitral Awards.

To this list one must evidently add the public policy of the country in which enforcement of the award is likely to be requested.[78]

Most of the items on this list are discussed elsewhere in this essay, but brief comments may be added about two of them. With regard to public international law, there is of course no question but that parties can expressly stipulate that their relationships shall be governed in whole or in part by public international law, and this does on occasion happen where one of the parties is a State or a State enterprise. The present author finds it hard to see why this fact should entail that the application of public international law in these instances should cause it to become part of an all-pervasive general law of commerce, applying between private parties even in the absence of express agreement; for the principles which are apposite to regulate the relationship between sovereigns are not a priori germane to the relationship between commercial persons or companies[79] and in practice, the express incorporation of public international law into ordinary day-to-day trading contracts is, as far as the present author's experience extends, entirely unknown.[80]

---

[76] *Supra*, n. 4.

[77] Quoting Fouchard (*supra*, n. 4.), Articles 575–630, and the same author, 'L'arbitrage internationale en France après le décret du 12 Mai 1981', Clunet (1982) 374, 395.

[78] Lando (*supra*, n. 4), 766. He refers in this context to Article 26 of the ICC Rules of Arbitration, 1976, which requires the arbitrator to 'make every effort to make sure that the award is enforceable at law'.

[79] See M. Virally, in *Étude Goldman*, 381.

[80] As to the relationship between Article 38 of the statute of the International Court of Justice and the *lex mercatoria*, see Goldman, 'Réalité et perspectives' 486, citing A. Broches.

The inclusion of uniform laws—such as the 1980 Convention on the International Sale of Goods—in the list of sources is qualified[81] by the suggestion that the arbitrator is bound to apply them only when the internal courts of those countries which are connected with the parties or the subject-matter of the dispute would be obliged to apply them, although in other cases the uniform laws may act as a guide to the arbitrator. If this is so, we have here another example of a 'micro' *lex mercatoria*, particularized in relation to the individual transaction.

WHAT ARE THE RULES OF THE *lex mercatoria*?

Plainly, it would be of great practical importance to the hypothetical adviser to know whether in any published work, and particularly in any published award, the view had been expressed that a particular rule forms part of the *lex mercatoria*. Setting aside for a moment the difficulties of time and access to the literature which the adviser would be likely to encounter, it seems that he would be able to put together a list somewhat on the following lines, as representing a tolerably complete account of the rules which are said to constitute the *lex mercatoria* in its present form.[82]

1. A general principle that contracts should prima facie be enforced according to their terms: *pacta sunt servanda*.[83] The emphasis given to this maxim in the literature suggests that it is regarded, not so much as one of the rules of the *lex mercatoria*, but as the fundamental principle of the entire system.
2. The first general principle is qualified at least in respect of certain long-term contracts, by an exception akin to *'rebus sic stantibus'*.[84] The interaction of the principle and the exception has yet to be fully worked out.
3. The first general principle may also be subject to the concept of *abus de droit*,[85] and to a rule that unfair and unconscionable contracts and clauses should not be enforced.[86]
4. There may be a doctrine of *culpa in contrahendo*.[87].
5. A contract should be performed in good faith.[88]
6. A contract obtained by bribes or other dishonest means is void, or

---

[81] Lando (*supra*, n. 4), 749.

[82] I have omitted from this list one or two rules, referred to in the literature, of a procedural nature (such as a rule that the arbitrator has power to adjudicate on his own jurisdiction) since the literature as a whole and the theoretical foundations which it proposes treat the *lex mercatoria* as a body of substantive law.

[83] So many authors have stated this principle, that citation would be superfluous. It is justly pointed out by M. Virally, in *Étude Goldman*, 381, that *pacta sunt servanda* is not really a rule on its own, but is merely a reflection of the nature of a contractual obligation. The problem is to decide when the rule admits of exceptions.

at least unenforceable.[89] So too if the contract creates a fictitious transactions designed to achieve an illegal object.[90]

7. A State entity cannot be permitted to evade the enforcement of its obligations by denying its own capacity to make a binding agreement to arbitrate, or by asserting that the agreement is unenforceable for want of procedural formalities to which the entity is subject.[91]

---

[84] The very guarded nature of this proposition is demanded by the uncertain state of the authorities. B. Goldman Clunet (1979), 475, 494, calls it a principle, or at least a presumption. The fact that *force majeure* and frustration are similar in some respects, but quite different in others, may have misled some arbitrators (see the comments of Cremades and Plehn (*supra*, n. 4), 342). There is often no problem where a 'micro' *lex mercatoria* is involved, as in ICC No. 1512, Clunet (1974; 908 (India and Pakistan). But on a wider canvas some of the decisions cannot command general acceptance. If ICC No. 1703 decides that long-term contracts are subject to an implied right of suspension in cases of *force majeure,* this is inconsistent with the common law. So too are the 'nombreuses sentences' referred to in Fouchard (*supra*, n. 4), Article 620. Other ICC awards, including Nos. 1782, 2139, 2142, 2216, 2478, and 3093, have been cited on this subject, but to the present author they seem either irrelevant or insufficient to enable any clear statement to be made as to the present relationship between the first two general principles. In any developed legal system this is a troublesome topic, but in the *lex mercatoria* it seems to be particularly difficult. (See a valiant attempt at a synthesis by Derains, Clunet (1974) 944, and also B. Goldman, Clunet (1979) 494.)

[85] Goldman, 'Frontiers' 184, [cites] from a treatise by Fouchard an unpublished award to this effect. In an *ad hoc* arbitration YBIL (1982) 77, the arbitrators were *amiable compositeurs,* but expressed themselves to be applying the *lex mercatoria* and applied the concept of *abus de droit* to the giving of notice to terminate a commercial relationship. This concept cannot form part of a 'macro' *lex mercatoria,* since it is not known to the common law.

[86] To this effect, see Lando (*supra*, n. 4), 765. There appears to be no authority for such a radical proposition in the reported awards, and although there are a very few traces of something similar in the common law (e.g. in relation to liquidated damages and penalties and the equity against forfeiture), it would not, as stated in the text, form part of a 'macro' *lex mercatoria.*

[87] See Derains, Clunet (1976) 947 citing unreported ICC Award No. 2540. The observations of the arbitrators appear to have been *obiter,* since they decided according to national law. The doctrine is not known to the common law.

[88] Goldman, '*Contemporary Problems*', 116; id., 'Réalités et perspectives', 492, and Loquin, *Apport.* The latter states that the principle is wider than principles which are applicable by national laws to 'les operations internes', and the references to awards suggest that it is a generalization from other rulcs. See e.g. ICC No. 2520, Clunet (1978) 992, and No. 2478, Clunet (1975) 925. The Norsolor case (*supra*, n. 73) is the most conspicuous example of this doctrine in operation.

[89] Loquin, 'L'Arbitrage', 765, citing ICC No. 1110, apparently unreported, but discussed in some detail in Lew, *Applicable Law* 553 (*supra*, n. 4), ff. Like ICC No. 3913, Clunet (1984) 920, and also No. 3916, Clunet (1984) 930 (which is to the opposite effect) this was a case on jurisdiction, and was therefore perhaps concerned with international *ordre public,* rather than the *lex mercatoria.* See also Lalive, *ICCA* 52, citing No. 2730, Clunet (1984) 914, also reported in 9 *YBCA* 105. The latter could have been, and perhaps was, decided by direct reference to Yugoslav law, or by the *ordre public* of the *lex fori.* I suspect that the same is likely to be true in most, if not all, cases in this category.

[90] See e.g. ICC No. 2730 and *supra,* n. 89. The transaction involved a fraud on the Yugoslav exchange control authorities.

[91] To this effect, Goldman, '*Contemporary Problems*', 123, and Lalive, *ICCA* Articles 136–7. There appear to be few if any reported arbitral awards on the point. Perhaps it should be classed as a principle of international *ordre public* rather than *lex mercatoria.*

8. The controlling interest of a group of companies is regarded as contracting on behalf of all members of the group, at least so far as concerns an agreement to arbitrate.[92]
9. If unforseen difficulties intervene in the performance of a contract, the parties should negotiate in good faith to overcome them, even if the contract contains no revision clause.[93]
10. 'Gold clause' agreements are valid and enforceable.[94] Perhaps in some cases either a gold clause or a 'hardship' revision clause may be implied.[95]
11. One party is entitled to treat itself as discharged from its obligations if the other has committed a breach, but only if the breach is substantial.[96]
12. No party can be allowed by its own act to bring about a non-performance of a condition precedent to its own obligation.[97]

---

[92] The broader version of this principle is extracted by Derains from ICC No. 2375, Clunet (1976) 973. See also Goldman, 'Réalités et perspectives, 496. This case and the Dow Chemical case were both concerned with the question of whether associated companies were bound by the arbitration clause. Nos. 2375 and 1434, Clunet (1976) 978, are also referred to. I believe that most of these cases could, without recourse to this very far-reaching doctrine, which is certainly not part of the common law, have been decided simply by enquiring whether a consent to arbitration as between the associated company and the other parties could be spelt out of their words and conduct. See No. 2138, Clunet (1975) 934.

[93] See Loquin, *Apport,* Article 39 and Goldman 'Réalités et perspectives', 492, citing ICC No. 2478, Clunet (1975) 925 (and note thereon by Derains), also No. 2291, Clunet (1976) 989. The former is an example of the promisee's duty to mitigate his loss; the latter is referred to at n. 95. *infra.*

[94] Cremades and Plehn (*supra,* n. 4), 346. There are several awards to this effect, including ICC No. 1512, Clunet (1974) 905; No. 1990, Clunet (1974) 897; No. 2748, Clunet (1975) 925; No. 2291, Clunet (1976) 989. It may be doubted whether this is a separate rule, rather than an application of *pacta sunt servanda.*

[95] A common lawyer must step delicately here. Much attention has been given to Soc. Européene d'Études v. Yugoslav Government (1959), J. de. Dr. Int. 1074, ad to ICC Award No. 2291, Clunet (1976) 989. Unfortunately, space does not permit a full discussion of these two awards and the interpretations which have been placed upon them. The former was a remarkable case in which the arbitrators implied into an engineering contract a guarantee against exchange losses, resulting in an award of twenty times the sum stipulated by the contract. This decision, described by Fouchard (*supra,* N. 4), Article 618 as 'audacieuse', could not be said to exemplify any *lex mercatoria* with claims to a world-wide perspective and one may detect a note of unease about it even among enthusiasts. The other award, ICC No. 2291, is an example of those cases where a commonplace dispute was given an extra dimension by unnecessary recourse to the *lex mercatoria.* It is, however, an instructive example of the dangers of making unsupported generalizations. In the award and commentary we find that Anglo-Saxon law is 'plus accessible à la revision des contrats en cas de déséquilibre même pour la cause économique (clause de hardship)', as well as reference to 'le présence presque automatique de clauses de ce type dans les contrats internationaux'. The former is not a correct statement of the common law; and the inclusion of hardship and similar clauses in the routine type of transportation contract with which the arbitrators were concerned is almost, if not entirely, unknown.

[96] Award ICC No. 2583, Clunet (1976) 950, and note Derains; No. 3540, Clunet (1981) 915, 7. YBCA 124.

[97] Fouchard (*supra,* n.4), 441, citing an unpublished award.

13. A tribunal is not bound by the characterization of the contract ascribed to it by the parties.[98]
14. Damages for breach of contract are limited to the forseeable consequences of the breach.[99]
15. A party which has suffered a breach of contract must take reasonable steps to mitigate its loss.[100]
16. Damages for non-delivery are calculated by reference to the market price of the goods and the price at which the buyer has purchased equivalent goods in replacement.[101]
17. A party must act promptly to enforce its rights, on pain of losing them by waiver.[102] This may be an instance of a more general rule, that each party must act in a diligent and practical manner to safeguard its own interests.[103]
18. A debtor may in certain circumstances set off his own cross-claims to extinguish or diminish his liability to the creditor.[104]
19. Contracts should be construed according to the principle *ut res magis valeat quam pereat*.[105]
20. Failure by one party to respond to a letter written to it by the other is regarded as evidence of assent to its terms.[106]

This list, incomplete as it may be, seems rather a modest haul for twenty-five years of international arbitration. The reader must form his own conclusions. The following comments may, however, suggest themselves.

First, the reported awards do not in all cases seem to sustain the wealth of commentary based upon them. By no means all of them make explicit reference to the *lex mercatoria* as an independent system of law. Those instances in which reference is made to commercial usage are equally explicable on the ground that the usage controlled the meaning of the contract, an approach which is just as consistent with national as with

---

[98] A contract describing itself as 'vente d'équipement' was treated as embracing a contract of services in ICC No. 3242, Clunet (1982) 968.

[99] ICC No. 2404, Clunet (1978) 995.

[100] This rule appears on all the lists. Various awards are cited in support, including ICC No. 2478, Clunet (1975) 925; No. 2103, Clunet (1974) 902; No. 3344, Clunet (1982) 978; No. 2412, Clunet (1974) 892. The awards on mitigation rarely call up the *lex mercatoria* in so many words; they merely treat the principle as obvious.

[101] Fouchard (*supra*, n. 4), 441, citing an unpublished award.

[102] ICC No. 3344, Clunet (1982) 978; No. 3243, Clunet (1982) 968; No. 2250, Clunet (1976) 992, have been cited in support.

[103] Commentary on ICC No. 2520 (*supra*, no. 102), citing No. 2291.

[104] ICC No. 3540 (*supra*, n. 96). As given in *YBCA* 131 the conditions for the exercise of a set-off resemble those for set-off in 'in law' under English law, but are more restrictive than those of the set-off 'in equity'.

[105] ICC No. 1434, Clunet (1976) 978.

[106] ICC No. 3344, Clunet (1982) 978. This conclusion, said to be 'fortement influencé par le droit français', is not consistent with the common law.

anational legal systems. Second, it may be said that 'whilst there can be found an abundance of sweeping formulation of legal principles, these are of little use for legal analysis'.[107] Third, where the rules are expressed more specifically, they cannot in every case be derived from any world-wide generalization of national laws.[108]

HOW IS THE *lex mercatoria* TO BE ASCERTAINED?

Under this heading, we must examine two distinct problems with which the adviser will be faced. First, how is he to discover the substantive content of the *lex mercatoria*? Second, how is he to predict, in a case where the relevant rule has not yet been firmly established by a consensus of opinion or by one or more reported arbitral awards what sources a tribunal will deploy when addressing the new issue of principle, and what conclusion it will reach?

The first question has been little addressed in the literature. Yet, mundane as it may seem, it is important in practice—and the practical superiority of the *lex mercatoria* is advanced by its proponents as the principal justification for its existence. Our hypothetical adviser is not an academic lawyer, established at an institution of learning in one of those European cities where the *lex* is most at home. Rather, he is a practitioner, established in a trade centre which may be in any part of the world, possessing such resources of time and knowledge and commanding access to such printed materials as can reasonably be expected of those holding themselves out as competent to advise on matters of international trade in the world-wide domain to which the *lex mercatoria* lays claim.

Here, the practitioner is likely to run into trouble at the outset. Some of the theoretical analysis is contained in periodicals which, if not available to him in his own country, might be forwarded to him by his correspondents. Assuming that he can read the language in which they are written, these articles give him a broad idea of the doctrine, but perhaps not a great deal of detail. For this he would have to follow up references in footnotes, which will often be to publications of limited circulation or to works of reference now out of print or to volumes of the Festschrift variety which were printed in restricted numbers and are mostly found in private libraries. Even if he had the time, the practitioner could not achieve a full conspectus.[109] This being so, he would be likely to look for concrete examples of situations in which the *lex mercatoria* has been applied through

---

[107] P. Schlosser, op cit, 107.

[108] There is, of course, a risk of unfairness here. It is too easy to say that if the rules form part of every nation's law, they are banal, and that if they do not, they cannot be the subject of a valid generalization.

[109] Even with the help of colleagues here and abroad and generous access to libraries, the present author was unable to follow up by any means all the references cited in the more readily available literature.

awards rendered in international commercial arbitrations. Here again he would be in difficulties. Thousands of such awards are made every year. Some are published under the auspices of certain arbitral institutions,[110] but most are not. Moreover, the published awards are almost without exception concerned with the application of national laws.[111] Few can be claimed as clear examples of the workings of the *lex mercatoria* in practice.

Closer to the point are awards made by tribunals which can be regarded as 'de-localized', assuming this concept to have meaning. How many of these there are is impossible to say; but once again, only a few are published. There have been a few *ad hoc* awards and ICSID awards and a limited number of awards springing from references conducted under the auspices of the ICC. The practitioner could look these up, but they would not take him very far. The publication of extracts from ICC awards began in Clunet, *Journal du droit International,* in 1974 and, with some overlapping, in the Yearbook of Commercial Arbitration (YBCA) in 1976. Since then, a total of about 130 awards have been published, some of them dating from the 1950s and 1960s. This is only a small proportion of the total number of ICC awards, in which the *lex mercatoria* might be expected to exert the greatest influence. Of these, not many are even claimed by commentators to have any connection with the *lex mercatoria.* Although the number cited is rather greater, the present author believes that not more than about twenty five are really concerned with it. Furthermore, as more than one author has pointed out,[112] the selection for publication is made, quite legitimately, to illuminate some aspect of the doctrine. The practitioner has no way of finding out whether there have been other awards in which the application of the *lex mercatoria* was raised and rejected, or never raised at all.[113] In addition, many reports are heavily edited, in the interests of confidentiality. For the commentator this is no hardship. But the practitioner or arbitrator who is asking himself whether a previous award is one which should be followed in the particular case before him will need to know: (i) the factual details of the dispute: (ii) the extent to which a non-mercatorist approach was advanced by the parties; (iii) the arguments addressed by the parties as to the mercatorist rule to be applied; and (iv) (and very importantly) the steps (if any) taken by the tribunal to inform itself accurately of the national laws from which it

---

[110] e.g., the Society of Maritime Arbitrators in the United States and various chambers of trade and arbitral institutions in Europe.

[111] Arbitral awards applying national laws, like the judgements of courts, form part of the corpus of national laws, from which, by a process of creative induction, an international arbitrator may derive the rules of the *lex mercatoria*; but the adviser cannot safely treat them as directly establishing these rules.

[112] e.g. Cremades and Plehn (*supra*, n. 4), 342, and J. Lew, *Lib. Am. Saunders,* 231. See also Derains, in Clunet (1977) 931, on the editorial principles of that journal.

[113] Among published awards ICC No. 4237, 10 *YBCA* 52, may be an isolated example.

proceeded to derive its generally accepted rules. Many extracts are deficient in this respect, and some are so brief as to be almost useless. The same comment may be made *a fortiori* about unreported awards which are referred to in footnotes or in systematic collections.[114]

To the academic lawyer these considerations may seem trifling. Either the *lex mercatoria* is part of an international legal order, or it is not. Either a rule forms part of the *lex* or it does not. The difficulties which practising lawyers in various parts of the world may experience when trying to search it out cannot alter the position. Nor, it may be said, it is a valid objection to the doctrine as an intellectual construct that the adviser may find it difficult, and often impossible, to predict whether a tribunal not yet appointed will decide to apply the *lex mercatoria*: or what kind of *lex mercatoria*, whether 'macro' or 'micro' or some other kind, it will be; or what sources the tribunal will consider of greatest importance; or what weight will be attached to prior awards on the same question, if any exist and can be found.

All this is true enough. If the contract expressly directs the arbitrator to apply the *lex mercatoria*, or if he conceives that the circumstances justify him in treating such a director as implicit, he will find a way of doing so, notwithstanding the fragmentary nature of the norms so far established. But this is only a small part of the story. The purpose of a commercial legal order is to regulate transactions, not awards or judgments. For the businessman, proceedings in court or arbitration are a wretched last resort, to be avoided at almost any cost—and in fact they are avoided in all but a minute proportion of cases. What he requires is a legal framework, sufficient to inform him before any dispute has arisen what he can or must do next. If a dispute does arise he needs to be told whether he can insist or must yield, and how much room he has for manoeuvre. When asking such a question, the last answer which a businessman wants to hear is that it is a good question.[115]

In the light of all these considerations one may take stock of the *lex mercatoria* as it stands today by asking, Does it provide the businessman with a set of rules which is sufficiently accessible and certain to permit the efficient conduct of his transactions? Is the *lex* manifestly superior, in its content and methodology, to established national systems of commercial law? If so, is its superiority so obvious that it can now be said to have imposed itself, whether by the very fact of its existence or by a notion of implied consent, on the international business community as a whole, and on all transactions in which it is not expressly excluded? In short, has the *lex mercatoria* stolen the international commercial scene, pushing national laws into the wings?

[114] Many instances are collected in J. Lew, *Applicable Law*, (*supra*, n. 4).
[115] See 'L'Objet essential du droit, la prévisibilité,' in Fouchard (*supra*, n. 4) 435.

In each case, the detached observer must, I believe, be driven to answer 'no'. More sympathetically, he might add '. . . or at least not yet'.[116] What the future holds is hard to forecast. The *lex* has established a tenacious academic foothold in Continental Europe, and its cause is being vigorously promoted elsewhere. The Norsolor and *Deutsche Schachtbau* is encouraging, even if it does not amount to the explicit endorsement which some have asserted. On the other hand, there appears to be no sign that the *lex* is gaining a foothold in ordinary day-to-day business, through the medium of an express choice. It has not yet been put to the test by enforcement proceedings in jurisdictions where the most resistance is likely to be encountered. The conscious decision of those who framed the UNCITRAL Model Law to adopt the expression 'the law determined by the conflict of laws rules which [the arbitral tribunal] considers applicable' in Article 28(2), in preference to looser words such as 'the rules of law',[117] must have been a great disappointment to mercatorists, and, if the Model Law is reproduced on any scale in national legislation, it will be a serious obstacle to the growth of the *lex*. It may also be sensed that the tide of economic opinion is hardly running in its favour. Essentially, the *lex mercatoria* is a doctrine of *laissez-faire*. In very many parts of the world it is considered that the exercise of free consent by individual parties must be subordinated to broader economic and political considerations bearing on international trade.[118] Furthermore, the disfavour with which 'transnational' groups or corporations are now regarded in some quarters cannot but hinder the general acceptance of a doctrine whose legitimacy is seen, rightly or wrongly, as derived at least in part from the existence of such bodies.

In addition, it is impossible to overlook the change in the character of arbitration which has occurred during recent decades. In the past, it might have been possible without excessive idealism, to see arbitration as a vehicle for the pacific settlement of disputes, producing awards which would be honoured either because it did not occur to the loser to do anything else, or because a default would have exposed him to the censure of his peers and to a damaging loss of reputation. We now live in a harsher

[116] Some large claims are made for the current acceptability of the *lex mercatoria*. For example, 'L'existence de règles transnationales qui régissent les relations économiques, notamment entre États et entreprises étrangères, n'est plus sérieusement contestable aujourd'hui' (P. Leboulanger, *Les Contrats entre états et enterprises étrangères* (1985), 221). It is however noteworthy that many commentators, including Goldman himself, express the position in much less extreme terms.

[117] There can be no doubt that the divergence between the language of Articles 28(1) and (2) was deliberate, and marks a real difference in meaning. See the Analytical Commentary on the draft text, prepared by the Secretariat of UNCITRAL, A/C No. 9/264, p. 62 and 63 (English version). A proposal to assimilate the language of Article 28(2) to that of Article 28(1) was discussed, but not adopted; see Analytical Compilation of Comments by Governments, A/C No. 9/263, p. 41 (English version).

[118] See e.g. Grigera Naón (*supra*, n. 11), 91.

world. Winning is what matters. Whether because of a change in commercial attitudes or simply because the stakes are so much higher, many arbitrations are now fought as intensely and with as much zeal for taking every available advantage, whether procedural or otherwise, as any action in court.[119] No longer can it be taken for granted that awards will be honoured.[120] In such a climate, one must ask whether the foundations of the *lex mercatoria* are sound enough to sustain the blasts to which it may be subjected.

I would not wish to end in such a negative vein. Two final suggestions may be more constructive. First, the growth and strengthening of international commercial arbitration, which everyone in the field strives to promote, is not dependent on a solution to the problems here discussed. In most instances, the parties and the arbitrator need never look beyond the contract and the facts to arrive at the outcome of a dispute. There is no call for recourse to law at all; or if there is, the principle is so clear as to be taken for granted. In very many cases the applicable law is nominated by the contract. Even if it is not, and even if the members of a tribunal come from different legal backgrounds, it is rare to find that their instinctive reactions to a situation diverge sufficiently to demand a formal appraisal and resolution. If a contract appears insufficiently explicit to furnish a direct statement of the parties' rights, duties, powers, and liberties, then the arbitrators will construe it and fill the gaps in it by recourse to their own knowledge of how commerce works in practice, and of how commercial men in the relevant field express themselves. Whether an arbitrator who approaches the matter in this way feels it necessary to employ the *lex mercatoria* or some established technique of a national system, such as the implication of a term, or whether he does not rationalize what he is doing, but simply goes ahead and does it, is unlikely to make any difference in all but a small minority of cases. What is important is that the arbitrator keep constantly in mind that he is concerned with international commerce, with all the breadth of horizon, flexibility, and practicality of approach which that demands. In keeping these features constantly in the public eye, the mercatorists perform a most valuable function.

Finally, the person whose interests lie at the heart of the *lex mercatoria* as of all commercial arbitration, is the businessman. All the debates proceed upon rival assumptions about his opinions and wishes on this or

[119] This is well recognized by Derains, Clunet (1977) 976 and Clunet (1980) 950, where he speaks of the 'banalisation' of arbitration.

[120] Of course, many awards are still honoured spontaneously. But it is much more common than it used to be for claimants to seek security for an eventual award, and the disapprobation of colleagues is not the force it was. Interestingly, a commentator (Cremades and Plehn (*supra*, N. 4), p. 325. n. 39) cites reinsurance as an example of a field where awards are spontaneously honoured. This was so in the past, when the market was narrow, and default could be fatal. Nowadays, in the experience of the present author, reinsurance is the most bitterly litigious of all areas of commercial activity.

that topic. Yet all the literature is written by lawyers. Perhaps the time has now arrived for the contestants to call a truce, and for the businessman to speak for himself.[121]

[121] Malynes, the first English author on the old *lex mercatoria,* was a merchant. His book, *Consueto, vel Lex Mercatoria* was addressed to a wide public. It was said to be of 'Necessary for Statesmen, Judges, Magistrates Temporal and Civil Lawyers, Mintmen, Merchants and all others negotiating in any parts of the World'.

12

Fault in the Common Law of Contract

by G. H. TREITEL

One of the significant points of contrast between the civil and the common law of contract is, or is said to be, that in the former fault is, while in the latter it is not, an ingredient of contractual liability. The general requirement of fault in civil law systems is, indeed, subject to many important exceptions, so that there is much support for the view that the civil law of contract has a greater area of strict liability than might at first sight appear from general statements of the requirement of fault;[1] and indeed the orthodox approach of a 'general' requirement of fault, subject to exceptions, has been viewed with scepticism by some civil lawyers.[2] The purpose of the discussion that follows is to consider the question from a common law perspective and to ask whether, even in the common law of contract, fault (in the sense of want of care, diligence or honesty) does not play a greater role than is usually supposed.

The common law has devoted little attention to the question whether fault is a requirement of contractual liability. There is little discussion in a contractual context of the standards of liability (strict liability, liability for negligence, liability for intentional wrong-doing) with which tort lawyers are so familiar. The general assumption seems to be that in contract there is no requirement of fault. Thus in England it has been said that 'In relation to a claim for damages for breach of contract it is, in general, immaterial why the defendant failed to fulfil his obligations and certainly no defence to plead that he had done his best.'[3] In the United States, there is, similarly, no reference to fault in the definition of breach given in the Restatement 2d, Contracts § 235(2): 'When performance of a duty under a contract is due any non-performance is a breach.' The definition of breach in § 312 of the first Restatement was, from this point of view, similar: 'A breach of contract is a non-performance of any contractual duty of immediate performance.' But § 314 of the first Restatement contained significant qualifications: 'A failure, *without justification*, to perform all or any part *of what is promised in a contract* is a breach thereof' (emphasis added). These

---

[1] See especially Zweigert, *Some Comparative Aspects of the Law Relating to Sale of Goods,* ICLQ Supplementary Publications No. 9, esp. at p. 3; von Marschall in *Kolloquium zum 65. Geburtstag von Ernst v. Caemmerer,* pp. 21-3.
[2] e.g. Gschnitzer, *Schuldrecht, Besonderer Teil und Schadenersatz,* p. 146.
[3] *Raineri* v. *Miles* [1981] AC 1050, 1086.

statements neither mention fault as a requirement, nor do they rule it out. The proposition that the failure in performance must occur 'without justification' leaves open the question whether lack of 'fault' can provide a justification; and the phrases 'duty under a contract' and 'failure . . . to perform . . . what is promised in a contract' similarly leave open the crucial questions what a party's duty is, or what he has promised: has he simply promised to perform, or only to make reasonable efforts (or to do his best) to that end? The English statement quoted above may reject the latter possibility, but it only does so 'in general'. In this respect, it reflects the assumption with which the common law starts, namely that liability for breach of contract is strict; but this general principle is subject to significant exceptions in which fault is an element of liability. In the discussion that follows, we shall see that it is a relatively simple matter to identify situations that fall respectively within the general principle of strict liability and within the exceptions in which liability depends on fault. The difficult (and most interesting) situations are, not surprisingly, those that lie on the borderline.

A. ILLUSTRATIONS OF THE PRINCIPLE OF STRICT LIABILITY

(1) *Inability to Pay Money*

The clearest illustration of the principle of strict liability is the general rule that inability to pay money is no excuse for failing to make the payment when due. The point is taken so much for granted that it is rarely litigated; but there is support for the application of the principle of strict liability in English and American cases which hold that a purchaser of land cannot avoid liability on the ground that he has been unable to raise the purchase money[4] or to raise it by the time at which the purchase ought to have been completed.[5] It makes no difference that the purchaser's inability to pay on the due day was in no way imputable to his fault; for instance, where it was brought about by the slow operation of the exchange control machinery of the country from which the money was to be transferred.[6] The legal theory is that the payment of money is never impossible: the debtor can always obtain funds, if only he is prepared to pay enough by way of interest.

For this reason, the rule has sometimes been explained in the United States by reference to the distinction, borrowed from the civil law, between 'objective' and 'subjective' impossibility.[7] It is said that impossibility is

---

[4] *Christy* v. *Pilkington* 273 SW 2d 533 (1954)
[5] *Universal Corporation* v. *Five Ways Properties Ltd.* [1979] 3 All ER 533, 554; cf. *Francis* v. *Cowcliffe* (1977) 33 P 4 CR 368; *Congimex SARL (Lisbon)* v. *Continental Grain Export Corp. (New York)* [1979] 2 Lloyd's Rep. 346, 353.
[6] As in *Universal Corporation* v. *Five Ways Properties Ltd.*, supra n. 5.
[7] See German Civil Code § 275.

objective when performance cannot be rendered by anyone and subjective when it cannot be rendered by the promisor, though it could be rendered by others. The distinction formerly had some vogue, being drawn in the treatises of Williston[8] and Corbin,[9] and in the first Restatement;[10] but it attracted criticism[11] and is no longer used in the Restatement 2d.[12] It could be argued that inability to pay money when due was merely subjective impossibility and therefore did not provide an excuse. Reference to the civil law origin of the distinction, however, casts some doubt on this explanation. Thus under § 275(2) of the German Civil Code supervening subjective impossibility (Unvermögen) can provide a contracting party with an excuse, but this rule does *not* apply to inability to pay money.[13] Modern English law, moreover, does not make use of the distinction between the two kinds of impossibility; but it nevertheless regards liability for inability to pay money as strict.

Inability to pay being no excuse, the same is, *a fortiori*, true where the debtor can only show that payment in accordance with the contract would cause him a high degree of inconvenience. In an American case it was accordingly held to be no defence that the business from which payments were to be made under a long-term contract had been discontinued because it could only have been run at a substantial loss.[14] The debtor can only wind up the business without liability if he made no definite promise to maintain the contractual relationship for the stipulated time.[15]

The general rule is thus well established, that inability to pay money is no excuse even though it occurs without the fault of the person who ought to have made the payment. But there are occasional hints of possible qualifications to the rule in cases in which one party's failure to make a payment, though not actually a breach, entitles the other party to bring the contract to an end, and so can lead to a forfeiture. Such a result can, for example, follow where a life insurance policy provides that the insurer can 'forfeit' the policy if a premium is not paid by the end of a stated period (often including days of grace). The English view is that the power to forfeit can be exercised even though the failure to pay on time is caused by events entirely outside the control of the person who ought to have made the payment: for example, by a war between the country in which that

---

[8] Williston on *Contracts*, 3rd ed., § 1932.
[9] Corbin on *Contracts*, 1325 where objective impossibility is also called 'absolute' but this should not be taken too literally, as one of Corbin's examples of 'absolute' impossibility shows: 'No one can go to the moon'.
[10] § 455, Comment (a).
[11] e.g. Patterson, *The Apportionment of Business Risks through Legal Devices* 24 Col. L. Rev. 355, 349-50.
[12] See § 261, Comment (e).
[13] See Larenz, *Lehrbuch des Schuldrechts*, Vol I, 13th ed., pp. 282, 294.
[14] *Martin v. Star Publishing Co.* 126 A. 2d. 238 (1956)
[15] e.g. *Rhodes v. Forwood* (1876) 1 App. Cas 256.

person resides and the country in which the insurance company carries on business.[16] But in the United States the courts did not apply this rule with its full rigour to cases arising out of the Civil War. In one such case[17] a New York insurance company issued a policy on the life of a person resident in Mississippi. He regularly paid the premiums until, in 1861, he was prevented from lawfully doing so by the outbreak of the Civil War. He died in July 1862 and it was held that the company could invoke a clause in the policy permitting forfeiture on failure to pay premiums when due. But the court evidently regarded this result as harsh and held that the company was, in spite of being entitled to forfeit, under an equitable obligation to make some payment to the estate of the assured. There is no English authority for equitable relief in cases of this kind; and the view that is not available is supported by recent decisions restricting relief against forfeiture to situations in which literal enforcement of a contract would deprive the party in breach of 'proprietary or possessory rights'.[18]

(2) *Inability to Deliver Generic Goods*

A second illustration of the principle of strict liability is that a seller of generic goods is liable if he fails to deliver them in accordance with the contract even though the failure is due to circumstances wholly beyond his control. Such a seller has, for example, been held liable where he was unable to deliver because he was unexpectedly let down by his own supplier,[19] where his inability to deliver was the result of crop failure leading to a general shortage of goods of the contract description,[20] or of governmental requisition of such goods,[21] or of other governmental acts such as prohibition of export.[22] It is, of course, possible for the seller to mitigate such liability by express provisions of the contract; but even such provisions may, on their true construction, leave him liable without fault. In one English case[23] frozen Chinese rabbits were sold on terms expressly protecting the sellers from liability on the occurrence of certain specified events (such as flood, fire, or storm) 'or any other causes beyond their

---

[16] McNair and Watts, *The Legal Effects of War*, 4th ed., pp. 280-4; MacGillivray and Parkington, *Insurance Law*, 7th edn. § 984.

[17] *New York Life Insurance Co.* v. *Statham* 93 US 24 (1876).

[18] *The Scaptrade* [1983] 2 AC 694, 702; *Sport International Bussum BV* v. *Inter-Footwear Ltd.* [1984] 1 WLR 776. A critique of the contrasting case of *B.I.C.C. plc* v. *Burndy Corp* [1985] Ch. 232 is beyond the scope of this paper.

[19] e.g. *El Rio Oils (Canada) Ltd.* v. *Pacific Coast Asphalt Co. Inc.* 213 P. 2d. 1 (1950); *Intertradex S.A.* v. *Lesieur Torteaux S.A.R.L.* [1978] 2 Lloyd's Rep. 509.

[20] e.g. *Hersman* v. *Shapiro* 1926 TPD 367 (South Africa).

[21] *Gelling* v. *Crispin* (1917) 23 CLR 443.

[22] As in many of the soyabean cases: see *infra*, at notes 29 to 41.

[23] *P. J. van der Zijden Wildhandel* v. *Tucker & Cross Ltd.* [1975] 2 Lloyd's Rep. 240; contrast *Ford* v. *Henry Leetham Ltd* (1915) 21 Com-Cas. 55, on the interpretation of a differently worded *force majeure* clause.

control.' They were let down by their Chinese suppliers but were nevertheless held liable to their buyers as they had failed to show that it was impossible for them to acquire goods of the contract description elsewhere. Even a total embargo on the export of frozen rabbits from China would not have brought the clause into operation unless the sellers had shown that they could not have brought frozen Chinese rabbits afloat (i.e. shipped before the embargo was imposed).

One possible explanation of the seller's liability in the present group of cases is that it *is* based on fault: he could have performed, and chose not to do so because of the extra difficulty or expense of doing so in the altered circumstances. But the better view is that liability in this type of case is strict: its basis is that the seller assumes the risk of being unable to deliver, just as in the cases previously discussed the buyer assumes the risk of being unable to pay. The civil law certainly regards liability for inability to deliver generic goods as an *exception* to its general requirement of fault;[24] and three arguments would seem to support the view that the common law similarly regards such liability as strict.

The first such argument is based on cases in which a seller fails to deliver because his anticipated source of supply fails: for example because his crop is wholly or partly destroyed by frost, drought, or disease,[25] or because his supply of milk fails when his cattle fall ill[26] or because he is cut off from a source of supply in a foreign country by war or other circumstances preventing export.[27] The questions principally discussed in the cases[28] are whether the contract expressly or by implication refers to that source of supply (so that the goods are not purely generic); or whether, although the contract contains no such reference, the source is within the "contemplation" of both parties. If there is such reference and the failure is not due to the seller's fault, he is excused; and the same may be true if there is such 'contemplation'. But if there is no such reference or contemplation, he is liable: the courts have not gone on to consider whether any alternative source of supply was available, or whether it would have been reasonable for the seller to resort to it. This would be the position where the contract was in terms for generic goods and only the seller had contemplated the source that had become unavailable; and *a fortiori* where even the seller had not contemplated a particular source but was merely prevented from performing by events affecting markets and the availability of supplies in

---

[24] e.g. German Civil Code § 279
[25] *Howell* v. *Coupland* (1976) 1 QBD 258.
[26] *Whitman* v. *Anglum* 103 A. 114 (1918).
[27] *Blackburn Bobbin Co. Ltd.* v. *T. W. Allen & Sons Ltd.* [1918] 1 KB 540, affd. [1918] 2 KB 467.

[28] In the growing crop cases, absence of fault is taken to be a necessary condition for the seller's exoneration in the sense that he can only escape liability if he cultivated his crop with due diligence: cf. *infra* at n. 123.

general. The point is illustrated by a number of the recent cases[29] in which United States soyabean meal had been sold on c.i.f. terms for June 1973 shipment. During that month the export of soyabean meal was (subject to certain exceptions) prohibited by the United States Government; but the sellers were in many of the cases[30] nevertheless held liable. They were not protected even by *force majeure* and prohibition of export clauses unless they could either show that they had intended to ship the goods themselves[31] or identify the person who was to ship the goods ('the relevant shipper')[32] which they were to acquire through string contracts in order to perform their contracts with the buyers. A seller who failed to show either of these things was simply one who had failed to make adequate arrangements to perform a contract for the sale of purely generic goods and was liable accordingly.[33] The cases do not rule out the possibility that the seller might have been able to rely on the prohibition or *force majeure* clause if he could have shown that no goods of the contract description (which would include a reference to the contractual shipment period[34]) could have been shipped; but this defence would have been based on unavailability or impossibility—not on lack of fault in the sense of the seller's having made all reasonable efforts to obtain a supply and on his having nevertheless failed.

It is, however, arguable that fault enters as an element into another aspect of these soyabean cases. This is concerned with the argument that, even if the sellers (or the relevant shippers) were prevented from *shipping* goods of the contract description, they were nevertheless bound to buy goods afloat (i.e. goods shipped in June 1973 before the imposition of the embargo) and to tender those to the buyers. That is certainly the normal position under a c.i.f. contract,[35] but in the soyabean cases it was held that, where shipment was prevented, there was no such duty to buy afloat.[36] This exception to the normal rule was based on a number of special circumstances in those cases, *viz.*, that the contracts specified the country

---

[29] These cases raised many issues, of which only one is our concern here. See generally *Benjamin's Sale of Goods,* 3rd edn., §§ 1590-8.

[30] *André & Cie. S.A.* v. *Tradax Export S.A.* [1983] 1 Lloyd's Rep. 254, 258 ('numerous . . . decisions against sellers in strings').

[31] As in *Bremer Handelsgesellschaft m.b.H.* v. *Vanden Avenne-Izegem P.V.B.A.* [1978] 2 Lloyd's Rep. 109.

[32] See *Bremer Handelsgesellschaft m.b.H.* v. *C. Mackprang Jr.* [1981] 1 Lloyd's Rep. 292, 297.

[33] e.g. *Bunge* v. *Deutsche Conti-Handelsgesellschaft* [1979] 2 Lloyd's Rep. 435.

[34] *Bowes* v. *Shand* (1877) 2 App. Cas. 445.

[35] *Benjamin's Sale of Goods,* 3rd edn., §§ 1620, 1721.

[36] *Tradax Export S.A.* v. *André - Cie.* [1976] 1 Lloyd's Rep. 416, 423; approved on this point in *Bremer Handelsgesellschaft m.b.H.* v. *Vanden Avenne-Izegem P.V.B.A.* [1978] 2 Lloyd's Rep. 109; cf. *André & Cie.* v. *Tradax Export S.A.* [1983] 1 Lloyd's Rep. 254 and *Cook Industries* v. *Tradax Export S.A.* [1985] 2 Lloyd's Rep. 454 for the similar position relating to sales of goods to be shipped in the month in which the embargo was lifted.

Fault in the Common Law of Contract

of origin; that they contained *force majeure* and prohibition of export clauses; that such a prohibition had prevented export for part of the shipment period; and that many of the contracts formed parts of 'strings' leading back to an original shipper who had, when the embargo was imposed, made, or undertaken to make, arrangements to ship goods that were to be appropriated to the contracts. Some goods of the contract description may have been shipped in the early part of the shipment period, before the embargo was imposed. But the courts held that sellers who (or whose relevant shippers) were prevented from shipping were not bound to acquire such goods afloat; for if each seller in each string (which 'might embrace over 100 traders')[37] attempted to do this, prices would, in view of the strictly limited quantities of goods afloat shipped in June, be driven up to 'unheard-of levels'.[38] Of course, any embargo (or *force majeure* event) is likely to cause an upward pressure on prices; but in the peculiar circumstances of the soyabean cases the application of the normal rule, obliging the sellers to buy afloat, would have made that pressure so severe that it could fairly have been called extreme; and it is this factor of commercial impracticability, rather than lack of fault, which brought the prohibition and *force majeure* clauses into operation in spite of the fact that the alternative method of performance (i.e., buying afloat) had not become impossible. According to one view, indeed, the issue in these cases was whether the sellers could have obtained goods of the contract description 'by the exercise of any means reasonably open to them';[39] and this could be read as suggesting that liability was based on failure to exercise due diligence. Even if this suggestion is accepted, however, it is a narrow one: it only bases a seller's liability on lack of due diligence in relation to one possible mode of performance (i.e. buying afloat). The very judgment in which the suggestion is made recognizes the strict liability of the seller who neither intended to ship himself nor identified the relevant shipper.[40] Any exception that may be recognized in the soyabean cases to the principle of strict liability is therefore of a limited nature and is based on the peculiar circumstances of those cases and on the special terms of the contracts. These cases certainly do not support the view that a seller of generic goods can, in general, escape liability merely by showing that he used due diligence to obtain and deliver the goods. Indeed, many of the soyabean cases *illustrate* the principle of strict liability; for it often happened that the sellers were liable because they could not identify the

---

[37] *André & Cie.* v. *Tradax Export S.A.* [1981] 2 Lloyd's Rep. 352, 355 (decision revsd. [1983] 1 Lloyd's Rep. 254).
[38] *Tradax Export S.A.* v. *André & Cie.* [1976] 1 Lloyd's Rep. 416, 423.
[39] *André & Cie.* v. *Tradax Export S.A.* [1983] 1 Lloyd's Rep. 254, 258 (*supra*, n. 36); cf. *Continental Grain Export Corp.* v. *S.T.M. Grain Ltd.* [1979] 2 Lloyd's Rep. 460, 473.
[40] *André & Cie.* v. *Tradax Export S.A.* [1983] 1 Lloyd's Rep. 254, 258.

'relevant shippers'.[41] In these cases no question of fault, or of 'the exercise of any means reasonably open to' the sellers arose.

The view that liability in the present group of cases is strict is also supported by the analogous situation in which the goods are available but delivery in accordance with the contract becomes impossible. In an English case[42] a contract was made for the sale of potatoes to be shipped between 14 and 24 April from Malta. No ship capable of carrying the goods left Malta during that period, so that the seller could not ship the goods within the contractual shipment period; and he was held liable in damages. The basis of the decision is not that he might in theory have chartered a ship for the purpose of performing the contract and that his failure to do so amounted to failure to exercise due diligence. He was held liable simply because he had taken the risk of certain events beyond his control: 'the seller being on an island . . . must . . . make sure that shipping space is available before he commits himself to an absolute contract'.[43] It is, of course, easy for the seller to protect himself by contracting expressly 'subject to shipment', and the fact that such provisions commonly occur in contracts of this kind is one ground for saying that, in their absence, liability should be strict. The position is similar under a charterparty with respect to the charterer's obligation to load. Unless qualified by the contract, the duty to supply a cargo is strict,[44] so that the charterer is not excused by inability to find a cargo.

The reference in the case of the Maltese potatoes to an 'absolute contract' is, however, probably too extreme, at least if that phrase is used in the sense of a contract which must be performed in *any* event. The point is most easily illustrated by supposing that the harbour at Malta had been destroyed by an earthquake before shipment and before the end of the shipment period. In that case the seller would no doubt have been discharged: he might have taken the risk of there being no ship, but not that of there being no harbour. The Maltese potato case may similarly be contrasted with cases in England[45] and in India[46] in which sellers were unable to ship because of Governmental requisition of *all* the available shipping space; and this was held to absolve them from liability. Such cases show that liability is not *absolute* but only *strict*: it does not depend on 'fault', but it is subject to the doctrine of supervening impossibility or (as it

[41] e.g. *Bremer Handelsgesellschaft m. b. H.* v. *C. Mackprang Jr.* [1981] 1 Lloyd's Rep. 292; *Cook Industries Inc.* v. *Meunerie Liégeois S.A.* [1981] 1 Lloyd's Rep. 359, 365; *Bremer Handelsgesellschaft m. b. H.* v. *Continental Grain Co.* [1983] 1 Lloyd's Rep. 269; *Bremer Handelsgesellschaft m. b. H.* v. *Bunge Corp.* [1983] 1 Lloyd's Rep. 476.
[42] *Lewis Emanuel Ltd.* v. *Sammut* [1959] 2 Lloyd's Rep. 629.   [43] Ibid., p. 642.
[44] *The Aello* [1961] AC 135 (overruled, but not on this point, in *The Johanna Oldendorff* [1974] AC 479); cf. *Hills* v. *Sughrue* (1846) 10 M. & W. 253 (shipowner's undertaking to find a cargo held to impose liability without fault).
[45] *Acetylene Co. of G.B.* v. *Canada Carbide Co.* (1921) 8 Ll. L. Rep. 456.
[46] *Hussainbhoy Karimji* v. *Haridas* AIR 1928 Sind. 21.

is called in English law[47]) frustration. The relationship between that doctrine and fault will be further discussed below.[48]

(3) *Defects in the Subject-matter*

At common law, the principle of strict liability applies where goods are defective in the sense that they do not comply with the seller's express or implied undertakings as to quality. For example, in *Frost* v. *Aylesbury Dairy Co.*[49] the plantiff became ill, as a result of drinking milk sold to him by the defendants, because the milk was infected with typhoid germs. The defendants were held liable in spite of the fact that they had taken all reasonable precautions (in the light of the contemporary state of scientific knowledge) to ensure that the milk was pure. A seller would similarly be liable if it was for some other reason impossible for him, as a practical matter, to discover the defect: e.g. because he was a retailer selling goods in packets sealed by the manufacturer.[50] These applications of the rule of strict liability can perhaps be explained on the ground that the price for which goods are sold 'may be assumed to represent their value'[51] so that the seller's undertaking as to quality is reflected in the price. If the buyer had been content to take a risk as to the quality of the goods at the time of sale, it is assumed that he would have paid a lower price.

In the English common law, it was doubtful whether the same standard applied to other contracts for the supply of goods, for example, to contracts of hire. The continuing nature of the contractual relationship would here make strict liability more onerous to the supplier than in cases of sale and could therefore be regarded as a ground for somewhat reducing the standard of the supplier's liability. There was some support for the view that the supplier was not liable if he was not himself at fault, and if the defect was such that it could not have been discovered by the exercise of due care on the part of someone connected with the performance of the contract.[52] But legislative formulations of the supplier's implied undertakings as to quality in, for example, contracts of hire, hire-purchase and

---

[47] In the United States, 'frustration' is used more narrowly to refer to cases of frustration of purpose, such as the 'coronation cases', in which the contract was discharged even though performance was not 'impossible'.
[48] See section C(1) of this discussion.
[49] [1905] 1 KB 608; cf. *Lockett* v. *A.M. Charles Ltd.* [1938] 4 All ER 170; *H. Parsons (Livestock) Ltd.* v. *Uttley Ingham & Co. Ltd.* [1978] QB 791, 799-800.
[50] e.g. *Daniels* v. *White & Son* [1938] 4 All ER 258.
[51] *Readhead* v. *Midland Ry.* (1869) LR 4 QB 379, 386.
[52] *Hyman* v. *Nye* (1871) 6 QBD 685; *Read* v. *Dean* [1949] 1 KB 188; *Astley Industrial Trust Ltd.* v. *Grimley* [1963] 1 WLR 584, 598. The same standard applied at common law to an occupier of premises who allowed members of the public to enter them under contract: *Francis* v. *Cockrell* (1870) LR 5 QB 501; see now Occupiers Liability Act 1957 s. 5(1).

exchange, indicate that the liability of the supplier for breach of these undertakings is no less strict than that of a seller.[53]

The principle of strict liability was not originally applied by common law systems where the subject-matter of a sale or lease of *land* was defective. On the contrary, in such cases the starting principle was *caveat emptor* (or lessee): the vendor or lessor was not considered to give any implied undertakings as to quality.[54] This original principle is now subject to many exceptions, both at common law[55] and by statute;[56] and the vendor or lessor may also be liable in tort.[57] Such tort liability clearly depends on fault; but the standard of liability based on implied contractual undertakings or on statute is less clear. In some cases such liability has been held to be strict,[58] while in other it has been assumed that liability depends on fault.[59] One reason why no consistent standard of liability has as yet emerged may be that common law courts are not used to thinking of standards of liability in a contractual context; another reason may be that the courts have been more concerned to break down the original *caveat emptor* principle, than to define the standard of liability.

B. THE BORDERLINE

The cases which lie on the borderline between strict liability and liability based on fault are those arising from contracts for the provision of services: here both standards of liability are recognized, and the difficult question is to determine where, and on what grounds, the line between them is to be drawn. In England, the Supply of Goods and Services Act 1982 provides that a person who supplies a service in the course of a business impliedly undertakes to 'carry out the service with reasonable care and skill'.[60] The effect of these words is clearly that liability for breach of the statutorily implied term is based on fault; but the Act also preserves 'any rule of law which imposes on the supplier a stricter duty'.[61] The question whether the

---

[53] Consumer Credit Act 1974 Sch. 4 para. 35; Supply of Goods and Services Act 1982 ss. 4, 9. The wording of these provisions resembles that of the corresponding undertakings implied into contracts for the sale of goods by Sale of Goods Act 1979 s. 14, liability for breach of which is clearly strict.
[54] e.g. *Robbins* v. *Jones* (1863) 15 CB (NS) 221, 240; Williston on *Contracts* 3rd ed. §926.
[55] e.g. *Collins* v. *Hopkins* [1923] 2 KB 617 (furnished letting); *Hancock* v. *B. W. Brazier (Annerley) Ltd.* [1966] 1 WLR 1317 (house in course of construction); Williston on *Contracts* 3rd ed. § 926A.
[56] e.g. Landlord and Tenant Act 1985 ss. 6, 8, (replacing earlier legislation); cf. Defective Premises Act 1972 ss. 1, 3.
[57] e.g. *Batty* v. *Metropolitan Realizations Ltd.* [1978] Q.B. 554.
[58] e.g. *Hancock* v. *B. W. Brazier (Annerley) Ltd. supra.* n. 55; cf. *Wettern Electric Ltd.* v. *Welsh Development Agency* [1983] QB 796 (strict liability for breach of implied undertaking in licence to occupy a factory that premises are fit for occupier's purpose).
[59] e.g. *Batty* v. *Metropolitan Realizations Ltd, supra.*   [60] S. 13   [61] S. 16(3) (a).

Fault in the Common Law of Contract

supplier's liability is strict or based on fault will therefore continue to depend on the common law rules with which the following discussion is concerned.

(1) Carriage of Goods by Sea: Seaworthiness

At common law, a shipowner who contracted to carry goods by sea was prima facie under an 'absolute' obligation to ensure that his ship was seaworthy.[62] The rule was not in practice very important in English law, which freely allowed carriers to contract out of it by use of wide exemption clauses.[63] Where the goods are carried under a bill of lading governed (as it generally will be) by the Hague or Hague-Visby Rules, the carrier's obligation is reduced to one to exercise due diligence to make the ship seaworthy.[64] This statutory rule is (as is well known) a negotiated compromise between cargo interests and shipping interests, so that no general deductions can be drawn from it as to the function of fault in determining contractual liability.

(2) Services together with Components

Where a contract involves the supply of both services and components,[65] a distinction must be drawn between cases in which the components, and those in which the services, are defective.

(i) Defects in the components

Liability for defects in components has in a number of cases been held to be strict. For example, in *G. H. Myers & Co.* v. *Brent Cross Service Station*[66] a car repairer was held liable when connecting rods fitted by him in a customer's car disintegrated, causing extensive damage. It was no defence that the rods had been supplied by a reputable manufacturer and that the defects in them were not discoverable by reasonable examination. In a more recent case, a ship repairer was said to be under a duty to ensure that reasonable care in buying components was exercised;[67] but as he had broken that duty the further question whether he might be strictly liable did not actually arise. The standard of strict liability has been applied to a builder in respect of latent defects in materials incorporated by him in the structure.[68] Perhaps the most striking case is *Young & Marten Ltd.* v.

---

[62] *Steel* v. *State Line S.S. Co.* (1872) 3 App. Cas. 72, 86; see further *infra*, at n. 76.

[63] Contrast the position in the United States, where such clauses could be struck down as contrary to public policy : see *infra*, n. 128.

[64] e.g. Carriage of Goods by Sea Act 1971 s. 3 and Sched., Art 3(1) (U.K.); Carriage of Goods by Sea Act 1936 s. 3(1) (U.S.).

[65] Supply of Goods and Services Act 1982 s. 12(3) (a) provides that such contracts are contracts for the supply of services for the purposes of the Act, but it does not specify the standard of liability.

[66] [1934] 1KB 46.   [67] *The Zinnia* [1984] 2 Lloyd's Rep. 211, 218.

[68] *Hancock* v. *B. W. Brazier (Annerley) Ltd.*, [1966] 1 WLR 1367.

McManus Childs Ltd.[69] where the House of Lords held that a roofing subcontractor was liable for latent defects in tiles fitted by him, even though the defects were not discoverable by reasonable examination and even though the tiles were supplied by the very manufacturer who had been nominated for that purpose in the contract.

One justification for the application of the principle of strict liability to these repairing and building contracts is that, so far as they relate to the supply of components or other materials, they have a close affinity with sale. Another is that the contractor has a remedy over against his supplier on the contract of sale between them; and so the first link is forged in a chain of liability which prima facie stretches back to the manufacturer on whom liability should ultimately rest. These factors were stressed by the House of Lords in the *Young & Marten* case, where the decision may also have been influenced by the English doctrine of privity of contract, under which only the parties to a contract acquire rights and are subject to liabilities under it. The manufacturer or other supplier of components to the contractor is under no *contractual* liability to the latter's *customer*; and the rule making the contractor strictly liable to the customer is therefore often necessary if the customer is to have any remedy at all. In English law as it stands at present, his only remedy against the manufacturer or supplier of the defective components is in tort and based on fault. The impending introduction of manufacturers' 'product liability'[70] to ultimate consumers will weaken this justification for the contractor's strict liability but will not (because of the restrictions on the scope of the proposed scheme) remove it altogether.

The 'chain of liability' argument referred to above is also open to an obvious objection, namely that the chain may be broken, before it reaches the manufacturer, by a valid exemption clause. In the *Young & Marten* case it was accordingly suggested that a contractor would not be strictly liable to his customer for defective components if the manufacturer were only willing to sell them on terms that excluded his liability and if this fact was known to the contractor and to the customer.[71] From this point of view, the *Young & Marten* case may be contrasted with the Australian *Helicopter Sales*[72] case, where a helicopter owned by the plaintiff was serviced by the defendant under a contract specifying that the work should comply with certain certification standards imposed by the Government. These were complied with and it was held that no further undertakings as to quality could be implied. It followed that the defendant was not liable when the helicopter crashed because of a latent defect in a bolt which had

[69] [1969] 1 AC 454.

[70] i.e. the proposed implementation of the EEC Directive, OJ 1985 L 210 p. 17: see Consumer Protection Bill 1986, Pt. I.

[71] [1969] 1 AC 454, 467.

[72] *Helicopter Sales (Australia) Pty Ltd.* v. *Rotor Works Pty Ltd.* (1974) ALJR 390.

been fitted by the defendant. The bolt had been obtained by the defendant from the Australian distributor for the American manufacturer. No doubt the High Court was influenced by the fact that the manufacturer had successfully excluded liability under its contract with the distributor, who would thus (perhaps inappropriately) have been left with the ultimate liability.[73]

(ii) *Defects in the services.*
Where a contract involves the supply of components and services, liability for defects in the services appears to be based on fault. Thus although (as we have seen) a car-repairer's liability for defective components is strict, his duty with regard to the safe-keeping of the customer's car is one of care only.[74] The standard of the building or repairing contractor's work with respect to the carrying out of the work also seems to be, at least prima facie, one of care only. In the *Young & Marten* case, a distinction was drawn between the sub-contractor's duty to supply and his duty to fit the tiles, and it was accepted that the latter duty was one of care only.[75] In Australia, statutory force has been given to this distinction in section 74(1) of the Trade Practices Act 1974. The subsection deals with contracts for the supply of services by a corporation in the course of a business to a consumer. It provides that in such contracts there are two implied warranties: (i) that the services will be rendered *with due care and skill*; and (ii) that any materials supplied in connection with those services *will be* reasonably fit for the purpose for which they were supplied. The first implied warranty imposes a duty of care and the second a duty that is strict.

(3) *Services Alone*

Where a person contracts to render or supply services alone, the general principle is that he undertakes no more than to exercise reasonable care and skill. The statutory formulation of this rule in England has already been noted;[76] and we have seen that it is subject at common law to an exception in the case of contracts for the carriage of goods by sea. No general principle can be deduced from this exception, which is based on a number of special grounds. One possible reason for the 'absolute' warranty of seaworthiness may be traced to the law of marine insurance: since the cargo-owner absolutely warranted to the insurer that the ship was

---

[73] The appeal against judgment for the plaintiff in the court below was brought by this distributor, who had been brought into the proceedings as a third party by the defendant.
[74] See *Hollier* v. *Rambler Motors (A.M.C.) Ltd.* [1977] 2 QB 71.
[75] [1969] 1 AC 454, 465, cf. *H. Parsons (Livestock) Ltd.* v. *Uttley Ingham & Co. Ltd.* [1978] QB 791, 800; *The Raphael* [1981] 2 Lloyd's Rep. 659, 665. The duty of a landlord to maintain and repair the 'common parts' of a block of flats has similarly been held to be one of reasonable care and skill only: *Liverpool City Council* v. *Irwin* [1977] AC 239.
[76] *Supra,* at n. 60.

seaworthy,[77] it was necessary for him to have a co-extensive undertaking from the carrier. Another possible reason for the rule is that the 'absolute' warranty of seaworthiness was a survival from the old principle of common carriers' strict liability. This seems to have been the view taken in *Readhead* v. *Midland Ry*[78] where the court refused to extend the absolute warranty to contracts for the carriage of passengers by rail and laid down the modern rule that, at common law, the carrier only undertakes to use reasonable care as to the fitness of the vehicle and of other parts of the railway system.

There are many illustrations of the general common law principle that a contract for the supply of services alone imposes no more than a duty to exercise reasonable care and skill. This is all that is required of many persons who render some professional service, such as lawyers, medical practitioners, brokers or accountants.[79] In some contracts of this kind, the person who undertakes to render the service plainly does not guarantee to produce results. This is most obviously true of the lawyer who is engaged to conduct litigation, since one party must inevitably lose. It is also generally true of the medical practitioner since most forms of medical treatment involve a known element of risk so that the common understanding is that the person providing it does not guarantee its success. The position is illustrated by two recent English cases[80] in which medical practitioners had carried out sterilization operations and were held not to have guaranteed that the patients would thereby have become *permanently* sterile. It was recognized that such a guarantee might be *expressly* given but held that a mere statement that the operation was 'irreversible' did not amount to such a guarantee. Liability in such cases is based on fault: in one of the sterilization cases, the doctor was held liable for negligence in failing to warn the patient of the known risk that sterility might not be permanent.[81] A medical man can also be strictly liable where the contract contains a significant supply of materials element. This standard of liability was, for example, applied where a dentist contracted to provide a set of false teeth which, when provided, did not fit.[82] Here the supply of materials element can be said to have predominated: indeed, one member of the Court regarded the transaction as a contract for the sale of goods.[83]

The distinction between contracts for services above and those for

[77] Arnould, *Marine Insurance*, 16th edn. § 708.
[78] (1869) LR 4 QB 379, 382, 390-1.
[79] e.g. *Clark* v. *Kirby-Smith* [1964] Ch. 506 (solicitor); *O'Connor* v. *Kirby* [1972] 1 QB 90 (insurance broker); *McNealy* v. *Pennine Insurance Co. Ltd.* [1978] 2 Lloyd's Rep. 18 (insurance broker); *Stafford* v. *Conti Commodity Services* [1981] 1 All ER 691 (commodity broker); for medical practitioners, see *infra*, at no. 80.
[80] *Eyre* v. *Measday* [1986] 1 All ER 488; *Thake* v. *Maurice* [1986] QB 644.
[81] *Thake* v. *Maurice*, *supra*; for such liability, cf. *Gold* v. *Harringey Health Authority*, The Times, 17 June, 1986.
[82] *Samuels* v. *Davies* [1943] 1 KB 526.   [83] du Parcq LJ, at pp. 528-9.

Fault in the Common Law of Contract

services and the supply of a thing can also be used to explain the position of the architect. The starting principle is that his duty is one of care only;[84] and one explanation for this is that his services do not result in the production *by him* of a physical thing that is sold or transferred to his client. An important part of the architect's function is to supervise the supply of work and materials by others; and in the exercise of this function he is not expected to do more than to exercise a reasonable degree of professional care and skill. But the same argument does not hold good where he commits an error, not of supervision, but of design. Here the architect's position is quite different from that of the lawyer or medical practitioner. His function so far as design is concerned is not regarded as inherently risky: the soundness of the structure and the stresses which it is intended to withstand are supposed to be governed by scientific principles which are capable of producing exactly predictable results. The expectation of the parties in such cases may well be that the architect will design a structure that will serve the agreed or contemplated purpose, not merely that he will take reasonable care to do so. If the end product is a tower that leans because of a defect of design, should he not be strictly liable?

There is English authority to support the view that liability for such defects is strict. In one case,[85] a warehouse was built under the supervision of a consulting engineer who knew that motor trucks would operate on an upper floor but made insufficient allowance in his design for the resultant vibrations, so that cracks developed in the structure. Lord Denning MR was prepared to hold that there was an 'absolute warranty'[86] that the structure would be fit for the owner's purpose; and he based this view on the engineer's knowledge of the owner's intended use of the premises. There is support for the same standard of liability in a later case[87] in which a television mast was designed and erected for the Independent Broadcasting Authority by engineering subcontractors who had assured the Authority that the mast would not 'oscillate dangerously'. This assurance was held to have no contractual force, so that there was no express guarantee of the soundness of the structure. When, some two and a half years later, the mast collapsed, the subcontractors were held liable on the ground that they had been negligent. But dicta[88] in the House of Lords also approve the principle that a person who contracts to design an article, knowing of the purpose for which it is to be used by the customer, is strictly liable if, through defects of design, the article is not fit for that purpose. The case of the ill-fitting false teeth[89] can also be explained on this ground. Some dicta, indeed, suggest that liability for design defects is *only* strict

---

[84] e.g. *Bagot* v. *Stevens, Scanlan & Co. Ltd.* [1966] QB 197.
[85] *Greaves & Co. (Contractors) Ltd.* v. *Baynham Meikle & Partners* [1975] 1 WLR 1095.
[86] Ibid., at p. 1101.
[87] *I.B.A.* v. *E.M.I. (Electronics) Ltd.* (1980) 14 Build. LR 1.
[88] Ibid., pp. 47-8.   [89] *Samuels* v. *Davies, supra,* n. 82.

where the contract is one for the supply of services and materials;[90] but this limitation on this incidence of strict liability may, with respect, be doubted. In some of the cases mentioned above,[91] no defect in the materials or components was alleged; and where a defendant is thus liable for defects in services alone, it would be strange if the standard of that liability depended on the existence of another obligation (i.e. to supply materials) in respect of which he was not in breach.

The reasoning on which Lord Denning MR based the 'absolute warranty' for defects in design is, again, reflected in the Australian Trade Practices Act 1974. Section 74(2) deals with the situation in which services are supplied by a corporation to a consumer who has made known to the corporation the particular purpose for which the services are required. Here the corporation impliedly warrants that the services and any materials supplied *will be* reasonably fit for that purpose: in other words, there is a strict duty in relation both to the services and the materials. Similarly, where the consumer makes known the result that he desires the service to achieve, there is a warranty that the services and the materials *are* of such a nature that they might reasonably be expected to achieve the result. Again, this is the language of strict liability. In cases falling within section 74(2) this standard is justified by the fact that the customer bargains not for skill but for an end-product; and the duty to achieve that product, or result, is not performed merely by exercising due care and skill.[92] These situations should be contrasted with those covered by section 74(1) to which reference is made above, and under which there is a strict duty in relation to the materials but only one of care in relation to the services. The contrast between the two subsections resembles the distinctions drawn in the English case-law.

C. OTHER ASPECTS OF FAULT

The preceding discussion has been concerned with standards of contractual duties of performance. Fault also enters into other aspects of the question whether failure to perform a contractual undertaking amounts to a breach. In particular, fault is relevant where it is alleged that supervening events have discharged a contract or have provided a party with an excuse for non-performance; or that performance has not become due by reason of the non-occurrence of a contingent condition precedent.

---

[90] *Basildon D.C.* v. *J. E. Lesser Properties* [1985] 1 All ER 20, 26; cf. *Cynat Properties Ltd.* v. *Landbuild (Investments & Property) Ltd.* [1984] 3 All ER 513, 523; *Wimpey Construction U.K. Ltd.* v. *D. V. Poole* [1984] 2 Lloyd's Rep. 499, 514.

[91] i.e. *Samuels* v. *Davies, supra,* n. 82; *I.B.A.* v. *E.M.I. (Electronics) Ltd., supra,* n. 87.

[92] Civil lawyers will be reminded of the French distinction between *obligation de moyens* and *obligation de résultat*: see Nicholas, *French Law of Contract,* pp. 48-54.

(1) Discharge by Supervening Events

The doctrine of discharge of contracts by events which make its performance 'impossible' or illegal, or which frustrate its purpose, shows that, even where liability is strict, it is not absolute. For the present purpose, the most important aspect of this doctrine of discharge is that the supervening event must not be brought about by the fault of the party relying on it. As Blackburn J. said in his original statement of the doctrine in *Taylor* v. *Caldwell*, the parties are to be excused 'in case, before breach, performance becomes impossible ... without the default of the contractor'.[93] In the United States, the same requirement that the event must occur without 'fault' is to be found in the Restatement[94] and in the Restatement 2d.[95] In modern English law, the point is put by saying that 'Reliance cannot be placed on self-induced frustration.'[96]

For this purpose, 'fault' would clearly include such acts as the deliberate or negligent destruction of the subject-matter: the defendants in *Taylor* v. *Caldwell*[97] would clearly not have been discharged if they had deliberately or negligently set fire to the music hall. Again, inability to use premises for the purpose contemplated by the parties can discharge the contract, as in the well-known coronation cases;[98] but it has been held not to excuse a party where it results from his failure to take reasonable steps to resist zoning restrictions,[99] or from the fact that a licence to use the premises for the contemplated purpose is refused because he had made false statements in his application for the licence.[100]

The rule that a party cannot rely on self-induced frustration may apply where the event is brought about by that party's deliberate act, even though that act is not, in itself, a breach of contract.[101] This aspect of the rule has given rise to particular difficulty in cases where an employee was prevented from performing his contractual obligation to work as a result of an event, to the occurrence of which his voluntary conduct was at least a contributory cause. A famous example, given in an English case, is that of the prima donna who cannot perform her engagement to sing because she has caught cold and lost her voice by carelessly sitting in a draught. Lord Simon inclined to the view that she could rely on the doctrine of frustration so long as the incapacity 'was not deliberately induced so as to get out of the engagement'.[102] In the United States the Restatement 2d in principle

---

[93] (1863) 3 B. & S. 826, 834.   [94] § 457.   [95] § 261.
[96] *Bank Line ltd.* v. *Arthur Capel & Co.* [1919] AC 435, 452.
[97] *Supra*, n. 93.   [98] e.g. *Krell* v. *Henry* [1903] 2 KB 740.
[99] *McNally* v. *Moser* 122 A. 2d 555 (1956).
[100] *United Societies Committee* v. *Madison Square Gardens Corp.* 59 NYS 2d 475 (1946).
[101] e.g. *Denmark Productions Ltd.* v. *Boscobel Productions Ltd.* [1969] 1 QB 699; cf. *Black Clauson International Ltd.* v. *Papierwerke Waldhof-Aschaffenburg A.G.* [1981] 2 Lloyd's Rep. 446, 457.
[102] *Joseph Constantine S.S. Line Ltd.* v. *Imperial Smelting Corp. Ltd.* [1942] AC 154, 166-7.

recognizes that such carelessness can be 'fault' for the present purpose, but rightly adds: 'it is often so difficult to foresee the effect of conduct on health that fault in bringing about disability must be clear in order to prevent the disability from resulting in discharge'.[103] It seems that 'clear' here refers to causal connection rather than (as in Lord Simon's statement) to motive. The difference can be illustrated by a perhaps extreme American case in which a person who had been charged with murder engaged a lawyer to defend him and then committed suicide before the trial was over. This was said to be a breach of contract,[104] the doctrine of discharge being presumably excluded by the client's fault. Another difficult group of cases concerns the imprisonment of employees for criminal offences that have no direct connection with their employment.[105] In a number of recent English cases it has been held or said that the doctrine of discharge was not excluded even though the employee's criminal conduct, leading to his imprisonment, was deliberate;[106] but it is important to stress the exact context in which the question of discharge arose. The claims were for unfair dismissal and one line of defence was that the employees had not been dismissed as the effect of the imprisonment was to discharge the contract by operation of law. It was to rebut this defence that the employees argued that discharge was excluded as their inability to serve resulted from their own fault. To allow this defence would have been to stand the rule relating to 'self-induced frustration' on its head. That rule means that a party cannot rely on frustration that he has himself induced—not that one party cannot rely on frustration induced by the other. From this point of view, the English cases are to be preferred to a nineteenth-century Massachusetts case[107] in which an employee who had been imprisoned for adultery nevertheless successfully sued for wages in respect of the period of his imprisonment. The Restatement[108] and Restatement 2d[109] rightly disapprove of this departure from the generally accepted view regarding the wages of sin. But it does not follow either from this disapproval or from the English unfair dismissal cases that an employee could have relied on his own imprisonment as a ground of frustration if his employer had brought an action against him on the

[103] § 262 Comment (a); cf. Corbin on *Contracts*, § 1329.

[104] *Begovitch* v. *Murphy* 101 NW 2d 278 (1960). An advance payment received by the lawyer was nevertheless held to be recoverable by the estate of the accused person.

[105] Where there is such connection, the employee should certainly not be able to rely on the doctrine of discharge. Cf. the analogous South African case of *Benjamin* v. *Myers* 1946 CPD 655 (tenant unable to perform covenant to sell petrol as his supplies had been cut off for contravening wartime rationing regulations).

[106] *Harrington* v. *Kent C.C.* [1980] IRLR 353; *F. C. Shepherd & Co. Ltd.* v. *Jerrom* [1986] 3 WLR 801; *Hare* v. *Murphy Bros* [1974] ICR 603, 607; *contra*, *Norris* v. *Southampton C.C.* [1982] ICR 177. Whether the imprisonment actually frustrates the contract depends on such factors as the length of the sentence: see *Chakki* v. *United Yeast Ltd.* [1982] ICR 140.

[107] *Hughes* v. *Wamsutta Mills* 11 Allen (Mass.) 201 (1865).

[108] § 458 Ill. 5.   [109] § 264 Ill. 5.

contract. Although such an action is unlikely in an ordinary employment context, one can imagine other situations in which it can be a realistic possibility: e.g. where heavy expenses are incurred by the organizers of a 'pop festival' in reliance on a contract with a singer who is then arrested on a drugs charge.

The argument so far is that fault in the sense of deliberate or careless conduct is sufficient to exclude the doctrine of discharge; but the further point must be made that fault *in this sense* is not necessary for this purpose. The point may be illustrated by American decisions to the effect that a contract for the sale of goods may be discharged if the seller is prevented from delivering by a court order restraining him from disposing of the subject-matter—but only if the order is not the result of his 'fault,'[110] as it would be if the goods were being taken in execution by one of his creditors.[111] Yet the execution may be due to his failure to perform an earlier contract imposing a duty of strict liability: for example, where his source of finance or of generic goods for the performance of that contract has failed without any fault on his part.[112] Again, a contract for the carriage of goods by sea may be frustrated if the ship is destroyed or seriously delayed[113]—but not if the destruction or delay is due to a prior breach of the contract of carriage by the party relying on frustration.[114] One such breach may be the shipowner's failure to provide a seaworthy ship, and such a breach can occur without any 'fault' on the shipowner's part.[115] To accommodate such cases, the Restatement 2d defines 'fault' for the present purpose so as to include 'not only "willful" wrongs but such other types of conduct as that amounting to *breach of contract* or to negligence'.[116] The reference to 'breach of contract' here is not as circular as may at first sight appear. It does not amount to saying that impossibility is not a breach unless it is a breach. The point is that impossibility is an excuse unless it is due to an antecedent breach; and such a breach may occur without 'fault' in the sense of want of care or diligence.

(2) *Excuses for Non-performance*

A supervening event may not be sufficiently drastic to lead to complete discharge under the rules just discussed; but it may nevertheless give one party (or sometimes both) a temporary or partial excuse for non-

---

[110] *Peckham v. Industrial Securities Co.* 113 A. 799 (1921)
[111] *Western Drug Supply, etc., Co. v. Board of Administration of Kansas* 187 P. 701 (1920).
[112] See sections A(1) and (2) of this paper.
[113] *Jackson v. Union Marine Insurance Co.* (1874) LR 10 CP 125.
[114] See *Joseph Constantine S.S. Line Ltd. v. Imperial Smelting Corp. Ltd.* [1942] AC 154; *Monarch S.S. Co. Ltd. v. Karlshamns Oljefabriker (A/B)* [1949] AC 196; *Ocean Tramp Tankers Corp. v. V/O Sovfracht (The Eugenia)* [1964] 2 QB 226.
[115] See section B(1) of this paper. [116] § 261, Comment (d); emphasis added.

performance. Such an excuse may be provided by law, or by the express terms of the contract.

An excuse is, for example, provided by law where temporary illness for a limited time prevents a party from rendering personal services, e.g. under a contract of employment. The employee in such a case is not in breach,[117] and may, indeed, be entitled to wages during sickness.[118] Conversely, an event may occur which gives the employer an excuse for refusing to allow the employee to work so as to earn his pay. In an English case,[119] a group of musicians had been employed to give variety performances at the Café de Paris (in London) for a month under a contract containing a 'no play, no pay' clause. During the month, King George V died and all places of public entertainment were closed for two days. It was held that the employers were justified in refusing to employ (and to pay) the musicians on those two days, but not for the remainder of the contract period. The same principle applies where a farmer agrees to sell a specified quantity of produce to be grown on designated land: if, as a result of drought or disease, the land yields only part of the agreed quantity, the seller has an excuse to the extent of the deficiency[120] but not beyond;[121] that is, the quantity actually produced must be delivered under the contract.[122]

The assumption underlying these examples is that the temporary or partial failure in performance occurred without any fault of the party who ought to have rendered it. Thus if the farmer's crop had failed because of lack of proper cultivation he would not have been excused,[123] but would have been liable in damages in respect of the full contractual quantity. Similarly, if in the Café de Paris case the musicians had been unable to perform because the owner had without justification refused their services, or had carelessly made the premises unfit for their performance, he would have been liable in damages.[124] The only doubt as to the effect of fault arises from the employment and similar cases in which the person who was to perform the services is temporarily prevented from doing so by illness. The question whether his fault in inducing the illness excludes the excuse here depends on the same factors that determine whether such fault excludes the doctrine of total discharge.[125] Thus the excuse should not be

[117] e.g. *Poussard v. Spiers & Pond* (1876) 1 QBD 410, 414.
[118] See *Marrison v. Bell* [1939] 2 KB 187; cf. *Mears v. Safecar Securities Ltd.* [1983] QB 54 (where the right to such wages was excluded by the terms of the contract).
[119] *Minnevitch v. Café de Paris (Londres) Ltd.* [1936] 1 All ER 884.
[120] *Howell v. Coupland* (1876) 1 QBD 258.
[121] *H. R. & S. Sainsbury Ltd. v. Street* [1972] 1 WLR 834.
[122] Even though that quantity is so small that it can only be harvested for more than the contract price: *International Paper Co. v. Rockefeller* 146 NYS 371 (1914).
[123] The fact that the crop failed without such fault is assumed in the cases referred to in n. 120–1 *supra*.
[124] See *Hathaway v. Sabin* 22 A. 633 (1891).
[125] *Supra*, at n. 102–4.

available where the illness was deliberately induced with a view to getting out of the duty to do the work; but it might be available where the conduct of the defendant, though perhaps imprudent, was not such as to make the resulting illness readily foreseeable.

Excuses for non-performance provided by the terms of the contract are commonly known as 'exceptions'. These may provide that a party is not to be responsible for failure in performance that is due to certain specified events, such as perils of the sea or strikes. Such exceptions typically apply to causes not within the control of the parties; and they can be regarded as an expression of a commercial point of view that there should be no liability without fault for such circumstances. This policy is reflected in the tendency of the courts to construe exceptions so as not to cover the situation in which the specified event is due to the fault of the person relying on it. For example, in a contract for the carriage of goods by sea the prima facie common law rule is that the carrier can only rely on an exception if the event or state of affairs covered by it is not brought about by his negligence.[126] In the English common law, this rule of construction can be excluded by an express contrary provision, e.g. by a clause excluding liability for perils of the sea even if they arise from the negligence of the master or crew;[127] but in the United States such negligence clauses have been held to be 'contrary to public policy and therefore void'.[128]

In English law, a distinction is drawn between 'exceptions' of the kind just discussed and exemption clauses. An 'exception' is said to limit a party's duty, so that non-performance in circumstances falling within the exception is not a breach at all. An exemption clause, on the other hand, operates where a breach is proved or admitted; it then excludes or restricts liability for that breach. The distinction between the two types of clauses is important because some of the rules that restrict the efficacy of exemption clauses do not apply to clauses which limit (and so define) a party's duties.[129] Clearly, for this purpose the wording of the clause is not decisive: what is called an 'exception' may be an 'exemption'; and the converse may also be true. There is support for the view that fault is a relevant factor in drawing the distinction, and hence in determining whether non-perform-

---

[126] *Re Polemis and Furness Withy & Co.* [1921] 3 KB 360; the decision remains authoritative on the point for which it is here cited, even though it is generally considered to have been overruled on the issue of remoteness of damage by *Overseas Tankship (U.K.) Ltd. v. Morts Dock & Engineering Co. Ltd (The Wagon Mound)* [1961] AC 388.

[127] *Blackburn v. Liverpool, Brazil & River Plate S.N. Co.* [1902] 1 KB 290; the position under the Hague and Hague–Visby Rules (*supra*, n. 64) is beyond the scope of this paper.

[128] *Liverpool and Great Western Steam Co. v. Phoenix Ins. Co.* 129 US 397, 461 (1888).

[129] This is true of statutory no less than of common law rules. The Unfair Contract Terms Act 1977 does not, except in two groups of exceptional cases specified in s. 13 (1), prevent a party from excluding or restricting *duties*, as opposed to *liabilities* for breaches of admitted or proved duties.

ance is excused or amounts to a breach. In *The Angelia*[130] charterers had undertaken to load a cargo of sulphate rock at Eilat; their obligation to load was subject to various 'exceptions' including 'shortage of . . . wagons . . . or other unavoidable hindrances in . . . loading . . . and any other causes or hindrances happening *without the fault*[131] of the charterers . . .'. There was a delay of about six weeks in loading because the land carriers whom the charterers had engaged to bring the rock down to Eilat had been unable to provide trucks for the purpose at the agreed time. The shipowners claimed that this delay entitled them to cancel the charterparty: they argued that it amounted to a fundamental breach[132] and relied on the rule that exemption clauses are prima facie not to be construed to apply to breaches of this character. One reason why the argument was rejected was that the charterers were not in breach at all as the clause was not an exemption clause, but an exception, providing an excuse for non-performance. The main reason given for this classification of the clause was that the events that could bring it into operation were (by its terms) beyond the control of the charterers and had occurred without their fault.[133] It is not suggested that this is the only relevant factor for drawing the distinction, or that it is necessarily decisive; but where it does govern, as in *The Angelia*, fault is a criterion for determining whether non-performance is excused or amounts to a breach.

(3) *Certain Conditional Contracts*

Where a contract is subject to a contingent condition[134] precedent, the principal obligations under it (e.g. to deliver goods, to pay a specified sum of money) do not accrue till the stipulated event has occurred. Such a contract may nevertheless impose certain subsidiary duties on the parties or on one of them; and it is in relation to these subsidiary duties that fault is sometimes relevant to liability.

(i) *Duty not to prevent occurrence of condition.*

Fault is, in the first place, relevant under the rule that a party may be in breach if he prevents the occurrence of the specified event. In an American case,[135] a man promised his future wife $20,000, provided that she should survive him. Some years after their marriage, he shot and killed her, at the same time inflicting a fatal wound on himself of which he died the next day. His estate was held liable to his wife's since it was his 'deliberate and

---

[130] *Trade & Transport Inc. v. Iino Kaiun Kaisha Ltd. (The Angelia)* [1973] 1 WLR 210.
[131] Emphasis added.
[132] The later development, or decline, of that doctrine is not our concern in this paper.
[133] [1973] 1 WLR 210, 230.
[134] i.e. to an event which neither party promises to bring about. The common law also (confusingly) uses condition in a 'promissory' sense, to refer to an event which a party promises to bring about, or to the performance of a party's undertaking.
[135] *Foreman State Trust & Savings Bank v. Tauber* 180 NE 827 (1932).

wrongful'[136] act which had prevented the fulfilment of the condition. In these circumstances, the condition was, by a fiction, deemed to have occurred, so that the wife's estate recovered the full $20,000, even though there was no certainty that she would have survived her husband if he had not killed her.[137] From this point of view, the case may be contrasted with an English case[138] in which a contract for the transfer of a professional footballer provided for payment of part of the transfer fee only after the player had scored twenty goals for the new club. That club dismissed him from its team before he had reached this total, and was held liable *in damages*. This view is also supported by American authorities according to which the remedy of the party prejudiced by the prevention of the fulfilment of the condition is by way of damages or *quantum meruit*, not by a claim for the agreed sum.[139] This solution seems to be preferable to the doctrine of fictional fulfilment,[140] which contains an undesirable element of penalty, being apparently applicable even though the chance that the condition would occur was so small that the promise was worth much less than its face value. The true position, it is submitted, is that the principal obligation has not accrued, but that there is liability for breach of a subsidiary obligation not to prevent the occurrence of the condition.

The relevance of fault in preventing the occurrence of a condition is further illustrated by a line of cases in which agents were engaged by prospective vendors of property on the terms that the agents were to be paid a commission out of the purchase price, or when the contract of sale was performed. If the vendor entered into a contract of sale with a person introduced by the agent and then without justification refused to perform it, he was in breach of contract not only with the purchaser but also with the agent.[141] But the vendor was under no liability to the agent where he was innocent of fault: e.g. where he could not perform because his title was defective but he in good faith and on reasonable grounds believed that he had a good title.[142] Whether a vendor who honestly but negligently believed that he had a good title would be liable to the agent remains an open question.

The duty not to prevent the occurrence of a condition is not of universal

---

[136] Ibid, p. 830. [137] Cf. Restatement 2d, § Ill. 5.
[138] *Bournemouth & Boscombe Athletic F.C.* v. *Manchester United F.C., The Times*, May 22, 1980. In *Mackay* v. *Dick* (1881) 6 App. Cas. 251 the action was for the agreed sum, but the only question discussed was the *liability* of the buyer. There is no discussion as to the *remedy*. Cf. also *infra*, n. 141.
[139] e.g. *Barron* v. *Cain* 4 S.E. 2d 618 (1939).
[140] For this doctrine in civil law, see e.g. French Civil Code, Art. 1178; German Civil Code, § 162(1).
[141] *Goldstein* v. *Rosenberg* 73 NE 2d. 171 (1947); Restatement 2d § Ill. 2; cf. *Alpha Trading Ltd.* v. *Dunshaw-Patten* [1981] QB 290 (where the seller settled his claim with the buyer and was held liable *in damages* to the agent).
[142] *Blau* v. *Friedman* 140 A. 2d. 193 (1958); *Blake & Co.* v. *Sohn* [1969] 1 WLR 1412.

application. It does not extend to certain cases in which contractual rights are expressed to be subject to the 'satisfaction' of one party with the subject-matter or with the performance of the other. A party is clearly not in breach merely because he does not express such satisfaction, or expresses dissatisfaction. But occasionally the standard of satisfaction is said to be objective, so that a party who acts capriciously or in bad faith may, for that reason, be in breach.[143] To this extent, fault may be an element of liability. But the objective test is only applicable if 'it is practicable to apply such a test'.[144] These words would exclude from its operation cases in which the contractual performance to be rendered by one party is to do something which is to please 'the personal taste, fancy or sensibility of the other'.[145] The objective test does not seem to apply to the ordinary sale on approval.[146] The reference to satisfaction may, finally, have the more radical effect of negativing contractual intention until satisfaction is expressed.[147] Where this is the case, and where the standard of satisfaction is subjective, it makes no sense to ask whether there is 'fault' in refusing to express satisfaction.

(ii) *Duty of diligence to bring about occurrence of condition*

A party may be not merely under the negative duty just discussed (not to prevent the occurrence of a condition) but also under a positive duty to make some effort to bring about the occurrence of the condition on which the principal obligations depend. For example, a house or land may be sold 'subject to' the buyer's being able to make the requisite financial arrangements, or to one party's obtaining the requisite approval of a public authority for the proposed use or development of the premises. In such cases, the party who has to make the arrangements or to obtain the approval is under a duty of diligence only: he is not liable if, in spite of making reasonable efforts, he fails to bring about the specified event.[148] If he does nothing, or fails to make such efforts as are reasonable, he is liable in damages,[149] unless he can show that such reasonable efforts as he was

---

[143] *Andrews* v. *Belfield* (1857) 9 CBNS 779, 789; *The John S. Darbyshire* [1977] 2 Lloyd's Rep. 457, 464; *B.V. Oliehandel Jongkind* v. *Coastal International Ltd.* [1983] 2 Lloyd's Rep. 463; *The Nissos Samos* [1985] 1 Lloyd's Rep. 378, 385; *McCartney* v. *Badovinac* 160 P. 190 (1916).

[144] Restatement 2d § 228.   [145] *Haymore* v. *Levinson* 328 P. 307, 309 (1958).

[146] Cf. Uniform Commercial Code s.2-326 Comment 1: 'One the point of "satisfaction" meaning "reasonable satisfaction" where an industrial machine is involved, this Article takes no position'.

[147] e.g. *Lee-Parker* v. *Izett (No. 2)* [1975] 1 WLR 775 ('subject to satisfactory mortgage'); *Astra Trust* v. *Adams & Williams* [1969] 1 Lloyd's Rep. 81 ('subject to satisfactory survey'), doubted in *The Merak* [1976] 2 Lloyd's Rep. 250, 254.

[148] e.g. *Hargraves Transport Ltd.* v. *Lynch* [1969] 1 WLR 215; Restatement 2d, § 225 Ill. 8 (reasonable efforts to obtain bank's approval required).

[149] e.g. *Zieme* v. *Gregory* [1963] VR 214; Restatement 2d § 245 Ill. 3.

Fault in the Common Law of Contract 209

bound to make would inevitably have been useless.[150] His liability is not for breach of the obligation to perform the conditional promise, as that has never become due, but for failure to perform the subsidiary duty to make reasonable efforts to bring about the condition.

Similar problems arise where a contract for the sale of goods can only be lawfully performed if the requisite export or import licence is obtained. Once it has been decided whether the duty to obtain such a licence is incumbent on the buyer or on the seller,[151] the question arises as to the standard of the duty. This depends, in the first place, on the terms of the contract, which may expressly provide that the duty is only one to make reasonable efforts;[152] and a stipulation that the contract is 'subject to licence' will normally be construed as having this effect.[153] But a contract may on its true construction impose an absolute obligation to obtain a licence. In one case,[154] a Finnish seller of ant eggs undertook to ship the goods 'as soon as export licence in order' and assured the buyer that this was a 'mere formality'. But licences to export ant eggs were issued only to members of the Ant Egg Exporters Association, of which the seller was not one, so that his efforts to obtain a licence were unsuccessful. He was held liable in damages on the ground that he had undertaken an absolute duty to obtain a licence. In deciding whether the duty is absolute, the court may also have regard to other terms of the contract: thus the fact that a *force majeure* clause expressly provided that it could not be invoked on failure to obtain the licence, has been relied on to support the conclusion that the duty was absolute.[155] Similarly, the fact that the seller's duty to obtain an export licence *was* subject to a *force majeure* clause, while the buyer's duty to obtain an import licence was *not,* has been relied on in holding that the latter duty was absolute.[156] Where the duty is of this character, the analysis of the liability as being for breach of a subsidiary duty is of crucial importance; for to hold a party liable for breach of the principal obligation would conflict with the general rule that damages will not be awarded for breach of an illegal contract.[157]

The most difficult of the export or import licence cases are those in which the express terms of the contract give no clue as to the standard of duty

---

[150] This qualification is supported by the export and import licence cases to be discussed below: see *Benjamin's Sale of Goods*, 3rd ed. § 1569.
[151] See *ibid.* § 1559.
[152] e.g. *Charles H. Windschuegl v. Alexander Pickering & Co. Ltd.* (1950) 84 Ll. LR 89.
[153] *Ibid.* at p. 93; *Brauer & Co. (Great Britain) Ltd. v. James Clark (Brush Materials) Ltd.* [1952] 2 All ER 497, 501.
[154] *Peter Cassidy Ltd. v. Osuustukkukaupa* [1957] 1 WLR 273.
[155] *C. Czarnikow Ltd. v. Centrala Handlu Zagranicznego 'Rolimpex'* [1979] AC 351, 371.
[156] *Congimex Companhia Geral, etc., S.A.R.L. v. Tradax Export S.A.* [1981] 2 Lloyd's Rep. 687, 693; affirmed [1983] 1 Lloyd's Rep. 250, 254.
[157] Cf. *Walton (Grain & Shipping) Ltd. v. British Italian Trading Co.* [1959] 1 Lloyd's Rep. 223, 236; *Johnson Matthey Bankers Ltd. v. The State Trading Corp. of India* [1984] 1 Lloyd's Rep. 427, 434.

imposed on the party who has to take steps to obtain the licence. In such cases, the prima facie rule is that the duty is only one to take reasonable steps;[158] but this rule can be displaced not only (as already noted) by the terms of the contract but also by extraneous circumstances. One such circumstance is the knowledge of the parties as to the existence and operation of the licensing system: if (for example) only the seller has such knowledge and has not expressly qualified his duty to deliver, then his duty to obtain the necessary licence will be regarded as strict;[159] but if the knowledge is equally available to both parties, then the duty will merely be one of diligence.[160] The extraneous circumstances are, in other words, used as a basis for drawing inferences as to the commercial expectations of the parties, and the standard of liability is adjusted accordingly.

D. CONCLUSION

The foregoing discussion is far from being an exhaustive account of the role played by fault in the common law of contract. Such an account would range over many further areas, such as mistake, misrepresentation, illegality and remedies. The purpose of this paper has been to concentrate on the question whether the common law regards fault as an essential ingredient of breach of contract. Unlike the civil law, the common law has never squarely asked itself this question; and it has certainly not adopted or evolved any general theory either of strict liability or of liability based on fault. To judge from the difficulties which the civil law has experienced with its theory based on fault, the approach of the common law is much to be preferred: it has enabled the courts to tackle the problem in their characteristically pragmatic manner, and to seek such solutions as will best accord with the reasonable commercial expectations of the parties, and with the courts' own sense of fairness.

---

[158] *Re Anglo-Russian Merchant Traders and John Batt (London) Ltd.* [1917] 2 KB 679.
[159] As in *K. C. Sethia Ltd.* v. *Partabmul Rameshwar* [1950] 1 All ER 51; affirmed [1951] 2 Lloyd's Rep. 89.
[160] As in the *Anglo Russian Merchant Traders* case, *supra*, no. 158 : : see *K. C. Sethia Ltd.* v. *Partabmul Rameshwar* [1950] 1 All ER at p. 58 ("manifest to both parties").

13

The Impact of Community Law on Indirect Taxation

by N. P. M. ELLES

During the last twenty-five years the European Community has given rise to a new legal order of international law, and the European Court of Justice has concluded that Community law not only imposes obligations on individuals, but also confers rights which form part of their legal heritage. The Court of Justice has also affirmed the supremacy of Community law in the event of a conflict between Community law and national law.

In his foreword to *Community Law Through the Cases*,[1] Lord Wilberforce commented that it was 'unlikely that more than a few have much conception of the intricacy and pervasiveness of the penetration of the law of the Communities into national systems'. Since then many more people have become aware of this ongoing development; and in 1974 Lord Denning MR in the well-known passage from his decision in *Bulmer* v. *Bollinger*[1] describes the EEC Treaty as being 'like an incoming tide, It flows into the estuaries and up the rivers. It cannot be held back.'[2]

What is perhaps remarkable is that much of the recent development in Community law has come about through decisions of the Court of Justice relating to indirect taxation. It is perhaps even more remarkable that one may now with a little imagination envisage a practitioner in value added tax, with the Sixth Council Directive in his left hand and a National Statute in his right hand, but perceiving that if there is a conflict between them it is the document in his left hand which may be dominant. How comes it, then, that indirect taxation has been of relative importance?

One good reason is that the very origin of value added tax lies in a Council Decision of May 1965, and that this tax has developed through a series of Council Directives, of which fourteen have already been adopted. Another good reason arises from the truism that fiscal, monetary and exchange rate aspects are central to the formulation of economic policy. The approximation of indirect tax has not been a sterile harmonization for its own sake, but an effective force in achieving some of the objects of the EEC Treaty. In this way some of the cases on indirect taxation decided by the Court of Justice have contributed to the general development of the unwritten law of the Community and to this new order of international law.

This essay examines the development of Community law in the light of

[1] By the present writer, Stevens/Matthew Bender, 1973. [2] [1974] Ch 401.

cases on indirect taxation; and in particular, the development of the law relating to the direct effect of Directives and the extent to which these Directives have given rise to rights of individuals against the executive. It will also dwell on some aspects of the unwritten law of the Community, including the law of proportionality and how the individual may be protected from adoption by the executive of measures which offend its general principles and which are wider than is strictly necessary to enforce a particular measure. It will also examine the impact of Community law on the deduction of input tax, with particular reference to the formative period of a business and the extent to which input tax may be claimed notwithstanding that a trader may not have begun to make taxable supplies. Finally, it will take note of a new and interesting development in the law relating to 'consideration' in the context of value added tax, although it is too early to judge how far-reaching this development may prove to be.

The written law of the Community is enshrined not only in the Treaties themselves, but also in the Regulations, Decisions, and Directives of the Council and of the Commission. Many of the provisions of the Treaties are expressed in the most general terms, and, in investigating how those general terms are to be interpreted, the Court of Justice has called in aid Article 164 of the EEC Treaty which states that 'The Court of Justice shall ensure that in the interpretation and application of this Treaty the law is observed.'

The Court of Justice has acted as an administrative court, and its approach may be traced to the traditions of legal control over administration which had been developed in the six original member States. The Court of Justice thus imposes a measure of judicial control. It is essential to comment, therefore, that the Court of Justice is concerned with legality, and not with the merits of a case as such. Lord Mackenzie Stuart made this point clear in his Hamlyn Lecture in 1977:

Legality in this context implies conformity with certain objective standards within which the administrative action was permissible and the existence in fact of the necessary circumstances which alone allowed the administrator to take action in the dispute. Judicial control may even require an examination of the various alternatives open to the administrators in order to see whether the one chosen was reasonable in proportion to the end to be achieved. Once, however, the administrative decision in question has passed the test of legality the Court's duties are over. It would not then substitute its own appreciation for that of the administrators. (The Hamlyn Lectures, 29th ser. (Stevens).)

It is from its role as an administrative court that the unwritten law of the Community has developed, by applying wide general principles in formulating decisions. The unwritten law of the Community underlies the

The Impact of Community Law on Indirect Taxation 213

approach of the Court of Justice. Sir Jean-Pierre Warner, the Advocate-General in *AM & S* v. *The Commission* expressed himself as follows:

This Court, however, has never regarded the absence of an express provision as precluding it from holding that a general principle of law could affect the application of Community legislation. Were it otherwise, Community law would admit, for example, of no principle of proportionality, of no protection for legitimate expectations, of no right to be heard (except where expressly provided for) and of no guarantee of fundamental human rights.[3]

The application of those general principles in Community law is in the process of constant development, and it might be said that the need to make the Community work effectively has acted as a catalyst in that development.

The basic need for such an administrative court was at an early stage made clear in the judgment of the Court of Justice in *Costa* v. *ENEL*:

The executive force of Community law cannot vary from one State to another in deference to subsequent domestic laws, without jeopardising the attainment of the objectives of the Treaty.... The obligations undertaken under the Treaty establishing the Community would not be unconditional, but merely contingent if they could be called in question by subsequent legislative acts of the signatories.[4]

This decision not only illustrates the need for an administrative court, but also establishes the supremacy of Community law over national laws.[5]

It is more than twenty years since the Court of Justice in *Van Gend en Loos* affirmed that the Community gave rise to a new legal order of international law for the benefit of which the States have limited their sovereign rights, albeit within limited fields. The subject-matter of this important case, dull and pedestrian in the extreme, concerned duty on 'aqueous emulsion of ureaformaldehyde'. Prior to the EEC Treaty, import duty of 3 per cent had been imposed thereon; the Treaty abolished import duties, but the Dutch Government none the less imposed a new duty of 10 per cent. Van Gend en Loos, the importers, appealed on the ground that this new duty had like effect to the import duty and having regard to Article 12 of the EEC Treaty, could not be levied. The Court of Justice reached the well-known conclusion:

The ojective of the EEC Treaty, which is to establish a Common Market, the functioning of which is of direct concern to interested parties in the Community, implies that this Treaty is more than an agreement which merely creates mutual obligations between the contracting states. This view is confirmed by the preamble

---

[3] Case 155/79 [1982] ECR 1575, 1631.
[4] Case 6/64 [1964] ECR 585, 594, [1964] CMLR 425, 455^{N}-6.
[5] On this point I would refer also to *Amministrazione delle Finanze dello Stato* v. *Simmenthal,* Case 106/77 [1978] ECR 629, in which it was held that no incompatible national measures may be applied by national judicial authorities.

to the Treaty which refers not only to governments but to peoples. It is also confirmed more specifically by the establishment of institutions endowed with sovereign rights, the exercise of which affects Member States and also their citizens.[6]

This judgment heralded a new beginning, which was not, and still is not, universally acclaimed, because, independently of the legislation of member States, Community law has been seen not only to impose obligations on individuals in certain limited fields, but also to confer on them rights which could be enforced in their national courts. The Court of Justice expressed itself as follows:

Independently of the legislation of Member States, Community Law therefore not only imposes obligations on individuals but is also intended to confer upon them rights which become part of their legal heritage. These rights arise not only where they are expressly granted by the Treaty, but also by reason of obligations which the Treaty imposes in a clearly defined way upon individuals as well as upon the Member States and upon the institutions of the Community.[7]

The draftsmen of the EEC Treaty expressed themselves as determining to establish an even closer union among European peoples, and, *inter alia,* directing their efforts to the essential purpose of constantly improving the living and working conditions of their peoples, anxious to strengthen the unity of their economies by reducing the differences existing between the various regions and mitigating the backwardness of the less favoured; in so doing, they realized the importance of harmonization in the creation of the EEC. By Article 99 the Commission was enjoined to consider 'in what way the law of the various Member States concerning turnover taxes, excise duties and other forms of indirect taxation, including compensatory measures applying to exchanges between Member States, could be harmonised in the interest of the Common Market'. Article 100 provided that the Council, acting by means of a unanimous vote on a proposal of the Commission, should issue directives for the approximation of such legislative and administrative provisions of the Member States as have a direct incidence on the establishment or functioning of the Common Market.

The Single Act of the European Communities of February 1986 amended the EEC Treaty, and in particular replaced Article 99 by a new Article 99 in the following terms:

[Article 99]
The Council shall, acting unanimously on a proposal from the Commission and after consulting the European Parliament, adopt provisions for the harmonization of legislation concerning turnover taxes, excise duties and other forms of indirect taxation to the extent that such harmonization is necessary to ensure the

---

[6] Case 26/62 [1963] ECR 12; [1963] CMLR 129. [7] *Supra,* n. 6.

The Impact of Community Law on Indirect Taxation

establishment and the functioning of the internal market within the time limit laid down in Article 8A.

While provisions to harmonize or approximate legislation concerning turnover taxes, excise duties, and other forms of indirect taxation still require unanimity, the time limit for such adoption is given as 31 December 1992.

A cynic might comment that the Single Act sets out to establish an 'internal market', and in reality goes not further than the EEC Treaty of 1957, which made provision for the establishment of just such a 'Common Market', which should have been realized by the original six member States by 1970. But now there are twelve member States, and it may be right that the wine should be put in new bottles, since it has become apparent that the old bottles were not proving effective.

Value added tax (VAT) is the principal vehicle of indirect tax in the Community, and its development may be traced through a series of Council Directives which have had, and continue to have, as their avowed objective the harmonization of indirect taxation among the participating member States. At the time of its inception, VAT was heralded as a simple tax. In the United Kingdom there was only one positive rate, at 10 per cent; but there was also a zero rate, and some supplies were exempt. The tax was to be charged on supply of goods or services for a consideration by a taxable person in the course of a business carried on or to be carried on by him. This apparently simple concept has been found, none the less, to accumulate difficulties when applied to the practical and commercial facts of life. The result is that this simple concept has developed into a tax of great complexity, full of traps for the unwary.

The sixth Council Directive[8] is expressed to be on 'the harmonization of Laws of Member States relating to turnover taxes—Common System of Value Added Tax—uniform basis of assessment'. The preamble deals in detail with the background and also with the reasons for such harmonization. This preamble is of the greatest importance, and stipulates the fields in which such harmonization is to be achieved, in particular, further progress in the effective removal of restrictions on the movement of persons, goods, services, and capital and the integration of national economies, and also to enhance the non-discriminatory nature of the tax with particular reference to the terms 'taxable persons and taxable transactions, and the place where taxable transactions are effected'. It also proposes harmonization of the taxable base, provision of a common list of exemptions, provisions for determining deductions, and the collection of taxes in a uniform manner. None the less, member States were to be allowed to retain special schemes for small businesses and a measure of

---

[8] Sixth Council Directive of the European Communities (77/388 EEC) of 17 May 1977.

derogation from this Directive in order to simplify the levying of the tax or to avoid fraud or tax avoidance. Some of these derogations have led to the development of the law of proportionality.[9]

Article 189 of the EEC Treaty provides that 'a Directive shall be binding, as to the result to be achieved, upon each member State to which it is addressed, but shall leave to the national authorities the choice of form and methods.' 'Directives' are contrasted with 'recommendations' and 'opinions' which are expressed to have no binding force.

DIRECT EFFECT OF DIRECTIVES

As a result of the twin principles of the direct effect of Directives and the supremacy of Community law, the basic law which governs value added tax is that of the Community, rather than the municipal law. In practice, effective action has been taken by most member States to enact legislation to conform with the Directives, but it sometimes happens that a member State has not done so within the time specified by a Directive, or has only implemented some part of what a Directive has made binding, or has done so in a defective manner.

The citizen and his advisers must at all times be prepared to meet such a shortfall, and to refer constantly to the Directive and to the decided cases of the Court of Justice which form part of the municipal law. A practitioner must always bear in mind the provisions of the sixth and other Directives, and remember that, where there is a conflict, the provisions of the sixth Directive may prevail.

This point first came before the Court of Justice in a series of cases which raised the question whether a German charge on transport by inland water traffic continued to be payable as well as VAT.[10] Member States had been directed to apply before 1 January 1972 the common value added system to replace the freight charge imposed on transport instead of turnover tax. In fact, the German Federal Republic had introduced VAT with effect from 1 January 1968, and had extended it to transport services. The plaintiffs in these actions maintained that the levy of the freight charge in addition to value added tax was contrary to the Council Decision and the Directives. The Court of Justice held that the German Federal Republic was free to levy the freight charge in addition to VAT for the period prior to 1 January 1972. It was held none the less, that the Council Decision of 13 May 1965 and the subsequent Directives imposed an unconditional obligation on member States which enabled individuals to invoke their provisions in the national courts, but that such rights did not become effective before 1

---

[9] See *infra*, nn. 27 and 28.
[10] e.g. *Franz Grad* v. *Traunstein*, Case 9/70 [1970] ECR 825; [1971] CMLR 1.

January 1972. The aim of the Decision and the Directives was to ensure that the value added tax system was applied throughout the Community by the specified date; but prior to that date member States retained their freedom of action.

The concept of direct effect was established by *Van Gend en Loos* in 1963.[11] In the years following this decision there was a difference of opinion in academic circles whether this concept could be extended to Directives; and even after the decision of the European Court of Justice in the transport cases,[12] doubts lingered on. The transport cases established the proposition that where a Directive has imposed on a State an obligation sufficiently clear and precise, it may also confer on individuals the right to invoke its provisions.

This concept has been developed by the Court of Justice in a number of cases, and is clearly formulated in the *Becker* case in the following terms:

> Thus, wherever the provisions of a directive appear, so far as the subject matter is concerned, to be unconditional and sufficiently precise those provisions may in the absence of implementing measures... be relied upon as against any national provision which is incompatible with the directive or in so far as the provisions define rights which individuals are able to assert against the State.[13]

Despite the clarity of this formulation, doubts still arise. Difficulties sometimes occur because one part of a Directive may not be sufficiently precise and unconditional. In the *Becker* case it had been contended that Article 13B(d)(1) of the sixth Council Directive was an integral part of the whole Scheme created by the Directive, but that in a number of respects no unconditional obligation was imposed on member States; thus the Directive was not unconditional so as to have direct effect. The Advocate-General, Sir Gordon Slynn, commented as follows:

> It does not seem to me that all the provisions of a directive have to be unconditional before some which are unconditional can be relied upon. Indeed the decision in the Nederlandse Ondernemingen case[14] seems to support the contrary view. If those provisions which appear unconditional are dependent on those which are conditional or discretionary, the unconditional ones might be themselves available to an individual. In the present case, the exemption from taxation... in no way hinges on the discretionary or conditional powers conferred on member States by other Articles.

The relevant parts of the Directive were held to have direct effect.

In *English-Speaking Union of the Commonwealth* v. *The Commissioners of Customs and Excise*,[15] the London Value Added Tax Tribunal was in

---

[11] See *supra*, n. 6. [12] *Supra*, n. 10.
[13] *Ursula Becker* v. *Finanzamt Münster Innenstadt*, Case 8/81 [1982] ECR 53; [1982] 1 CMLR 499.
[14] Case 51/76 [1977] ECR 113; [1977] 1 CMLR 413. [15] [1980] VATTR 184, 201, 202.

some doubt as to whether Article 13A1(a) of the sixth Council Directive had direct effect, the result of which would have been to exempt the Union from the charge to tax; the tribunal, with some hesitation, reached the conclusion that it did not have direct effect. Its reason was that although the exemptions were clear in themselves, they were subject to a proviso that the exemption was 'not likely to cause distortion of competition'. The question before the Tribunal was whether the English-Speaking Union was to be treated as 'not carrying on a business for tax purposes as a body with objects in the public domain where members obtained no facility or advantage other than the right to participate in the management or receive reports on its activities'. On the facts before it, the Tribunal held that the Union should be treated as carrying on a business so that the supplies made to a member for his subscription were chargeable to tax. The Tribunal was in some doubt whether this proviso resulted in the exemptions not having direct effect, but decided not to make a reference to the Court of Justice under Article 177 because both parties requested that this should not be done.

In *Open University* v. *The Commissioners of Customs and Excise*,[16] the London Tribunal considered whether Article 13A1(i) had direct effect. This exemption extended, *inter alia*, to 'university education, vocational training or retraining, including the supply of services and of goods closely related thereto'. On the facts before it, the Tribunal concluded that for the payment to the BBC by the Open University, the BBC was not providing university education, but was supplying the services of preparing, producing, presenting, and reproducing the University's programmes on radio and television. The London Tribunal expressed the view that the services and goods supplied by the BBC were 'closely related' to the supply of university education, but were not themselves education.

For that reason the Tribunal further considered the words in the subparagraph (i) including 'the supply of services' and of 'goods closely related thereto'. On that point the Tribunal asked the question whether the exemption extended to services and goods supplied by a person providing education, or as extending to services supplied by a third party. The Tribunal preferred the former construction; so that the exemption was granted to supplies of services and goods closely related thereto, only if made by the body governed by public law providing the education, vocational training, or retraining. In the light of the *Yoga for Health Foundation* case, it might be asked whether the Tribunal should have applied the purposive, or teleological, test applied in the latter case. In *Yoga for Health Foundation* v. *Commissioners of Customs and Excise*,[17] the divisional court (Nolan J.) did not disagree with the London Value Added Tax Tribunal, which had accepted, but not decided, that the

[16] [1982] VATTR 29.   [17] [1984] STC 650, (1983) VATTR 297.

exemptions provided by Article 13A1(b), (g), and (m) of the sixth Council Directive had direct effect. The case proceeded on the basis that these exemptions had direct effect in English law. The London Tribunal then construed in a conventional manner the exempting provisions of the sixth Directive and dismissed the appeal of the Foundation. But the divisional court overruled the London Tribunal by adopting a European approach to the Article, rather than the traditionally English approach. Nolan J. adopted what 'was often called a purposive or sometimes a teleological' method of construction.

In *P. J. Parkinson v. The Commissioners of Customs and Excise*,[18] it was held by the London Tribunal that on the true construction of Item 1 of Group 1 in Schedule 6 to the Value Added Tax Act 1983 and of paragraph (b) of Article 13B of the sixth Council Directive, the United Kingdom was empowered to exclude from the basic exemption applying to the grant, assignment, or surrender of any interest or right over land or of any licence to occupy land, the leasing or letting of a fishery or fishing rights. This power to derogate did not extend to the transfer of an estate in fee-simple possession of the bed of a river. The London Tribunal held that Article 13B of the sixth Council Directive had direct effect in the United Kingdom. The result was that, despite the purported exclusion of the granting of any right to take game or fish from the exemption contained in Item 1 of Group 1 to Schedule 6 of the Value Added Tax Act, 1983, no tax was chargeable. It is however, understood that the Commissioners of Customs and Excise have appealed against this decision.

It would be a bold man who at this stage forecast how far the purposive, or teleological, approach may become a general canon of interpretation. In *Black-Clawson Ltd. v. Papierwerke AG*,[19] the point at issue was whether a report of a committee presented to Parliament should be taken into account in the interpretation of a statute. Lord Wilberforce expressed himself as follows:

My Lords, we are entitled, in my opinion, to approach the interpretation of the subsection, and of the 1933 Act as a whole, from the background of the law as it stood, or was thought to stand, in 1933 and of the legislative intention. As to these matters the report to which my noble and learned friend, Lord Reid, has referred is of assistance. He has set out in his opinion the basis on which the courts may consult such documents. I agree with his reasoning and I only desire to add an observation of my own on one point. In my opinion it is not proper or desirable to make use of such a document as a committee or commission report, or for that matter of anything reported as said in Parliament, or any official notes on clauses, for a direct statement of what a proposed enactment is to mean or of what the committee or commission thought it means: on this point I am in agreement with my noble and learned friend Lord Diplock. To be concrete, in a case where a

---

[18] (1985) VATTR 219.   [19] [1975] AC 591 at 629; [1975] 2 All ER 513 at 533.

committee prepared a draft bill and accompanies that by a clause by clause commentary, it ought not to be permissible, even if the proposed bill is enacted without variation, to take the meaning of the bill from the commentary. There are, to my mind, two kinds of reason for this. The first is the practical one, that if this process were allowed the courts would merely have to interpret, as in argument we were invited to interpret, two documents instead of one—the bill and the commentary on it, in particular Annex V, para 13. The second is one of constitutional principle. Legislation in England is passed by Parliament, and put in the form of written words. This legislation is given legal effect on subjects by virtue of judicial decision, and it is the function of the courts to say what the application of the words used to particular cases or individuals is to be. This power which has been devolved on the judges from the earliest times is an essential part of the constitutional process by which subjects are brought under the rule of law—as distinct from the rule of the King or the rule of Parliament; and it would be a degradation of that process if the courts were to be merely a reflecting mirror of what some other interpretation agency might say. The saying that it is the function of the courts to ascertain the will or intention of Parliament is often enough repeated, so often indeed as to have become an incantation. If too often or unreflectingly stated, it leads to neglect of the important element of judicial construction; an element not confined to a mechanical analysis of today's words, but, if this task is to be properly done, related to such matters as intelligibility to the citizen, constitutional propriety, consideration of history, comity of nations, reasonable and non-retroactive effect and, no doubt, in some contexts, to social needs.

It is sound enough to ascertain, if that can be done, the objectives of any particular measure, and the background of the enactment; but to take the opinion, whether of a Minister or an official or a committee, as to the intended meaning in particular applications of a clause or a phrase, would be a stunting of the law and not a healthy development.

Except possibly, in the interpretation of Community law, the purposive or teleological, approach may also be limited by other considerations. It was for instance settled by the House of Lords in *Davies* v. *Johnson*,[20] that *Hansard* may not be invoked in the interpretation of a domestic statute.

Despite the development of the concept of the direct effect of Directives, Sir Gordon Slynn has sounded a warning note,[21] and raised doubts whether the concept applies as between two individuals as well as between an individual and a defaulting government. He referred to the *Ratti* case,[22] in which it had been held (in the context of the free movement of goods) that a manufacturer could not be prosecuted under a national law which ought to have been amended pursuant to a Directive, where the manufacturer had complied with the Directive. He also referred to the *Becker* case[23] in which a credit negotiator has been able to rely on an

[20] [1979] AC 264; [1978] All ER 553.
[21] *International and Comparative Law Quarterly Review*, 33: 408 at 419.
[22] Case 148/78 [1979] ECR 1629.   [23] *Supra*, n. 13.

exemption from VAT contained in Article 13 of the sixth Council Directive, where the Directive had not been implemented in Germany.

Sir Gordon Slynn pointed out that, if a Directive could be held to have direct effect as between individuals, this would blur the distinction between Regulations and Directives, with the consequence (which he considered unacceptable) that an instrument addressed only to member States, and published in the Official Journal only for information would be binding on an individual to whom it had not been addressed. This point awaits consideration in some future case, but perhaps the concept of direct effect of Directives should be limited to cases where a defaulting government has sought to enforce a national law when it was in breach of Community obligation to change that law.

Article 177 of the EEC Treaty confers on the Court of Justice jurisdiction to give preliminary rulings on the interpretation of the Treaty and on the validity and interpretation of acts of the institutions of the Community, including Regulations of both the Council and the Commission. It is mainly through such references that the Court of Justice has interpreted the law, although in some cases it has given its rulings under Article 169 in proceedings by the Commission against member States for failure to fulfil their obligations under the Treaty. In these proceedings, and also under Article 173, the Court of Justice may review the lawfulness of acts of the Council and the Commission.

It was held by the Court of Justice in *SPA International Chemical Corporation v. Administrazione delle Finanze dello Stato*[24] that the scope of its judgments should be viewed in the light of the aims of Article 177 and the place it occupies in the entire system of judicial protection established by the Treaties. I quote from the judgment:

The main purpose of the powers accorded to the Court by Article 177 is to ensure that Community law is applied uniformly by national courts. Uniform application of Community law is imperative not only when a national court is faced with a rule of Community law the meaning and scope of which needs to be defined; it is just as imperative when the Court is confronted by a dispute as to the validity of an act of the institutions.

THE PRINCIPLE OF PROPORTIONALITY

The principle of proportionality appears to have originated from German administrative law, and this principle requires that the legislative means adopted to promote a legitimate end must be no more onerous than is required to achieve that end. This principle was considered in the opinion of the Advocate General in *Internationale Handelsgesellschaft m.b.H.v. Einfuhr-und Vorratsstelle für Getreide und Futtermitte.*[25]

[24] [1983] 2 CMLR 593, 617. [25] [1970] CMLR 294.

In fact the fundamental right invoked here,—that the individual should not have his freedom of action limited beyond the degree necessary for the general interest—is already generated both by the general principles of Community law, the compliance with which is ensured by the Court, and by the express provisions of the Treaty.

This principle was again considered in *Schluter* v. *Hauptzollamt Lörrach*.[26] This case was concerned with a temporary measure adopted for fixing compensatory amounts in the exchange rate between the D-Mark and the US dollar. The challenge failed in this case because the Court of Justice was not satisfied that the Council had imposed burdens on traders which were manifestly out of proportion with the object in view. In *Customs and Excise Commissioners* v. *Samex*,[27] Bingham J, the High Court of Justice applied the principles of proportionality and decided to refer the case to the Court of Justice.

This principle has been developed in recent cases and in particular in *National Panasonic U.K. Ltd.* v. *EC Commission*,[28] in *EC Commission* v. *Kingdom of Belgium*[29] (VAT on cars) and in *Direct Cosmetics Ltd.* v. *The Commissioners of Customs and Excise*.[30]

In the *National Panasonic* case it was claimed that the principle of proportionality was infringed, because no warning was given of an investigation, and the decision to investigate did not list any reasons to justify such an investigation without any warning. The challenge failed, however, because secrecy was held to be necessary in competition cases of this kind in order to forestall the possible destruction of or concealment of evidence, and so the measures taken by the Commission were held not to be disproportionate. The application of this principle is more clearly illustrated in the VAT on cars case and in the *Direct Cosmetics* case. In the former Advocate General, Pieter VerLoren van Themaat, expressed himself as follows:

In principle, however, I share the Commission's view that the special measures permitted exceptionally by Article 27 should not by nature derogate further from the normal rule than is justified by the objectives mentioned in the Article. The 'special measures for derogation from the provisions of this directive' may only be retained pursuant to paragraph 1, to which paragraph 5 refers, 'in order to simplify the procedure for charging the tax or to prevent certain types of tax evasion or avoidance'. The logical interpretation of this provision requires in fact that derogations from the provisions of the directive shall not go further than is justified by the special objectives. In other words, in the present case there must be an absolutely compelling connection between the end and the means of the measures for preventing tax evasion; the main objectives of the directive cannot, in my opinion, be substantially jeopardised further even by measures in derogations.

[26] Case 9/73 [1973] ECR 1135.   [27] [1983] 1 All ER 1042.
[28] Case 136/79 [1980] ECR 2033.   [29] Case 328/82 [1984] ECR 1861.
[30] Case 5/84 [1985] STC 479; [1985] 2 CMLR 145.

In this case the Belgian Government, prior to the coming into force of the sixth Directive, had adopted specific measures to ensure that what it considered a proper amount of VAT should be levied on cars which had been withdrawn for private use by motor manufacturers and dealers. Thus, if such a car was to be sold within six months, value added tax was to be charged on the full catalogue price of the car; if sold after six months but before eighteen months, tax was to be charged at a price midway between the catalogue price and the sale price; and if sold after eighteen months, the normal rates would apply.

The Belgian Government was aware that this charge to tax constituted a derogation from Article 27 of the sixth Directive, and accordingly notified the Commission under Article 27(5) in the current manner that it wished to retain the tax. In due course, however, the Commission informed the Belgian Government that in its opinion the Belgian provisions were incompatible with those of the sixth Directive, and in particular of Article 2 on the taxable amount for VAT, and that it could not accept the reliance of Belgium on the derogation provisions of Article 27(5) on the basis of measures taken to prevent tax evasion on new or imported cars and simplification measures relating to 'voitures de direction'. It was contended by the Commission that the measures adopted by the Belgian Government were of too general a nature and were disproportionate to the achievement of the desired objective. But in the opinion of the advocate-general, the measures adopted by the Belgian Government were not disproportionate to the end to be achieved, and the action of the Commission should be dismissed.

The Court took a different view. It was contended by the Belgian Government that the Directive did not lay down any restrictive criteria for national provisions intended to prevent tax evasion or avoidance, so there could be a derogation from the entire Directive, including the taxable amounts defined by Article 2, and the principle of proportionality could not be evoked. The Belgian Government further contended that, even if that principle did apply, it was satisfied because of the large-scale tax evasion which existed in the car sector. This evasion took the form, *inter alisa*, of the seller stating an incorrect price for new cars, particularly when used cars were part-exchanged, and in the deduction of input tax which had not been paid by the buyer. Such evasion was said to play a large part in the budget deficit and also to distort competition.

The Court of Justice accepted that the Belgian Government had reason to consider that there was a real risk of tax evasion, but the measures notified must not in principle derogate from the requirement to have regard to the taxable amount for VAT referred to by Article 2 'except within the limits which are strictly necessary to achieve that objective'. The Court of Justice reached the conclusion that, since the Belgian provisions, by applying the catalogue price to all new cars, altered the taxable amount in such an absolute and general manner, it could not be accepted that the provisions were limited to the derogations necessary to prevent the risk of tax evasion or avoidance. In particular, the determination of the taxable amount by reference to the catalogue price had the effect of eliminating any form of discount or rebate. The measures were therefore disproportionate to the desired objective and were void.

In the *Direct Cosmetics* case the appellant purchased cosmetics and toiletries and sold them by a direct selling method through agents who were not taxable persons. It fixed the prices at which its agents were to sell the goods, but allowed them to retain a discount expressed to be a discount of 20 per cent 'for prompt payment'. The agents were mainly women working at hospitals, offices, and factories who effected sales to their colléagues during lunch breaks. The Commissioners of Customs and Excise made a direction on the appellant company that the value of the supplies made by it shall be taken as their open market value on sale by retail. It is common ground that the Commissioners under Article 27 of the sixth Directive prior to 1 January 1978 properly notified to the Commission the original derogation which they wished to implement, and that no objection was taken thereto. This derogation followed the wording of paragraph 3 of Schedule 3 to the Finance Act, 1972, 'for the protection of the revenue'. Following on the decision of the London Tribunal in *Club Centre of Leeds* v. *The Commissioners of Customs and Excise*,[31] in which it was held that there was no tax evasion and no intention to avoid tax, the wording of paragraph 3 was amended, *inter alia*, by deleting the words 'for the protection of the revenue'. This amendment was not notified to the Commission as a new special measure.

The appellant company challenged the validity of the amendment to paragraph 3. The Commissioners contended that this amendment did not constitute a new special measure, and that, even if it did, the mere failure to notify the Commission should not result in the invalidity of the derogation. Questions of Community law were raised which the London Tribunal was not able to decide without making a reference to the Court of Justice for its opinion under Article 177 of the EEC Treaty.

On 13 February 1985 the Court of Justice gave judgment, holding that the amendment of paragraph 3 effected by the Finance Act, 1981, and in particular, the omission of the words 'for the protection of the revenue', amounted to a new special measure and that, since this had not been notified to the Commission, the derogation was void. The Court of Justice further held that the appellant company was entitled to rely on Article 11 of the sixth Directive. The matter was then referred back to the London Tribunal, which allowed the appeal of the appellant company so that VAT

[31] (1980) VATTR 135.

was chargeable in accordance with Article 2 of the sixth directive only on the consideration actually received by it for the sale of the goods. The tax authorities of the member State were bound to observe all the provisions of the sixth Directive in so far as a derogation had not been established in accordance with Article 27; such tax authorities could therefore not rely, as against a taxable person, on a provision derogating from the Scheme of the Direction without disregarding that member State's obligations under the third paragraph of Article 189 of the Treaty.

It was also contended by the appellant company, not only that the deletion of the words 'for the protection of the revenue' constituted a new measure within the meaning of Article 27, but that such a measure went well beyond the limits permitted by the Article in so far as such measures may not derogate from the basis for charging VAT set out in Article 2 of the sixth Directive, except to the extent strictly necessary for preventing tax evasion or avoidance. It was stressed by *Direct Cosmetics* that the Court of Justice had reached this conclusion as a point of principle in its judgment of 10 April 1984 in *EC Commission v. Kingdom of Belgium*[32] I quote from the judgment of the Court of Justice:

It follows from the foregoing that new special measures derogating from the directive do not accord with Community law unless, on the one hand, they remain within the limits of the aims referred to in Article 27(1) and, on the other hand, they have been notified to the Commission and have been implied by or expressly authorised by the Council as to circumstances specified in paragraphs (1) to (4) of Article 27.

The Court of Justice based its decision on the failure to notify the new special measure, and did not expressly found any part of its judgment on the question whether the derogation was within the limits of the aims referred to in Article 27(1). This latter point constitutes the subject-matter of further references to the Court of Justice in the cases of *Direct Cosmetics v. The Commissioners of Customs and Excise*[33] and *Laughtons Photographs Ltd. v. The Commissioners of Customs and Excise*[34] These cases came before the London Tribunal in November 1985; it gave its respective decisions on 18 and 19 December.

The Commissioners of Customs and Excise made their new Directions under paragraph 3 to Schedule 4 of the Value Added Tax Act, 1983:

In pursuance of paragraph 3 of Schedule 4 to the Value Added Tax Act 1983 the Commissioners of Customs and Excise hereby DIRECT that after 8 July 1985, the value by reference to which Value Added Tax is charged on any taxable supply of goods:
(a) by you to persons who are not taxable persons within the meaning of Section 2 of the Value Added Tax Act 1983,

[32] *Supra*, n. 29.   [33] LON/85/377, unreported.   [34] (1986) VATTR 13.

(b) to be sold, whether by persons mentioned in (a) above or others, by retail, shall be taken to be its open marked value on a sale by retail.

The facts as found by the London Tribunal did not differ materially from those which it had found in relation to the previous appeal by Direct Cosmetics Ltd. It was contended by Direct Cosmetics Ltd. and Laughtons Photographs Ltd. that these respective Directions were both invalid, because paragraph 3 was a provision 'outside the limits of the aims referred to in Article 27(1) of the sixth Directive'. Accordingly it was contended that the derogation obtained by the United Kingdom Government was of no effect, and that the appellant company could rely upon the rule in Article 11(A)1(a) that VAT was due upon the consideration eventually obtained.

The London Tribunal reached the conclusion that it was unable to reach a decision without reference to the Court of Justice under Article 177 for an opinion whether a measure such as that contained in paragraph 3 of Schedule 4 of the Value Added Tax Act, 1983, was within the limits allowed by Article 27 of the sixth Directive, or whether it was wider than was strictly necessary. The decision of the Court of Justice on the question asked by the London Tribunal will mark one further step in the development of the law of proportionality relating to VAT.

DEDUTION OF INPUT TAX AND PARTIAL EXEMPTION

In taxation it is wise to examine all angles, including the obverse of any problem. In direct taxation it is as well to bear in mind the impact of losses as well as of profits and gains; in all taxation it is important not only to master the technique of one tax, but to bear in mind its correlation with other taxes, because that is often when real difficulties begin. Value added tax is not directly concerned with gains or losses, but with turnover. The consequence is that, as in any multi-stage tax, the output of one taxable person may be the input of another, and claims for repayment of input tax are often of crucial importance. Thus questions are always arising whether there has been a taxable supply to a taxable person used or to be used for the purpose of any business carried on, or to be carried on, and in relation to which input tax may be reclaimed. Thus the terms 'business', 'business carried on or to be carried on', and 'consideration', fall to be examined in a large number of cases.

It is basic that input tax cannot be reclaimed in relation to an exempt supply, and that a trader who makes both taxable and exempt supplies in the course of a business carried on or to be carried on by him, or, in the language of the second and sixth Directives, in the course of an 'economic activity', will find that he can only reclaim input tax of a proportionate part of the tax related to taxable supplies. In *Morrison's Academy Boarding Houses Association* v. *The Commissioners of Customs and Excise*[35] the expression 'business' has come close to meaning 'the making of taxable supplies', although this conclusion may call for some qualification.

Some of the cases already referred to indicate problems which have arisen in deciding whether and to what extent the exempting provisions of the sixth Council Directive have direct effect; and doubtless, further problems will arise. Another point is the extent to which input tax may be deducted prior to the actual making of taxable supplies. Section 14 of the Value Added Tax Act 1983 envisages that input tax may in a proper case be claimed before taxable supplies have actually been made. This is suggested by the words 'business carried on or to be carried on'.

In formulating their practice the Commissioners of Customs and Excise appear none the less to have adopted the principle that no input tax may be reclaimed unless taxable supplies have actually been made. This was the line which was adopted by the Dutch fiscal authority in *D. A. Rompelman* v. *Minister van Financien*.[36] In this case the meaning of 'business carried on or to be carried on' was considered by the Dutch Court of Justice. This was a case in which there was a contract to purchase a building which had not yet been completed and the dealing in which would be held to constitute an economic activity. The question which arose was whether entering into a binding contract to acquire a building in the course of construction formed part of the economic activity in question under Article 4 of the sixth Council Directive, and whether this entitled the trader to deduct input tax at a preparatory stage, notwithstanding that no taxable supplies had at that stage been made.

The Dutch fiscal authorities refused to grant the refund, because the exploitation of the property had not in fact begun—in other words, because no taxable supplies had been made. Article 4 described 'economic activities' as comprising 'all activities of producers, traders and persons supplying services including mining and agricultural activities and activities of the professions. The exploitation of tangible and intangible property for the purpose of obtaining income on a continuing basis shall also be considered an economic activity.'

It was contended by the Rompelmans that the exploitation of an asset starts as soon as a right over it is acquired and that such a preparatory act must be considered part of the exercise of such economic activity, because it is a necessary condition for the taking place of the activity. The case was referred to the Court of Justice at Luxembourg. The Court of Justice concluded that the essence of the question submitted by the national court was whether the acquisition of a right to obtain the future transfer of the

[35] [1978] STC 1.
[36] Case 268/83 [1985] ECR, [1985] 3 CMLR 202.

title to part of an immoveable asset which had yet to be built, with the intention of letting such part in due course, could be considered to be an 'economic activity' within the meaning of Article 4(1) of the sixth Directive. It was observed by the Court of Justice, referring to the case of *Gaston Schul*,[37] that it was a fundamental characteristic of VAT that the tax was chargeable only after deduction of the amount of tax borne directly by the cost of the various components of the price of goods and services, and that the procedure of deduction was so arranged that any taxable persons were authorized to deduct from the VAT for which they were liable, the VAT which the goods and services had already borne.

It was provided by Article 17 of the sixth Council Directive, however, that the right to deduct arose 'at the time when the deductible tax becomes chargeable' and that Article 2 allowed a taxable person, to the extent that the goods or services are to be used for the purpose of his operation subject to tax, 'to deduct from tax that he is liable to pay, the VAT due or paid in respect of goods or services supplied or to be supplied by him by another taxable person'. The Court of Justice concluded that the first investment expenditure incurred for the needs of, and with a view of carrying out, an undertaking would be considered as an economic activity, and that it would be wrong to decide that the economic activities do not start until the moment when the asset is actually exploited—that is, when the taxable income is first generated.

CONSIDERATION

'Consideration' is a term of art in English law, and means an act or forbearance of one party, or the promise thereof, for which the act or promise of the other party is bought. Doubts have, however, recently arisen whether the meaning of the term 'consideration' as used in the second and sixth Directives has the same meaning as in English law. This may give rise to questions of fundamental importance, and in particular whether in a particular case there is a taxable supply, or even a 'supply' at all, because a supply of services for no consideration does not fall within the definition of a 'taxable supply'. This point arose in sharp focus in the recent decision of the House of Lords in the *Apple and Pear Development Council* v. *The Commissioners of Customs and Excise*.[38] The word 'consideration' was defined in the second Council Directive as '(a) in the case of supply of goods and of the provision of services, everything which makes up the consideration for the supply of the goods or the provision of services, including all expenses and taxes except the value added tax itself'.

---

[37] Case 15/81 [1982] ECR 1409; [1982] 3 CMLR 229.
[38] [1986] STC 192.

Annex A of paragraph 13 in relation to Article 8(a) provided that the expression 'consideration' meant everything received in return for the supply of goods or the provision of services, including incidental expenses (packing, transport, insurance, etc.) that is to say, not only the cash amount charged, but also, for example, the value of the goods received in exchange or, in the case of goods or services supplied by order of a public authority, the amount of the compensation received'.

The definition of 'consideration' was not repeated in the sixth Council Directive, and the word 'consideration' is used in a number of places in that Directive apart from Article 2. The House of Lords inferred that the word 'consideration' still had the same meaning as it was given in Annex A to Article 8(a) of the second Council Directive.

In *Staatssecretaris van Financien* v. *Cooperatieve Vereniging 'Cooperatieve Aardappelenbewaarplaats GA,* [39] the definition contained in Article 8(a) was considered by the Court of Justice. In that case a co-operative stored potatoes for its members at a constant temperature in such manner that each member had the right to deposit 1,000 kilograms of potatoes for each share held by him against the payment of a food storage charge. The co-operative imposed no storage charge in the years 1975 and 1976 and included nothing in respect of storage in its turnover tax declaration. The Dutch fiscal authorities considered that a benefit would arise to the holders of shares on the basis that 'the person for whose benefit the service of storage was effected had provided something in return'. The matter was referred to the Court of Justice under Article 177, which decided that since there was no payment within the meaning of Article 2(a) of the Directive, there was nothing which could be described as consideration for the service provided within the meaning of Article 8, and nothing that could be described as 'received by the Association' within the meaning of Article 13 of Annex A.

In the High Court and in the Court of Appeal the *Apple and Pear* case had proceeded on the basis that, in relation to the general apple and pear scheme, financed by a statutory levy on apple- and pear-growers, there was no consideration, so that no output tax was chargeable on the Apple and Pear Council for the services which it rendered. The House of Lords concluded that the definition of 'consideration' set out in Article 8(a) was close to, but not necessarily the same as, the ordinary meaning in English law. In the absence of any clear case-law of the European Court of Justice which was decisive of the matter, the House of Lords decided that it was appropriate for their Lordships' House to refer to the European Court a question raising this point. The decision of the Court of Justice is awaited with interest.

---

[39] Case 154/80 [1981] 3 CMLR 337.

In *Boots Company plc* v. *The Commissioners of Customs and Excise*,[40] difficult questions relating to 'consideration' have again been raised. In that case the question arose whether certain vouchers or coupons surrendered to Boots formed part of the consideration for the goods supplied at prices discounted by the face value of the coupon or voucher. The London Tribunal held that it was bound by the decision of the House of Lords in *Chappell & Co. Ltd.* v. *Nestle Co. Ltd.*[41] to hold that the vouchers or coupons formed part of the consideration. In that case Lord Reid said:

It is to my mind illegitimate to argue—this is a sale, the consideration for a sale is the price, price can only include money or something which can be readily converted into an ascertainable sum of money, therefore anything like wrappers which have no money value when delivered cannot be part of the consideration.

The respondents avoid this difficulty by submitting that acquiring and delivering the wrappers was merely a condition which gave a qualification to buy and was not part of the consideration for sale.

Lord Somervell expressed himself as follows:

The question, then, is whether the three wrappers were part of the consideration or, as Jenkins LJ held, a condition of making the purchase, like a ticket entitling a member to buy at a co-operative store.

I think that they are part of the consideration. They are so described in the offer. 'They', the wrappers, 'will help you to get smash hit recordings.' They are so described in the record itself—'all you have to do to get [such new] record is to send three wrappers from Nestle's 6d milk chocolate bars, together with postal order for 1s 6d.' This is not conclusive but, however described, they are, in my view, in law part of the consideration. It is said that, when received, the wrappers are of no value to Nestle's. This I would have thought irrelevant. A contracting party can stipulate for what consideration he chooses. A peppercorn does not cease to be good consideration if it is established that the promisee does not like pepper and will throw away the corn. As the whole object of selling the record, if it is a sale, was to increase the sales of chocolate, it seems to me wrong not to treat the stipulated evidence of such sales as part of the consideration.

The London Tribunal was led to the conclusion, under section 10(3) of the Value Added Tax Act 1983, that, since the consideration consisted not wholly of money (part of it consisted of the coupon), that the value of the supply had to be taken as its open market value. The Boots Company has appealed against the decision of the London Tribunal, which was made prior to the hearing of the *Apple and Pear* case in the House of Lords; and it is too early to conjecture whether the decision of the Court of Justice in that case may have some bearing on the outcome of the appeal by Boots Company plc.

[40] (1986) VATTR 49.   [41] [1960] AC 87; [1959] 2 All ER 701.

I have referred above to the well-known passage in the judgment of Lord Denning in *Bulmer* v. *Bollinger*,[42] where he describes the EEC Treaty as being 'like an incoming tide. It flows into the estuaries and up the rivers. It cannot be held back.' And yet, while it cannot perhaps be held back, its impact is limited to relatively few fields, and, as Lord Mackenzie Stuart pointed out in the Hamlyn Lecture for 1977, too much should not be expected of the Court of Justice as an instrument of European integration, 'because neither the court nor any other court may usurp the role of the legislature or of the executive'. It is none the less possible that, viewed from the middle of the twenty-first century, the cases referred to above may appear to have called in a new order of international law to redress the balance of the old.

[42] Supra, n. 2.

PART V
Public Law

14

Lord Wilberforce and Administrative Law

by D. G. T. WILLIAMS

INTRODUCTION

Administrative law in England and Wales has been transformed over the past twenty years. The transformation is evident in legislation (primary and subordinate) affecting remedies in judicial review, in the development of complaints procedures and the continuing expansion of tribunals, in the increasing academic and professional literature, and in a series of influential decisions in the courts, and especially in the House of Lords. Some judges—notably Lords Reid, Diplock, and Denning—are frequently and openly linked with the expansion of administrative law. Others, particularly Lord Wilberforce, have underwritten the expansion by ensuring that several of the new departures in the law have been made only with due respect for the lessons of the past, in accordance with the wishes (where expressed) of Parliament, and against a background of constitutional propriety. This chapter seeks to identify the distinctive features of Lord Wilberforce's contribution to administrative law and, from time to time, wider areas of constitutional law.

Lord Wilberforce's approach to issues of law and administration is nowhere better illustrated than in *Burmah Oil Co. Ltd. v. Bank of England*.[1] In that case Burmah Oil was seeking access to a number of documents, all relating to matters of policy 'of the highest national and political importance',[2] for the purpose of its lawsuit against the Bank; and the Chief Secretary to the Treasury objected on the ground that they belonged to classes of documents which ought to be protected in the public interest. The House of Lords, by a majority, decided to inspect the disputed documents; but it was eventually agreed that none of them contained 'matter of such evidential value as to make an order for their disclosure, in all the circumstances, necessary for disposing fairly of the case'.[3] Lord Wilberforce, in a minority of one, rejected the need for inspection at all:

---

[1] [1980] AC 1090. [2] Ibid. 1109, per Lord Wilberforce.
[3] Ibid. 1136, per Lord Keith.

'In the end, I regard this as a plain case: of public interest immunity properly claimed on grounds of high policy on the one hand in terms which cannot be called in question; of nothing of any substance to put in the scale on the other.'[4]

Lord Wilberforce's speech is significant for a number of reasons. In the first place, it shows a disinclination to adopt easy or fashionable assumptions about the attitudes and processes of government. The 'lengthy and detailed' certificate of the Chief Secretary was seen as providing 'manifestly solid grounds' for the claim of immunity;[5] the 'need for candour in communication between those concerned with policy making' was firmly accepted, with the additional comment that the argument of candour had of late 'received an excessive dose of cold water';[6] and the claim that out of 'fluid discussions' between the Bank and the Government, there might emerge material to support Burmah's case was treated with a considerable measure of scepticism.[7] Secondly, Lord Wilberforce's speech shows a dislike of speculative demands for disclosure. As opposed to the views of the majority, who were willing to take a 'judicial peep' at the withheld documents once it was established that it was 'likely' or 'very likely' or 'on the cards' that they would contain material substantially useful to the party seeking discovery,[8] his Lordship was not prepared to yield to the 'siren song' that inspection would do no harm.[9] On principle and on the basis of the authorities, Lord Wilberforce asserted that the court should not assume the task of inspection 'except in rare instances where a strong positive case is made out, certainly not upon a bare unsupported assertion by the party seeking production that something to help him may be found, or upon some unsupported, viz. speculative, hunch of its own'.[10]

In the later case of *Air Canada* v. *Secretary of State for Trade*,[11] Lord Wilberforce was able to merge the majority and minority formulae adopted in *Burmah Oil*. He saw the difference of opinion in *Burmah Oil* as stemming from the facts of the particular case; and he was now content to accept phrases such as 'likely' or 'reasonable probability' as meaning 'something beyond speculation, some concrete ground for belief which takes the case beyond a mere 'fishing' expedition'.[12] This does seem to involve a shift in emphasis—from the requirement of a 'strong positive case' to a requirement of 'likelihood'—and it is characteristic of Lord Wilberforce that he was prepared to move to middle ground in order to avoid what could become mere arguments of semantics or terminology—

---

[4] Ibid. 1117.   [5] Ibid. 1108 and 1113 respectively.

[6] Ibid. 1112. His Lordship also noted that it is now 'rather fashionable' to decry the argument, but he felt that to 'remove protection from revelation in court in this case at least could well deter frank and full expression in similar cases in the future'.

[7] Ibid. 1116.   [8] See esp. the speech of Lord Edmund-Davies, ibid. 1122 ff.
[9] Ibid. 1116.   [10] Ibid. 1117.   [11] [1983] 2 AC 394.
[12] Ibid. 439

or, as he once put it, 'narrow verbal distinctions'.[13] A similar shift of emphasis is seen in his speeches in the well-known *Zamir* and *Khawaja*[14] cases. In *Zamir* the House of Lords, through the leading speech of Lord Wilberforce, held that the decision by an immigration officer (acting in 'a statutory and para-statutory framework'[15]) that someone should be removed from the country as an 'illegal entrant' could be judicially questioned only if "there was no evidence on which he could reach his decision, or that no reasonable person in this position could have reached it'.[16] Less than three years later, in *Khawaja*, the House of Lords (including Lord Wilberforce) unanimously departed from that view, having been 'persuaded in principle that the power of the court to review the detention and summary removal of an alleged illegal entrant ... was too narrowly stated in *Zamir*'s case and must include power to decide whether the applicant for relief is or is not in fact an illegal entrant'.[17] Nevertheless, Lord Wilberforce, as in *Burmah Oil*, understandably drew attention to the linguistic, or terminological, difficulties involved in formulating appropriate tests for judicial review in particular statutory contexts; and again, understandably, he stressed that the power to review a determination that someone is an illegal entrant must have limits, including 'the fact that of necessity extensive fact-finding operations have to be carried out by the immigration authorities which cannot be repeated by the reviewing court'.[18]

THE LIMITS OF JUDICIAL REVIEW

Indeed, a third significant feature of Lord Wilberforce's speech in *Burmah Oil* is his evident determination to ensure that the courts should be aware of necessary limits upon power of judicial review or intervention. In the course of his speech he claimed that it is not for the courts 'to assume the role of advocates for open government',[19] that 'judicial review is not a 'bonum in se', it is a part, and a valuable one, of democratic government in which other responsibilities coexist';[20] and that to overrule the Minister's view on public interest immunity on 'unsupported contentions' would 'be to do precisely what the courts will not countenance in the actions of ministers'.[21] Allowance should be made, in other words, for the special knowledge and attributes of statutory bodies. The tribunal in *Anisminic Ltd. v. Foreign Compensation Commission*[22] was a specialized body with power to decide questions of law and with 'a wide measure of finality'

---

[13] In *Malloch v. Aberdeen Corp.* [1971] 2 All ER 1278, 1293 (HL).
[14] *R. v. Home Secretary, ex p. Zamir* [1980] AC 930; *R. v. Home Secretary, ex p. Khawaja* [1984] AC 74.
[15] [1980] AC 948.   [16] Ibid.
[17] [1984] AC 125, per Lord Bridge.   [18] Ibid. 104.
[19] *Supra*, n. 1, [1980] AC 1112.   [20] Ibid. 1117.
[21] Ibid.   [22] [1969] 2 AC 147.

attaching to its decisions.[23] The Minister in *Secretary of State for Education and Science* v. *Metropolitan Borough of Tameside*[24] 'must be given credit for having the background . . . well in mind, and must be taken to be properly and professionally informed . . . His opinion, based as it must be, on that of a strong and expert department, is not to be lightly overridden.'[25] The courts in *Bromley London Borough Council* v. *Greater London Council*[26] 'will give full recognition to the wide discretion conferred upon the council by Parliament and will not lightly interfere with its exercise'.[27]

It is not uncommon for judges to preface their rulings in administrative law with protestations of judicial restraint and reminders of administrative expertise. For Lord Wilberforce, however, the rhetoric of judicial restraint was muted, and instead he consistently took the opportunity to stress the overriding authority of Parliament. Hence the 'essential point' in *Anisminic* is 'that the tribunal has a derived authority, derived, that is, from statute'; and it would be 'misdescription' to state judicial enforcement of the intention of the legislature 'in terms of a struggle between the courts and the executive'.[28] Likewise, in the *Bromley* case, Lord Wilberforce coupled recognition of the wide discretion assigned to the Greater London Council with insistence that the council 'though a powerful body, with an electorate larger and a budget more considerable than those of many nation states, is the creation of statute and only has powers given to it by statute'.[29] Such statements are a corrective to easy arguments about the 'democratic' or 'non-democratic' implications of judicial review. In *Tameside* Lord Wilberforce saw it as 'vital' to bear in mind that the discretionary power of the Minister under the relevant provision of the Education Act, 1944, involved 'reviewing the action of another public body which itself has discretionary powers and duties. . . The authority . . . is itself elected, and is given specific powers as to the kind of schools it wants in its area.'[30]

A dispassionate respect for the limits of discretionary authority allowed by statute explains Lord Wilberforce's readiness in *Tameside* and *Bromley* respectively to hold against a Minister of the Crown and a leading local authority. The *Tameside* case was concerned with a Minister's intervention in questions of school reorganization. His intervention was based on a statutory provision framed in 'subjective' terms (if 'the Secretary of State is satisfied . . . that any local education authority . . . have acted or are proposing to act unreasonably . . . he may . . . give such directions . . . as appear to him to be expedient'), but Lord Wilberforce denied that judicial review was thereby excluded.[31] He looked carefully at the structure of that

[23] Ibid. 207.   [24] [1977] AC 1014.   [25] Ibid. 1048.
[26] [1983] 1 AC 768.   [27] Ibid. 813–14.
[28] *Supra*, n. 22, 207–8.   [29]*Supra*, n. 26, 813.   [30] *Supra*, n. 24, 1047.   [31] Ibid.

'notable statute', the Education Act, 1944,[32] and, after a detailed consideration of the actual events in Tameside, concluded that if the Minister

had exercised his judgment on the basis of the factual situation in which this newly elected authority was placed—with a policy approved by its electorate, and massively supported by the parents—there was no ground, however much he might disagree with the new policy, and regret such administrative dislocation as was brought about by the change, upon which he could find that the authority was acting or proposing to act unreasonably.[33]

In the *Bromley* case, which concerned a far-reaching fare reduction policy on buses and the Underground, Lord Wilberforce looked at the construction of the Transport (London) Act, 1969, and concluded that, while 'a large degree of autonomy'[34] was allowed by the statute, the Greater London Council and the London Transport Executive were required 'to operate subject to the interlocking restraints spelt out in it'.[35] These restraints, it was held in the House of Lords, had not been observed. Lord Wilberforce, like other members of the House, declared that approval by the electorate could not confer validity on *ultra vires* action;[36] he also endorsed the so-called fiduciary duty to ratepayers expressed years earlier in *Prescott* v. *Birmingham Corporation*[37] ('a decision which remains valid in principle'[38]) and *Roberts* v. *Hopwood*[39] ('which also remains authoritative as to principle although social considerations may have changed since 1925'[40]).

Some aspects of the *Tameside* and *Bromley* decisions, especially when read together, do appear to raise difficulties. In the earlier case, however, Lord Wilberforce reminded us that 'there is no universal rule as to the principles on which the exercise of a discretion may be reviewed: each statute or type of statute must be individually looked at.'[41] Perhaps the most criticized aspect of the *Bromley* case is the resurrection of the concept of a fiduciary duty to ratepayers; and in a later case Ormrod, LJ, was reluctant to see the concept of such a duty as opening up 'a route by which the courts can investigate and, if thought appropriate, interfere with any exercise of their discretionary powers by local authorities'.[42] In his speech in *Bromley*, Lord Wilberforce was, it should be stressed, utilizing the concept of a fiduciary duty as an aid to interpretation, rather than as an independent basis of challenge—a further reminder of the extent to which his analyses in administrative law cases are, as far as possible, tied closely

---

[32] Ibid. 1046.   [33] Ibid. 1052.   [34]*Supra*, n. 26, 819.
[35] Ibid.   [36] Ibid. 814.   [37] [1955] Ch. 210.
[38] *Supra*, n. 26, 815.   [39] [1925] AC 578.
[40] *Supra*, n. 26, 815.   [41] *Supra*, n. 24, 1047.
[42] *Pickwell* v. *London Borough of Camden* [1983] QB 962, 1004. See the comments in J. A. G. Griffith, *The Politics of the Judiciary*, 3rd edn. (1985), 142 ff., esp. 145.

to a process of statutory construction. In each statutory context a special factor may influence the manner in which the courts examine the exercise of discretionary power. In *Tameside* the special factor was the meaning of 'unreasonable', which (in the words of Lord Diplock) was seen as 'a term of legal art';[43] in *Bromley* the House of Lords was (in the words of Lord Scarman) 'invited to construe the Act in the light of the principle that a local authority owes a fiduciary duty to its ratepayers'.[44] The injection of these special factors into judicial review of discretionary power helps to explain why there is 'no universal rule' as to the application of the relevant principles.

WORDS OF DESCRIPTION

That Lord Wilberforce was not dazzled by theoretical and conceptual arguments, however, is a fourth feature of his speech in *Burmah Oil*, and another aspect of his dislike of vague or speculative assertions. Those who seek, in the face of a strong claim of public interest immunity, 'to demonstrate the existence of a counteracting interest calling for disclosure of particular documents' must give the courts something 'very definite' upon which to proceed;[45] and Lord Wilberforce has on more than one occasion called for a 'common sense' approach to the facts of particular cases.[46] His broader hesitancy in the face of efforts to categorize arguments is seen in *Calvin* v. *Carr,* where he referred to 'the difficult area of what is void and what is voidable, as to which some confusion exists in the authorities'.[47] and in *Anisminic,* where he commenced his analysis 'in non-technical terms, avoiding for the moment such words as "jurisdiction," "error" and "nullity" which create many problems'.[48] Later in *Anisminic* Lord Wilberforce spoke of the dangers of the word 'nullity' if it brings with it 'the difficult distinction between what is void and what is voidable, and I certainly do not wish to recognise that this distinction exists or to analyse it if it does'.[49] His Lordship added that the term may be convenient 'as a word of description rather than in itself a touchstone'.[50] It is noteworthy in this regard that Lord Wilberforce, in *London and*

---

[43] *Supra*, n. 24, 1064, per Lord Diplock. To fall within the term, he added, the conduct must be such 'which no sensible authority acting with due appreciation of its responsibilities would have decided to adopt'. Lord Russell of Killowen said (1075: 'History is replete with genuine accusations of unreasonableness when all that is involved is disagreement, perhaps passionate, between reasonable people. In summary, my Lords, 'unreasonably' is a very strong word indeed, the strength of which may easily fail to be recognized.'

[44] *Supra*, n. 26, 837. Lord Scarman gave full attention to the concept of a fiduciary duty (838–9).

[45] *Supra*, n. 1, 1113–14.   [46] *Supra*, n. 11, 439.
[47] [1980] AC 574, 589 (PC).   [48] *Supra*, n. 22, 207.
[49] Ibid. 208   [50] Ibid.

Clydeside Estates Ltd. v. *Aberdeen District Council*[51] agreed with both Lord Hailsham, LC and Lord Keith of Kinkel in warning against the confusing use of such expressions as 'void' and 'voidable'. Lord Hailsham, in particular, wished to discourage 'rigid legal classifications' and 'stark categories' such as 'mandátory' and 'directory', 'void' and 'voidable', a 'nullity', and 'purely regulatory': such language could be useful (presumably for descriptive purposes), but could also be misleading 'in so far as it may be supposed to present a court with the necessity of fitting a particular case into one or other of mutually exclusive and starkly contrasted compartments'.[52] Several years earlier, in an important case on natural justice, Lord Wilberforce spoke of 'the risk of a compartmental approach which, although convenient as a solvent, may lead to narrower distinctions than are appropriate to the broader issues of administrative law'.[53]

Lord Wilberforce's rejection of 'rigid legal classifications' is vividly seen in *Davy* v. *Spelthorne Borough Council*,[54] where the issue facing the House of Lords was the application of the general rule in *O'Reilly* v. *Mackman*.[55] The issue before the House related 'to the circumstances in which a person with a cause of action against a public authority, which is connected with the performance of its public duty, is entitled to proceed against the authority by way of an ordinary action, as distinct from an application for judicial review'.[56] The plaintiff sought damages against a local council, alleging that he had been negligently advised of his rights under planning law. All members of the House of Lords agreed that the action for negligence could proceed, but Lord Wilberforce took the opportunity to pour a cautious measure of cold water on the new-fangled terminology of 'public' and 'private' law which had gained widespread respectability in the wake of *O'Reilly* v. *Mackman*. Prefacing his remarks with the assertion that local authorities may 'in certain limited circumstances' become liable for common-law negligence in the performance of their duties,[57] he was reluctant to introduce a new and rigid classification into the law:

The expressions 'private law' and 'public law' have recently been imported into the law of England from countries which, unlike our own, have separate systems concerning public law and private law. No doubt they are convenient expressions for descriptive purposes. In this country they must be used with caution, for, typically, English law fastens not upon principles but upon remedies ... We have not yet reached the point at which mere characterisation of a claim as a claim in public law is sufficient to exclude it from consideration by the ordinary courts: to permit this would be to create a dual system of law with the rigidity and procedural hardship for plaintiffs which it was the purpose of the recent reforms to remove.[58]

[51] [1979] 3 All ER 876 (HL).
[52] Ibid. 883, per Lord Hailsham, LC.
[53] *Malloch* v. *Aberdeen Corp.* [1971] 2 All ER 1278, 1294 (HL).
[54] [1984] AC 262.   [55] [1983] 2 AC 237.
[56] *Supra*, n. 54, 269, per Lord Fraser.   [57] Ibid. 276.   [58] Ibid.

The reforms to which Lord Wilberforce referred in that passage were those achieved through the Supreme Court Act, 1981 (s. 31), and the relevant statutory rules incorporated in Order 53 of the Rules of the Supreme Court since 1977. In his view any 'public law' element in the plaintiff's action in *Davy* was 'peripheral'; but, more generally (and in terms which tend to qualify *O'Reilly* v. *Mackman*), he emphasized that there was no statutory provision indicating that the procedure under Order 53 'was the only procedure which could be followed in cases where it applied', and that the onus lay on the defendant to show an abuse of the process of the court.[59] Once again, Lord Wilberforce's strict adherence to the proper interpretation of statutes could be coupled with his dislike of the adoption of rigid legal categories. His approach to change in the law was sometimes pragmatic—as in his Parliamentary support for the Lord Chancellor's amended proposal (in the Administration of Justice Bill) concerning the leave requirement in judicial review,[60] or in his judicial reservations in the *Rossminster* case over the suggested introduction of interim declarations[61]—but in general he preferred legal advances to be achieved, if not by legislation, then by scrupulous regard for precedent (where available) and for principle (where formulated).

PRECEDENTS AND BASELINES

A characteristic feature of Lord Wilberforce's speech in *Burmah Oil* was his regard for precedent, combined with a readiness to move forward cautiously from a baseline of authority. Hence *Conway* v. *Rimmer*[62] was seen as the proper starting-point in the balancing process needed in cases of public interest immunity. Even so, it 'does not profess to cover every case, nor has it frozen the law', and his Lordship was prepared in *Burmah Oil* to concede 'that the courts may, in a suitable case, decide that a high level governmental public interest must give way to the interests of the administration of justice'.[63] His readiness to unfreeze the law in suitable cases is well demonstrated in *Anisminic,* which concerned the hallowed distinction 'between a usurpation of a jurisdiction which someone has not got, and the wrong exercise of a jurisdiction which someone has got'.[64] A 'rigorous and powerful analysis' on traditional lines had been set out by

---

[59] Ibid. 278–9.
[60] See *Parl. Deb., HL,* 461, cols. 443 ff., esp. 456–57, 19 Mar. 1985.
[61] *R.* v. *Inland Revenue Commissioners, ex p. Rossminster Ltd* [1980] AC 952, 1001. Lord Wilberforce added in this regard that 'sensible limits have to be set on the courts' powers of judicial review of administrative action'.
[62] [1968] AC 910.   [63] *Supra,* n. 1, 1113.
[64] *Supra,* n. 22, 193, per Lord Morris of Borth-y-Gest, referring to the speech of Lord Sumner in *R.* v. *Nat. Bell Liquors Ltd.* [1922] 2 AC 128.

Diplock, LJ, in a unanimous Court of Appeal; but the decision was reversed in the House of Lords, with Lord Wilberforce as one of the majority, 'on a wider and more modulated view of what is jurisdictional error'.[65] In the course of his speech in *Anisminic* Lord Wilberforce said, after looking at a selection of earlier decisions, that 'the cases in which a tribunal has been held to have passed outside its proper limits are not limited to those in which it had no power to enter on its inquiry or its jurisdiction, or has not satisfied a condition precedent'.[66] Problems of jurisdictional error were by no means solved by *Anisminic,* but it provided the opportunity for Lord Diplock, in a 'generous depature from the initial legalism' of his approach'[67] and Lord Denning MR, to seek the effective abolition of any distinction between errors of law which go to 'jurisdiction' and errors of law which do not.[68] In *Anisminic* Lord Wilberforce—who had played no part in the earlier 'landmark' cases of 1968, namely *Conway v. Rimmer*[69] and *Padfield v. Minister of Agriculture, Fisheries and Food*[70]—was conscious that we had reached an important stage 'in our administrative law',[71] and that it was time to move forward.

In a similar vein Lord Wilberforce, again with dutiful regard to decisions in the past, was prepared in *Anns v. London Borough of Merton*[72] to extend the general duty of care to the sphere of statutory functions of public bodies. Building on the earlier case of *Dorset Yacht Co. Ltd. v. Home office*[73] his Lordship—recognizing incidentally, that the powers and duties of a local authority 'are definable in terms of public not private law'[74]—set out the much-discussed distinction between the policy area and the operational area of decisions taken by public authorities or bodies, though he accepted that the distinction is one of degree. To speak of questions of degree, of course, is consistent with Lord Wilberforce's dislike of rigid categories; and in the leading case of *locus standi* in administrative law (the *Fleet Street Casuals* case[75]), where differing views were put forward in the House of Lords, Lord Wilberforce—though adopting a conservative view on standing—was not prepared to assert, for instance, 'that, in a case of sufficient gravity, the court might not be able to hold that another taxpayer or other taxpayers could challenge them'.[76] This concept of 'sufficient gravity' was echoed by two other members of the House of

---

[65] The quotations are taken from Lord Wilberforce's short note on 'Lord Diplock and Administrative Law', in [1986] PL 6.
[66] *Supra,* n. 22, 210.   [67] See Lord Wilberforce (*supra,* 65) 7.
[68] See *O'Reilly v. Mackman,* (*supra,* n. 55) (Lord Diplock) and *Bulk Gas Users Group v. Attorney-General* [1983] NZLR 129 (Cooke J.).
[69] *Supra,* n. 62.   [70] [1968] AC 997.   [71] *Supra,* n. 22, 209.
[72] [1978] AC 728.   [73] [1970] AC 1004.
[74] *Supra,* n. 72, 754.
[75] *R. v. Inland Revenue Commissioners, ex p. National Federation of Self-Employed and Small Businesses Ltd.* [1982] AC 617.
[76] Ibid. 633.

Lords,[77] though it falls short of the more ambitious views of standing put forward by Lords Diplock and Scarman.[78]

In the course of his speech in *Fleet Street Casuals* Lord Wilberforce showed the cautious side of his concern for precedent. Indeed, he denied that the 'threshold requirement' of 'sufficient interest' in Order 53 meant that the test of standing was to be the same for all the forms of remedy allowed. As a matter of common sense, he insisted, the rules of standing may reflect the different character of the relief sought, and we should not go too far 'in our enthusiasm for liberation from procedural fetters'.[79] Another warning against straining 'the power of judicial innovation' was issued by Lord Wilberforce in *Gouriet* v. *Union of Post Office Workers*,[80] where Lord Wilberforce took account both of 'a long, uniform and respected series of authorities' and of the constitutional validity of the view that it is 'the exclusive right of the Attorney-General to represent the public interest—even where individuals might be interested in a larger view of the matter'.[81]

CONSTITUTIONAL DELICACIES

The constitutional nature of the issues in *Gouriet* was referred to several times by Lord Wilberforce: in speaking of the remedy of private prosecutions as 'a valuable constitutional safeguard against inertia or partiality on the part of authority';[82] in stating that, in 'terms of constitutional law', the rights of the public are vested in the Crown and that the Attorney-General enforces them as an officer of the Crown;[83] in dismissing as 'unimpressive support' the citation of Canadian and United States cases arising in different constitutional frameworks;[84] and (implicitly) in recognizing that the right of the Attorney-General to invoke the assistance of the civil courts in aid of the criminal law as 'exceptional' and a jurisdiction of 'great delicacy.'[85] A similar awareness of the constitutional background is evident in *Burmah Oil,* in which Lord Wilberforce accorded considerable respect to the Minister's definition of the public interest;[86] and in *Air Canada*, apart from recognizing 'the high level status and confidentiality' of the documents sought, he incidentally referred to 'a powerful convention' which prevents ministers from having access to papers of their predecessors.[87]

On occasion Lord Wilberforce was directly confronted by written constitutions. In *Minister of Home Affairs* v. *Fisher*,[88] for example, he was

---

[77] Lord Fraser and Lord Roskill, ibid. 647 and 662 respectively.
[78] Ibid. 636 ff. and 647 ff. respectively.   [79] Ibid. 631.
[80] [1978] AC 435, 478.   [81] Ibid. 478 and 481.   [82] Ibid. 477.
[83] Ibid.   [84] Ibid. 480.   [85] Ibid. 481.   [86] *Supra*, n. 1., 1117.
[87] *Supra*, n. 11, 437.   [88] [1980] AC 319.

prepared to interpret the Bermuda Constitution broadly, 'without necessary acceptance of all the presumptions that are relevant to legislation of private law'.[89] In the absence of a written constitution and particularly a Bill of Rights, Lord Wilberforce understandably attached importance to the statutory wording; but this did not exclude presumptions in favour of individuals. *Raymond* v. *Honey*[90] was concerned in part with alleged contempt of court by a prison governor in denying a prisoner's right of access to the courts. Lord Wilberforce pointed out that nothing in the Prison Act 1952 conferred power to make regulations interfering with access to a court: the prison rules had to be interpreted accordingly, or be regarded as *ultra vires*, and standing orders could not confer any greater powers than the regulations. In his dissenting speech in *Hoffman-La Roche & Co.* v. *Secretary of State for Trade and Industry*,[91] which concerned an interlocutory injunction sought to prevent charging for the drugs librium and valium in excess of prices provided for in subordinate legislation, Lord Wilberforce was anxious as far as possible to avoid injustice to private individuals because of the general rule that there is in England—as opposed to 'more developed legal systems'—no right of compensation for illegal acts of the administration.

Arguments about wider principles of free speech or personal freedom were not permitted to override the dictates of Parliament or to lead to the creation of 'rights' or 'immunities' without the most careful consideration. In the troublesome area of the law relating to 'obscenity', Lord Wilberforce spoke sharply of the definition of 'obscene' in the Obscene Publications Act 1959 (it could 'only have been the pressure of Parliamentary compromise which can have produced a test so difficult for the courts'[92])—and somewhat wryly of the purposes of the defence of the public good, introducing 'a new type of equation—possibly between incommensurables—between immediate and direct effect on people's conduct or character (s. 1) and inherent impersonal values of a less transient character assumed, optimistically perhaps, to be of general concern (s. 4)'.[93] Despite reservations about the legislation of 1959, however, Lord Wilberforce sought to interpret its provisions so as to meet Parliament's intentions as far as possible.[94] The constitutional implications of freedom of speech, particularly of freedom of the Press, were directly faced in *British Steel Corporation* v. *Granada Television Ltd.*[95] That case concerned the identity of the person who had submitted secret or confidential documents to

---

[89] Ibid. 329. [90] [1983] 1 AC 1. [91] [1975] AC 295.
[92] *Director of Public Prosecutions* v. *Whyte* [1972] AC 849, 862.
[93] *Director of Public Prosecutions* v. *Jordan* [1977] AC 699, 719. In *Science Research Council* v. *Nassé* [1980] AC 1028, 1067, Lord Wilberforce noted in a different context that balancing 'can only take place between commensurables'.
[94] *Gold Star Publications Ltd.* v. *Director of Public Prosecutions* [1981] 2 All ER 257 (HL).
[95] [1981] AC 1096.

Granada. The House of Lords by a majority ruled that Granada should disclose the informant's identity to British Steel. Lord Wilberforce, one of the majority, was not impressed by 'appeals, made in vigorous tones to such broad principles as the freedom of the press, the right to a free flow of information, the public's right to know'. Of course, he added, he favoured a free press 'who indeed would not?'—but the use of the term '*right* to know' would 'not conduce to an understanding of the legal position', and in any event 'there is a wide difference between what is interesting to the public and what it is in the public interest to make known'.[96] There was an echo of his Lordship's views in *Burmah Oil* when he asserted that a 'general proposition that leaks should be encouraged, or at least not discouraged, cannot be made without weighing the detriments in loss of mutual confidence and co-operation which they involve';[97] and he was not prepared, as was Lord Salmon in his dissent, to grant a wide immunity to the Press against revealing its sources of information. The case, in his view, did not touch on freedom of the Press 'even at its periphery'[98] a statement which illustrates Lord Wilberforce's preference for resisting easy categorization at the level of rights and freedoms as much as in relation to concepts such as 'void' and 'voidable' and 'public law'.

The issue of personal freedom arose in the *Rossminster* case,[99] which concerned the search of property by officers of the Inland Revenue. In the court below Lord Denning MR had claimed that there had been no search and seizure like it 'since that Saturday, 30th April 1763, when the Secretary of State issued a general warrant by which he authorised the King's messengers to arrest John Wilkes and seize all his books and papers', an action struck down in the courts as 'worse than the Spanish inquisition'.[100] Lord Wilberforce was unimpressed. He accepted that a 'formidable number of officials now have powers to enter people's premises, and to take property away', and that the courts have the duty to supervise 'critically, even jealously, the legality of any purported exercise of these powers'. But such supervision must be 'in the context of the times', and appeals to eighteenth-century precedents of arbitrary action 'do nothing to throw light on the issue'. Moreover, it is not for the courts 'to restrict or impede the working of legislation, even of unpopular legislation; to do so would be to weaken, rather than to advance, the democratic process'.[101] Lord Wilberforce thereupon proceeded, along with a majority of the House of Lords, to hold in favour of the Inland Revenue, both as to the validity of the search warrant and on the 'reasonable cause' for seizure of property, though leaving open the possibility of later litigation on the question of 'reasonable cause'.

[96] Ibid. 1168.
[97] Ibid. 1174.   [98] Ibid. 1168.
[99] *Supra*, n. 61.   [100] Ibid. 970, CA.   [101] Ibid. 997–8, per Lord Wilberforce.

THE SEARCH FOR CLARITY

Many of Lord Wilberforce's judicial remarks, in a variety of cases, display a determination to offer clear guidance through simple rules when advising lower courts. His Lordship regretted the absence of such clear guidance in the terms of the 'illogical and unscientific' Obscene Publications Act;[102] and he recognized perforce in a Privy Council case 'that no clear and absolute rule can be laid down on the question whether defects in natural justice appearing at an original hearing, whether administrative or quasi-judicial, can be 'cured' through appeal proceedings'.[103] The latter remark is a reflection of the considerable variability of principles of administrative law. Nevertheless, Lord Wilberforce's search for clear guidance accounts as much as anything else for his disagreement with the majority of the House of Lords in *Burmah Oil*. Bearing in mind that decisions on public interest immunity have to be made at first instance by judges or masters in chambers, he stated:

They should be able to make these decisions according to simple rules: these are provided by the law as it stands. To invite a general procedure of inspection is to embark the courts on a dangerous course: they have not in general the time nor the experience to carry out in every case a careful inspection of documents and thereafter a weighing process. The results of such a process may, indeed are likely to be, variable from court to court and from case to case. This case provides an example of opposite conclusions come to upon identical materials . . . This inevitable uncertainty is not likely to do credit to the administration of justice and is bound to encourage appeals.[104]

Such an affirmation is not unlike the assertion by the Radcliffe Committee on Ministerial Memoirs, reporting in the wake of the *Crossman Diaries* case,[105] that 'the most useful principles of law for public purposes are those that can be ascertained without, not through, litigation'.[106] The Committee saw it as 'a genuine disadvantage' that the law would have to be applied on a case-by-case basis.[107] Lord Wilberforce was fully aware of the inevitability of case-by-case development in many circumstances, but he also strove for rationalization and clarity wherever possible; and his outstanding contribution to constitutional, and particularly administrative, law has been to combine the impetus in that direction with a careful adherence to statute and an awareness of the necessary limitations upon what can be achieved through the courts. Writing recently about Lord Diplock, he

[102] *Supra*, n. 92, 862, per Lord Wilberforce.
[103] *Calvin v. Carr* [1980] AC 574, 592, per Lord Wilberforce.
[104] *Supra*, n. 1, 1117, per Lord Wilberforce.
[105] *Attorney General v. Cape (Jonathan) Ltd.* [1976] QB 752.
[106] Report of the Committee of Privy Counsellors on Ministerial Memoirs, Cmnd. 6386 (1976) para. 65.
[107] Ibid.

spoke of 'cautious moves within established principle';[108] and that phrase could well be applied to his own approach. But Lord Wilberforce was not afraid of new territory, as was amply demonstrated in *Anisminic* and *Tameside*, and there is a distinctive assurance, based on controlled constitutional assumptions, in his judicial decisions. He offered an invaluable corrective to the uninhibited expansion of the jurisdiction of the courts in matters of 'public law'.

[108] [1986] PL 6.

Index

Abus de droit 174
Act of State doctrine 77–8, 84
Aerospace plane 24, 29
 development of 24, 29
Aggression 18
Air law 42
Alliances, military 14
Amiable composition, see *Lex mercatoria*
Anti-ballistic missiles 33
Anti-satellite weapons (ASAT's) 32, 34, 37–8
Antitrust-proceedings
 United States 88, 132–3
Arbitration
 commercial 112 *et seq.*, 149 *et seq.*
 judicial review 125–6, *passim*,
 English a. law 120 *et seq.*
  Commercial Court 121–2, *passim*
  London Court of International Arbitration 127, *passim*
 transnational 153
Arms
 control 20
 production and trade 20
 race 14

Commercial arbitration, see Arbitration
Commercial disputes 111 *et seq.*
Commercial law
 and see *Lex mercatoria* 111 *et seq.*
Common heritage of mankind 46
Common law 111 *et seq.*
 contract, c.l. of 185 *et seq.*
Common law of mankind 49
Confiscation 138 *et seq.*
Consideration 228 *et seq.*
Contract, see Common law
Corporate veil, see State corporations
Culpa in contrahendo 174

Damages 177
Détente, process of 13–14
Diplomacy 94–5, 104
 Diplomatic immunity 105–6
Disarmament 19, 20
Discovery 132
 evidence abroad 87 *et seq.*
Drainage basin
 international 54 *et seq.*
 obligation to negotiate 58

Economic order
 more equitable 20
 New International 41

Equity 111, 149, 155, 166–7
European Community law 211 *et seq.*
 direct effect of directives 212, 216 *et seq.*
 supremacy over national law 211, 213
European Defence Initiative 29
Evidence
 abroad, see Discovery
 disclosure of documents 235–6
Extraterritorial effect of State jurisdiction 87 *et seq.*

Fault
 common law of contract 185 *et seq.*
Force
 definition 18
 non-use of 13 *et seq.*
Force majeure 139, 145–7
Forum non conveniens 86 *et seq.*

General principles of law 47, 173, 213
Gold clause 176
Government
 recognition as a 77
 unrecognised 80

Immunity, see Diplomacy; Interest; State
Independence
 economic 15
 political 19
Indians native peoples of North America 47
Integrity
 territorial 19
Interdependence 50
Interest (policy), public 88, 132, 140, 144, 236, 240, 242, 244, 247
International law (and see Wilberforce, Lord)
 challenge of 40
 classical 44, 49
 codification and progressive development 50
 customary 43, 46, 47, 48
 domestic courts and 40
 European tradition 40, 42, 44, 92
 Grotian tradition 41, 45, 47, 50
 historical origins 40, 43, 44, 50–1
 India, ancient 91 *et seq.*
 Islamic fundamentalism 42
 Latin America and 45
 Muslim i.l. 92, 107
 nihilistic approach to 15
 regional variations 41
 scope and content 39
 sea, i.l. of the 46, 50
 socialist 42

International law (*cont.*)
  United States and 45
  universal i.l. 39 *et seq.*, 91 *et seq.*
Interpretation
  purposive (teleological) 219, 220–1
  statutory 125, 219–20
  ut res magis valeat quam pereat 177
Intertemporal law 45
Investment problems 49

Jurisdiction, see State
Jus cogens 48

Law
  sanctions and 95, 97
  supremacy of 96 *et seq.*
Lex mercatoria
  amiable composition and 162, 166
  applicability 162 *et seq.*
  definition 150 *et seq.*
  equity and 166–7
  juridical status 160–1
  macro 156 *passim*
  micro 157 *passim*, 174
  national law and 167–72
  rules of 174–8
  scope 165–6
  sources 155 *et seq.*, 172 *et seq.*
Liability
  contractual 185 *et seq.*
  strict 185 *et seq.*
Liberation
  colonial domination (l. from) 19
Locus standi
  in administrative law 243–4

Mercenaries 19
Moon and other celestial bodies
  emplacement of defensive weapons 37
  testing of weapons 35
  use for exclusively peaceful purposes 35

Natural law 149
Natural resources, *see* Sovereignty
Non-intervention 19
Nuclear weapons 14, 19

Occupation of territory 19, 47
Ordre public 134, 139, 140, 144, 169

Pacta sunt servanda 95 *et seq.*, 167, 174
Peace
  breach of 18
  threat to 18
Peace-keeping system 16
Poverty 20
Public interest (policy), see Interest

Rebus sic stantibus 174
Reprisals
  armed 20
Resources (and see Sovereignty)
  deep-sea and seabed 49
Rivers, see Watercourses

Satellite
  global s. system 61 *et seq.*
  regional s. systems 67 *et seq.*
  —telecommunication, see Space
Sea, see International law
Security
  collective s. 16
Self-defence 16, 18, 20
Self-determination 15, 20
Settlement of disputes, peaceful 16, 18
Sovereign immunity
  State organisations 133 *et seq.*
  States 77, 81 *et seq.*
Sovereignty
  limited s. (doctrines of) 16
  natural resources (s. over) 15, 49
  people (s. of the) 101
Space
  law of outer 41–2
  militarisation 27
  reconnaissance 28, 32
  remote sensing 28, 32
  Space Defense Initiative (SDI) 27, 29, 37
  telecommunications 25–6, 28, 32, 61 *et seq.*
  transportation 25
  weather observation 28, 32
Space shuttle 24
Space-stations 23 *et seq.*
  commercial, scientific use of 23
  defensive weapons 32–3
  demilitarisation 29
  legal status 30
  military use of 23 *et seq.*
  permanent 25, 26
State
  jurisdiction 77, 87 *et seq.*, 118
  State immunity, see Sovereign immunity
  unrecognised States 77, 80
State corporations 131 *et seq.*
  corporate veil 137 *et seq.*
  discovery, see Discovery
  identification with State 147 *et seq.*
  public policy, see Interest
  set-off against State claims 141 *et seq.*
State succession 46
Subversion 19

Taxation, indirect 211 *et seq.*

Index

Territory
  acquisition by occupation 47
  desert areas inhabited by nomadic tribes 48
  res nulliûs 47
Terrorism 19
Transnationalism 152–4, *passim*

War
  just 97–8
  law of 92 *et seq.*
Water
  diversion of 53 *et seq.*
  equitable utilisation 53 *et seq.*
Watercourses
  artificial waterway 56
  international 53 *et seq.*
Weapons of mass-destruction 31–2
Wilberforce, Lord
  administrative law 235 *et seq.*
  All Souls, Fellow of 3
  capital gains tax 5
  career 3 *et seq.*, 111
  children, position of 7
  codification 7
  constitutional law 244–6
  European Community law 211
  evidence
    disclosure of documents 235–6
  family relations law 7
  force majeure 145
  foreign currency
    damages in 6
    f.c. obligation 6
  freedom of speech 244–5
  international law 77 *et seq.*
  interpretation of statute 7, 219–20, 241
  judicial office
    judicial innovation 244
    judicial 'legislation' 5
    limitations 4, 236, 237–40
  law reform 6, 7
  natural justice 8, 241
  personal freedom 246
  precedent, regard for 242, 244
  property rights 7
  'public' and 'private' law 241
  revenue law 5
  State corporations 145
World
  government 103
  State 99

X-ray lasers 33–4